LIBRARY LOG

The Diary of A Public
Library Director

LIBRARY LOG

The Diary of A Public Library Director

ROBERT S. ALVAREZ, Ph.D.

ADMINISTRATOR'S DIGEST PRESS

I would like to dedicate this book to my fellow staff members at the Nashville Public Library who made everything reported in this Diary both possible and most enjoyable, and to David R. Allen, the "library school" student at the University of Maryland who is responsible for the publication of this material so many years later.

Copyright © 1991 by Robert S. Alvarez

Published by Administrator's Digest Press
719 San Miguel Lane, Foster City, CA 94404

Printed in the United States of America
Library of Congress Catalog Card No. 90-080439

ISBN 0-9618247-2-7

CONTENTS

INTRODUCTION

When a library school student wrote me in August '89 to suggest I write a book telling what it's really like running a small or medium-sized library—since he could find nothing like this in his survey of professional literature—I thought of my old "Library Log." This was a daily record, or diary, of my first two years as the director of the Nashville Public Library in Tennessee.

Two or three nights a week I would write down everything of significance that transpired since my last writing: my thoughts about what we should be doing to revitalize this interesting old library, and about the staff, the library board, the public, the local politicians, and everything else that came to mind. It reported our problems and accomplishments, our frustrations and our joys.

When I stopped writing this "Log," it amounted to 385 double-spaced typewritten pages. I had written it as anyone writing a diary, not for publication but simply because I felt this was going to be one of the high points of my life and I wanted a record of the total experience. And once I started it I found I truly enjoyed writing it.

In reviewing what I'd written in the summer of '48 it hit me that this was interesting material. Nobody had ever done anything like this, to my knowledge, and why wouldn't it provide a good and helpful read for anyone interested in library management? So I sent the first 25 pages to a library publisher. When they rejected it, the whole manuscript was dumped in a closet, and there it stayed. It moved with us to five subsequent homes, but I never thought of it again until this fall—41 years later.

As I re-read these weathered old pages I was struck with the fact that there's really nothing old about their contents. If I were to eliminate the dates on the pages I don't believe it would occur to anyone reading them that they were not of current origin. The bulk of the happenings, and all my thinking, could have taken place in the 1980's just as well as in the 1940's. The only two things that reveal the earlier date are (1) the figures that are given for staff salaries and the price of material at the time, and (2) the use of the word "Negro" instead of "black"—as in "Negro Librarian" and "Negro Branch." That was the terminology of that period and I have tried to keep the manuscript just as it was written and edited in the 1940's.

Whether or not this is the first or only "library log" ever kept by a public library administrator, or at least the first one ever published, I don't believe there was ever a more eventful time in the history of a particular library. It was a perfect time to be appointed the director of a public library in a perfect location—the City of Nashville—which I immediately fell in love with on my visit there to be interviewed by the Library Board. Reading their telegram back in Cleveland, Ohio, that offered me the Nashville job was the happiest moment in my life and the two years that followed were the most wonderful I ever spent.

I couldn't have picked a more challenging work situation or one that provided more problems or opportunities. The Library, with its colorless downtown building and its equally drab and lifeless three branches, was at the bottom of every ranking of public libraries serving U.S. cities of over 100,000 population. Its budget was only 25¢ per capita, when most libraries had $1.50, and its circulation was less than 1 volume per capita. The only way to go was up. In short, it was an ideal spot for a young librarian interested in building library service.

And the greatest thing about it was the people involved. First and foremost, there was the happy dispositioned staff that had never experienced a budget increase or a salary raise in 17 years, nor known any public attention or praise. They were ready to follow without question any new leader who seemed to offer a real change in direction and tempo, and a more dynamic library in which they could take pride.

Secondly, there was the corporate library board with its community leaders who held title to the library property as the Carnegie Library of Nashville, Inc. The City provided the money to operate the Library but the Board controlled its operation in every way. And being successful business people, for the most part, they were too busy and too sensible to involve themselves in the goings-on at the library. They were happy to delegate the job of running the library to their new, young library director. He'd been a public library director before, and had business experience in both the personnel and public relations fields, and had written to each board member after his interview with them to outline the major needs that he saw in the Nashville library picture and to indicate what he would want to attempt to do if he was appointed the Librarian. The Board members were enthusiastic about his ideas and were prepared to let him go ahead and do these things.

No library director was ever given more freedom to do his job, which is a major reason why the Nashville Library did so many new things and why the "Library Log" *should be* interesting reading. Unlike the great majority of library administrators, I could hire anybody I wanted at any time, give raises whenever they were deserved—even though the individual had received one only a few months earlier, move or paint any section of the library, offer any new service or library program, and purchase anything I thought was needed on first seeing or hearing of it. I knew of course that I should always stay within the total library budget, and I always did. I feel sad when Librarians with far more money to spend than I ever had, tell me that they can't order our *Business Information* newsletter until they get the approval of their library board.

The Library Board not only gave their director free rein and favored him with their complete trust and support; they recognized the results of his leadership and rewarded him accordingly. In his first seven months on the job he received two raises, for a total salary increase of 50 percent. The library not only paid for his membership in the Kiwanis Club but for all his weekly luncheons as well. And when they saw how much driving their director was doing, visiting branches, city councilmen and community leaders, etc., they bought him a library car and regularly paid for the insurance and repairs on it, and permitted him to drive it to and from work. Very few families had two cars in those days and this unusual library perk was much appreciated.

So it truly was a unique and delightful situation in many ways. But that isn't enough to make this library diary worth reading 42 years later. What *does* give this account current value for any present or would-be administrator are the many interesting innovations which it tells about—some of which are still fairly new to many libraries today—and the picture of what can be accomplished through imagination, positive thinking, and a supportive library staff and library board.

For instance, we were perhaps the first library to add color, painting the floors, walls, bookshelves, etc., adding some bright-colored furniture, and covering the tops of the long, dark reading room tables with an ivory-colored material. Basement storerooms were transformed into attractive Young Moderns Dens, for teenagers, in every library, with the first Young Moderns Council—with two student representatives from each high school in the area. Also in 1946–47, our Children's Room was transformed into what visiting librarians and salesmen would say was ''the most attractive children's room they ever saw.'' Its weekly marionette shows were for many years unmatched in a library setting.

x

In the same years the Library was the second in the country to operate self-service "booketerias" in local supermarkets, circulating books at the lowest unit cost of any time or place. A few libraries are now moving into this field, 40 years later. We also started displaying all our new books full front out—in '46—and many libraries are just now attempting this. Many others are still trying to get their counties to pay for free service to their county residents and so should be interested in the unique arrangement that effected this for Nashville-Davidson County in 1948. In the same year we started floodlighting the front of the main library at night, installed an attractive neon sign to clearly identify the building, built a bookmobile with the shelves in the middle and windows all the way around the outside, and did many other things in the actual operation of the library that were different then and still largely are today. I mention these things only to suggest that there might be a good deal of information in this book that is still useful today.

But whatever real value there may be in reading this *Library Log* stems more, I believe, from what it pictures of the general library atmosphere . . . the improved staff morale and their increased productivity as every library operation was streamlined and the chief emphasis was placed on quality service to each customer. There is much about a library director's philosophy of service, and his or her many opportunities for improving the library and relating better to everyone in the community. It is hoped that the reader will feel the constant movement of the library, and see the importance of the individual staff member and his or her development.

Many book-reviewers will downgrade this book simply because it was written years ago, and many librarians will pass it by for the same reason, even though they may never have read anything like it before. Certainly, there have been important changes in libraries in the past forty years, mainly due to the advent of the computer, but libraries—like schools, department stores, museums, and other well-established institutions—are basically much the same as they were in the 1940's. They are still trying to serve the book and informational needs of their customers. And to the extent that this "Library Log" shows how one library was transformed to meet these needs it should prove of interest and value to all administrators facing today's more complex challenges. They might be encouraged to read about a well-established library that doubled its circulation in two years while its staff was reduced by 25 percent.

And hopefully it will provide the sort of picture that the library school student was seeking as to "what it's like to run a library." In essence, it's a great experience and there are few limits for the person who knows what he or she wants to do and believes that Everything is Possible.

LIBRARY LOG

The Diary of A Public Library Director

INVITATION

If, after reading this book, you think you'd like a subscription to *Library Administrator's Digest*—and don't already have one—just write to Box 993, So. San Francisco, CA 94080 and say you would like to continue on from *Library Log*, and a one-year trial subscription will be yours for only $19.95.

No publication has a finer and more creative and enthusiastic group of subscribers. The following is a sample of the unsolicited comments that we have received from some of them in the past year. As you can see, these are dedicated, caring librarians who are continually seeking ways to improve the quality of their service. If you have the same interest, do come and join the *LAD* family.

"LAD is my first priority in professional reading. Thanks."
Hilma Cooper, Dir., Cheltenham Twp. Libs., Glenside, PA

"Thanks for the many hours of creative thought your *Library Administrator's Digest* has inspired in me."
Marilyn Hinshaw, Dir., Eastern Okla. Dist. Library System

"I think *LAD* is a super publication."
Donald Fought, Dir., Public Library, Port Clinton, Ohio

"The *LAD* is still my favorite reading of the month."
Alan Woodland, Chief Ln., New Westminster, Br. Columbia

"I thoroughly enjoy *LAD*. It is an informative, eye-opening publication, which always provides some good ideas."
George Needham, Dir. of Communications, Ohio Library Assn.

"I enjoy your newsletter, and while I don't always agree with what you say, it does make me think."
Michael Golrick, Director, Wilton Library Assn., CT

"Your publication does more to renew my library spirits than any one other thing I can find. Thanks for sharing with us your enthusiasm for the good ideas you hear about."
Mrs. Lou Hewlett, Assoc. Dir., Jackson-George Reg. Lib., MS

"I've been getting your Digest for several years and never fail to find some good idea that we can use. It's one of my most valuable resources."
LaVonne Leitner, Dir., Rampart Regional Lib. Dist., CO

"I love *LAD*. It is one of only two library journals which actually has practical ideas. I can count at least 5 in the last year that were a real help, and lots of others that were interesting and provocative. I wouldn't miss it."
Carol Hole, Outreach Supervisor, Alachua Co. Library Dist., FL

"All of the staff enjoy this publication."
Agnes Fansler, Librarian, Sun City Public Library, Arizona

CHAPTER I

Getting the Library Moving

June 1, 1946: Nashville now has a new City Librarian—and most happy am I to be he!! Mr. D. left the Library yesterday to enter the ranks of the Retired, and so, after three very pleasant weeks of working with him and learning my way around here, the grand old institution is now my responsibility and opportunity.

It's a great time to take over, too. The Library has just been hanging on for the past twelve years—until it is now about as weak as an institution can be and still continue to give service. Any action we take now must mean a step upward.

The Library does only a fourth of the business it should do. It circulates no more books than most libraries in cities one-third its size. I never thought our Brockton circulation was very high, but it was over seven times as high per capita as the Nashville figure.

When one compares the forty cities between 100,000 and 200,000 population whose library statistics are recorded in the latest ALA report, Nashville is seen to occupy the tail-end position on every count. In circulation, number of borrowers, library support, expenditures per capita, money for books, and circulation per capita, the Nashville Library is right at the bottom. It is the only one circulating less than one volume per capita.

I don't believe the public has any idea of this condition. In fact, I don't believe that the majority of Nashvillians ever give any thought to their library. The Library never does anything, or says anything, to occasion such attention. The average citizen doesn't even know where the Nashville Public Library is. Half a dozen times, when arranging with real estate agents to meet me at the library, I have been asked where the institution was located. "Oh Yes," they would say, "that's across from East High School" (where stands our East Branch), or "Do you mean the Joint University Library?" (located on the Vanderbilt campus). Perhaps they would have responded better to the name of "Carnegie Library" which is on the outside of the building and apparently better known.

However, if the public is not aware of the backward state of their library, the same thing can not be said of the librarians I met at the state meeting in Chattanooga last week. More than a few of them asked me: "What are you going to do about the Nashville Library? That's the deadest library I know."

To all of them my answer was the same: That we were aware of the situation, but that the Library had never had the money with which to do a good job. There is a lot of truth in that, and certainly that explains the situation as well as anything else, but we can't continue through the years with the same excuse—good as it may sound.

We do need more money—but whether we get it or not, there is still a tremendous amount that can be done. No library has ever approached the saturation point as far as use of the books it does have is concerned. We have a great many books—new and readable—that stand on our shelves most of the time for lack of readers. In short, we have sufficient books and library staff to do a much greater business; our trouble seems to be a shortage of readers, rather than a shortage of the wherewithal to serve them.

We librarians are always bemoaning our lack of funds to buy books. Maybe, however, we should make greater use of the books we have. Then we should have a better chance of getting the money we feel we so greatly need.

The answer at Nashville, as in most places, would seem to lie in a better job of advertising and selling what the library does have. A library can not go ahead without a certain amount of publicity, any more than a department store can. In fact, the library has the greater need for advertising. Most people already know what they can expect to find in a department store and have certain things in mind when they visit one. On the other hand, most of them are only slightly familiar with a library's resources and services and are not led there by such definite and known needs.

Many people will visit the library to pick up a specific title that is called to their attention—on a subject of particular interest to them—but the title must first be brought to their attention. This can be done in a great many different ways—but it must be done somehow if the books are going to be used.

The Nashville Library has had almost no publicity in recent years. No talks by the Librarian to local groups, no column in the newspapers, no direct-mail advertising, and little in the way of displays and exhibits. The Librarian has been too busy with the day-to-day details of his job to engage in public relations work, and there has been nobody on the staff to do such work for him.

That is the situation in most libraries. The staff go about their individual desk jobs and leave the planning and public relations work to the Librarian. The Librarian, in turn, seldom has the time, the inclination, or the know-how to develop a public relations program. And so everybody limits themselves to serving the people who come to the library and little is done about getting out and bringing in new customers.

It is so very easy to procrastinate on this public relations business. It is so much easier to settle down in one's comfortable office or let oneself become involved in the many fascinating little jobs of library administration—while the time flies by. The first thing one knows, another very enjoyable day is over—but nothing has been done about that bigger and more important job of library promotion.

Yes, it is hard for the Librarian to get himself away from the library for a few hours of personal contact work—selling the library to this individual or that organization. It isn't that the Librarian dislikes talking to people about the library; it's just that it takes a certain amount of energy to get out and through the business district—either walking, or driving and looking for parking places.

We do want to have a good column in the newspaper talking about the interesting new material that the library has. The Brockton paper was very generous in allowing me several full columns every Thursday, in a good position in the paper. I don't expect to be quite so fortunate here, particularly since the column will probably have to run in the Sunday Tennessean.

I hope to be able to sell the paper on the idea, and feel sure that I can make such a column more interesting and useful than the present series of long reviews which may create some interest but serve only those readers with sufficient money to be able to buy the books that sound good to them. The library column would be easier to read and would have the great advantage of locating the books it "sold," for everyone to come and get.

Perhaps later we can find someone who is capable of devoting full time to library publicity, exhibits and displays. The Library greatly needs such a person, as do most libraries. If such an individual could help to bring about an increase of 10 or 15 per cent in the library's circulation, while increasing the library's expenditures by from 2 to 4 per cent, his or her employment would appear to be a good investment.

■   ■   ■   ■   ■

June 3, 1946: Our biggest problem is one of personnel. This is to be expected, since the people who staff a library constitute its most important element. They are more important than the bookstock, or the building.

A well-trained, live-wire staff can build a real service institution out of any reasonable collection of books. Conversely, the best book collection will fall into relative disuse if manned by an ill-equipped group of library attendants. It takes people with book knowledge, imagination, and a pleasing and helpful personality, to get people coming to a library in any number.

I am afraid Mr. D feels that I made a great mistake in not snapping up some librarians who have expressed an interest in working in the Nashville Library this summer. But that is something I will never do: hire a librarian just because I need somebody when I would never choose her if there were other people available. A library appointment is apt to be a lifetime contract. And it is too difficult, if not impossible sometimes, to get rid of those who prove to be second-rate material. It is much better to make no appointment until the right person for the job comes along; one can usually struggle along some way while waiting for the person to appear.

Building a first-rate library staff is the Librarian's most important and most satisfying job. If he succeeds in this, most of his problems are over, or at least greatly minimized. Each good person he adds to his staff will make a certain part of his machine come to life. Every new appointee will, in turn, proceed to solve many lesser problems that fall in his or her area of service.

To me, building a library staff is like building a winning professional baseball team. It involves a close looking over of the young people coming up from the bush-leagues (library schools) and careful consideration of the possibility of trades with other clubs in the league to get experienced people. The Librarian should always be looking for the best person to play each position on his staff. He must always be alive to the possibility of strengthening his staff at different points—perhaps adding extra punch at his Reference desk, or in his Children's Department, or at some other strategic point.

Any Librarian would do well to appoint only those people he felt were so good that he knew he would not be able to keep them for long: they would either get married and leave or be enticed away by another library offering more money. For such a Librarian would always have an alert, vigorous staff, bringing new ideas and fresh viewpoints with them; at the same time he would be relatively free of the great superannuation problem that handicaps so many institutions.

At the present time, all of the Nashville Library's department heads and branch librarians are over the retirement age. The Board of Trustees is quite concerned over this situation, believing that these people should be retired but having no retirement allowance to offer them. The Library is outside the City government, being a private corporation, and hence library employees are not city employees and thus do not come under the city's retirement plan. Members of the library staff must work until they drop, unless they have an independent means of support. Since it is almost impossible for anyone to save any money out of a librarian's salary—in Nashville anyway—the older members of the staff can look forward to nothing but continued years of work. They certainly deserve a permanent vacation, with time to get outdoors and relax a bit, and we will have to find some answer to this problem.

■   ■   ■   ■   ■

June 4, 1946: Visited George Peabody Library School again, looking for good staff material. There must be fifty or more students there, but not more than four or five likely-looking prospects. Professional schools tend to draw a more studious-appearing student body. It is always such a pleasure to sight an attractive, animated individual among all the others; you feel that if you can get her for your staff, they can keep the rest of the school.

It's not beauty that I'm looking for, but I do want "my" library represented by interesting, happy, personable people. Certainly all those who are going to meet the public should be the type of people the public will enjoy meeting. It's not enough that they "love books" or that they have graduated from a library school.

As far as the public is concerned, the circulation desk is the library. The young people they encounter there represent the library to them. They are the only "librarians" that most readers ever meet. The rest of the staff, and the profession of librarianship, is judged largely by the performance of the circulation desk attendants.

If these young people know their job, if they are pleasant and make the "customer" feel welcome and at ease, and if they do more than merely check books in and out, the public will enjoy coming to the library and will feel that it is a "good library."

We have just lost a charming, uninhibited young lady who was the Acting Head of our Circulation Department and the perfect example of what a circulation librarian should be. Although with the library for less than a year she knew most of the patrons by name and would greet each one as if she were especially delighted to see him, or her. She would make each one feel as if he or she was the most important person in Nashville; you could almost see them puff up with delight and come alive under her treatment.

Such a person is as great a delight to the Librarian as she is to the people who visit the library. A few of them can brighten up a library and add years to the Librarian's life. It means so much to have people on the staff who are eager and responsive, who have a sense of humor, who are full of ideas, who are ready to try anything once, who are vitally interested in seeing the library go ahead, and with whom it is a real pleasure to discuss the problems and the future of the library.

I believe the average Librarian greatly misses having someone to talk things over with from time to time. Being a Librarian is apt to be a rather lonely position for most men. In the majority of cities under 100,000 population, the Librarian is the only man on the library staff. His contacts are pretty-much confined to women. There is nobody he can run out to lunch with—and talk shop.

For the last three years I have been out of the library field. The thing I welcomed most in the business world was my constant association with men, most of them my own age. And I enjoyed having a group of them from the office to eat with every day, instead of taking a hurried bite alone. Library work has many other attractions, but the absence of other men on the scene is one serious disadvantage.

To get back to the library school, I did pick out a few young ladies for interviews. With all of them I had to over-come a certain lack of interest in public library work. The group is certainly not public-library minded. Each one had first to be sold on this field of librarianship—which isn't too hard a job ordinarily, considering the variety of opportunities open to the public librarian. Most of this group, however, had visited the Nashville Library and, to be perfectly honest, it looks pretty uninteresting compared to the new Joint University Library's building serving Vanderbilt University and George Peabody and Scarritt Colleges.

To me, however, the attraction of the Nashville situation lies in the fact that it *is* so dead. There is so much to be done! The thing has almost no limitations. All the pleasures of planning and reorganizing and seeing something grow—and the sense of accomplishment that goes with that—are there in abundance.

The head of a public library has so much greater oppor-tunity than his colleagues in other fields of librarianship. He serves so many different kinds of people, he serves so many more of them, he serves them in so many different ways, and then there are always so many more unserved thousands awaiting his attention. Furthermore, he can experiment with new ideas and institute whatever new services seem to hold possibilities for increasing the library's business. He is a more independent operator than the head of a college or institu-tional library whose ideas must conform in large part to those of the administrative officer, or faculty group.

In short, public library work offers the greatest scope, the greatest amount and variety of opportunity, the greatest freedom of action, the greatest number of people to reach and the widest service area in which to work. And many of these advantages can be passed down to the lowest-ranking members of the staff. This is particularly true in a small library such as Nashville's where one can get into any work that interests him and develop it to the full without conflict with other staff members. In such a library, staff members are closer to the Librarian, closer to the public, and closer to the library's real problems.

I tried to make the point that salary is not everything, and that some jobs are much more interesting and exciting than others. One of these young people might be given a branch to run in a small library system, and that might be immensely more satisfying and happy an assignment than being just another assistant in a particular department of a large library.

I told these girls that we would be having several jobs of this calibre available very soon, and that meanwhile I was looking for some administrative assistants. This is the sort of position that should be established in every good-sized library. It offers the most interesting and varied experience that a young librarian can get.

We need one or two of these general assistants who will be available to handle special assignments, undertake new services, cover the schedule at the circulation desk in emergencies, and do whatever else is required from day to day. Generally, when a Librarian gets an idea, he has nobody that can be assigned to the thing, and consequently nothing comes of it. He should have someone to whom he can throw the proposal and say: "It seems to me we ought to . . . Why don't you take the thing and see if you can't get something underway for us."

Many of the Librarian's problems fall between departments, and many of his ideas are quite outside the present library organization. He needs assistants who are not tied to a particular department and who are thus free to follow-up new ideas, make surveys and special studies, plan displays and exhibits, and do a hundred other things that he lacks the time to do himself.

I went on to tell them that whatever department or aspect of the work was assigned to them, that would be entirely theirs to do with. They could experiment with every idea they had. I would expect them to plan for their department and make the necessary decisions concerning it. They would have all the authority and support they needed.

Authority must always accompany responsibility. It is impossible to do a job without the necessary authority. I feel very strongly about this after two years as head of a library in New England where I carried the responsibility for the library but did not have the authority to control the situation or take the action required in particular situations. I did not have the authority to hire and fire, to make certain decisions of a professional nature, or even to see that members of the staff carried out their assignments. If a staff member did not want to do a particular job he simply refused, and generally complained to the president of the Board of Trustees who then jumped on the Librarian at the next Board meeting.

The Librarian has to back up his staff members. Even more than that, he has to build up his people—with encouragement, praise and the opportunity to express themselves and make their own decisions. They must know where they stand, the importance of what they are doing, and something of what the future holds for them. Care must also be taken to insure that everyone is advised in advance of changes that may affect them, with a satisfactory explanation of the reasons for these changes so that there is no feeling of insecurity or fear.

Talking to these students, however, was somewhat of a hopeless assignment. Almost everyone in the graduating class this year is starting out with a salary of $2100 or more— a good bit above the Nashville Library's starting salary of

$1,500. I considered offering $1800, which is more than any member of the Nashville staff now receives, but it is dangerous, as well as unfair, to offer inexperienced people more than experienced department heads and branch librarians are getting.

■   ■   ■   ■   ■

June 5, 1946: Just heard that the young lady we most wanted from the Peabody graduating class signed up with Rex Potterf and is ticketed for Fort Wayne. What if the Fort Wayne Public Library *does* do seven times the business the Nashville Library does? I still think she would have a more interesting time helping to put this place on its feet. She would doubtless have more to think about and a greater feeling of accomplishment upon leaving the building at night.

This salary problem is going to be a tough one to crack. We are certainly not able to raise all professional salaries at this time to a minimum of $2100. Hence we are going to have to pay new people more than our older, experienced employees—or decide to do without any more trained librarians and get along with our present thinned-out staff. With only thirteen people remaining of the twenty who were on the staff in April, we are temporarily shorthanded. However, if the employment agency finds us a good Secretary, and we can dig up one more good circulation assistant somewhere, we ought to get by fairly well. By streamlining our library routines and eliminating unnecessary tasks we ought to be able to do away with a number of positions and save the cost of replacing the people who resigned this Spring.

For instance, the Circulation Department has been filing the book cards by author and classification number, instead of by date. It takes practically the full-time of an assistant to pull up and examine every card each day to see what books have become overdue. The cards are now being rearranged by date, doing away with a long, tedious daily task, and giving us—in effect—an additional circulation assistant.

The idea behind the old arrangement seemed to be to facilitate answering a patron who wanted to know whether a certain book was in circulation, and possibly also, who had the book. To me, the important thing is whether or not the desired book is available. If the books is not to be found on the shelves it should be sufficient to tell the customer that you are sorry but apparently someone else has the book.

It should not be necessary, and serves no purpose, to check the circulation records to insure that the book is in circulation. It is out, as far as the customer is concerned. And as for telling him the name of the borrower having the book, that would seem to be none of his business—to put it bluntly.

■   ■   ■   ■   ■

June 6, 1946: We ought to save $600 or more next year by getting better discounts on our books. In the past, the Library has purchased most of its books through local bookstores, receiving a 20 per cent discount. With our small book budget, however, we must do a good deal better than that. Hence I have arranged with the Personal Bookshop in Boston to supply most of our new books at a discount of 33 and ⅓rd per cent or better. They will of course pay transportation costs.

I expect to order the majority of the new books a month or more in advance of their publication dates to facilitate their earliest arrival in the library. In so far as possible, new books should be on the shelves by their publication dates. That is the time when the public is reading announcements and reviews and wanting to get hold of a copy.

The average book has a very short "life." If a library waits until a new title is two months old before getting the book into circulation it has simply lost a good part of the service of that book. It has also wasted book money, since a book worth $2.50 on publication date is not worth that several months later.

There is no reason in the world why a library can't have most of the new books available on their birth-date. For one thing, it can simply get its orders in earlier. There is no need for waiting to see a new book before you buy a copy, unless it happens to be a technical or an expensive book. The sort of books that a library this size buys are easily recognized and evaluated. One look at the author, or an indication of the subject content of the book, is generally enough to tell any bookwise librarian whether or not the book should be checked for purchase. Certain authors are "must" authors. A new novel by one of this group may be quite mediocre, yet one knows that the public will be demanding to see it and that, therefore, several copies will have to be provided anyway.

In the field of non-fiction the percentage of obvious choices is even greater. In such cases, one doesn't care too much who wrote the book or how he wrote it—he just knows that people will be interested in reading a book of that type. Then there are all the subjects that need better coverage in the library. There is a real need for a good book, or at least a new book, on a hundred different topics, and librarians know what these are.

In short, there is little guesswork or risk in selecting books for the average public library. If the Librarian considered only the amount of advertising and promotion given each new novel, and bought accordingly, he wouldn't be far wrong. Publishers are pretty good business men and they don't spend $5,000 or more pushing a lemon; when one reads about a big promotional campaign to sell a particular book, he can generally mark that book down as a strong candidate for the best seller lists. Furthermore, he can be certain that most book club selections are going to be "big books" in the life of his Circulation Department, although the Book of the Month Club has made some poor selections recently. A tremendous amount of time is wasted in the larger libraries, having new books read prior to their purchase. It is not only a great waste of staff time, spent reading, writing reviews, typing cards, and keeping files of the reviews, but more than that, it delays the purchase of the books and keeps them out of the hands of the public for an important period of time.

Some libraries, to be sure, have to be particularly careful what kinds of books they buy. A Librarian in a conservative New England city may constantly be afraid someone will run across a risqué passage in one of the books on the open shelves. For instance, when I was in Massachusetts I was attacked both publicly and at library board meetings for putting "Gone With the Wind" and "The Good Earth" (by Pearl Buck) on the open shelf. The third month I was in town, the headline of the local scandal sheet screamed forth: "Dr. Alvarez Filling Library With Dirty Books." The three big lines of type stretching across the page filled the top third of the front page.

But the Librarian has plenty of help in recognizing the titles that are likely to prove objectionable to some of his patrons. There are a dozen reviews available on all the big books and many of them will suggest that a particular title is "not for the conservative library." The Librarian generally knows well in advance of publication date which titles are what were called in Brockton "red-star books."

Up there, every book that contained any expressions, passages, scenes, or thoughts that were considered unfit for the reader of high school age was immediately marked with a red star and placed on special shelves directly behind the circulation desk. These books were then listed in what was widely known as the "red star book," and this book was well thumbed by the adult population.

My first move, on arriving in Brockton, was to remove this suggestive little book from the circulation counter. I could see no point in going out of our way to advertise these books by calling attention to them in such a list. We were in effect saying to the public: "We have gone over all our books and picked out the risqué ones for you . . . and here they are." And the public responded just as one would expect—just as they have to that fourth-rate movie, "The Outlaw." There was always a constant stream of requests for red-star books. Didn't make any difference what the story, or who the author. "Just give me two red-star books," people would say.

Any Librarian who finds himself checking many titles for order in the main body of the *Publishers Weekly* or *The Retail Bookseller* should wake up to the fact that he is getting behind in his ordering. By the time that a book appears in these annotated lists it is well on its way to publication. It should have been ordered considerably before this—from publishers' catalogs and announcements, from the advertising sections of the above two periodicals, from the Virginia Kirkus reviews and many other sources.

Not all of the new books entering the library need be there by publication date, however. Only the titles that are being advertised and that will be talked and read about and hence demanded at that particular time. Less important fiction and many non-fiction titles can be received six weeks after publication date without disappointing any readers. These are the books that people are glad to find in the library but not those they come looking for. And the only point in putting off receipt of some of these volumes is that the library can get a 40 per cent discount on the fiction by taking slightly-used copies from the Personal Bookshop's rental collection. We hope to save some money this way in ordering our mysteries, westerns, and light romances.

■   ■   ■   ■   ■

June 7, 1946: Signed myself up to teach a course in public library administration this summer at Peabody Library School—much against my better judgement. Don't know when I'll find the time to prepare for it, organize the work and put the thing over as I'd like to. I'll be too busy at the Library to give it any thought during the day. And I hate to take the time from my family on evenings and weekends, particularly so as I haven't been with them for ten months.

Certainly the teaching stipend isn't enough to compensate for having the course on my mind for the next two and a half months, as it surely will be. I shouldn't be doing it at this time, but took the thing just because of the chance it offered to get acquainted with a number of library school students and sell them on the idea of working at the Nashville Library.

My main objective is to teach these young people to think. Library schools don't always teach their students to use their heads, to question everything they do to see whether it is really necessary, and to try to find more efficient and productive methods. I want to turn out young people who will be keen and alert, always looking for ways to improve their work, and with no resistance to change.

Such an attitude of mind is a much greater asset than a good knowledge of reference titles and cataloging routines. Furthermore, I am more interested in broadening their horizons of librarianship, and increasing their understanding of administrative library problems, than I am in teaching them how to run a library. By the law of averages, no more than one or two members of the group will ever head a public library. Thus it should be more helpful to try and make good assistants out of them—to help each one become more the sort of professional librarian that other people who are library administrators will be very thankful to have on their staff.

Of course I may be thrown out by the rest of the faculty. If my students start asking their other instructors, "Why?", and demanding reasons for performing each step of various library routines, I may be viewed with some alarm by my teaching colleagues, nice and co-operative as they are.

.   .   .   .   .

June 10, 1946: Had a special meeting of the Nashville Library Board this afternoon to consider what might be done about the financial plight of the Library. With the cost of books up 15 or 20 per cent, the cost of binding up 50 per cent or more, and the cost of personnel up 50 per cent, the Library— with its stationary budget—is in a tough spot.

I pointed out the difficulty of competing with other libraries for new staff members. For instance, Mr. D. offered a girl a job for $115 a month—and got back a letter saying that the youngster was taking a position with the Memphis Library "for almost twice that amount." And then there was the attractive librarian from the Knoxville Public Library, whom I met at Chattanooga, who was getting about $2400 and was only an *Assistant* in the Reference Department there.

Also pointed out the fact that both Chattanooga and Knoxville, smaller Tennessee cities, had almost four times the circulation we did, and were serving their entire counties. As a matter of fact, we have a girl helping us out this week who formerly worked in Knoxville; she says the Nashville Library "can't hold a candle to Knoxville." And of course Chattanooga looks pretty good with their new library building.

Everyone was agreed that the Library desperately needs more money. They felt equally sure, however, that the Library is not going to get any appreciable increase this year. The City is short of funds, and other departments can make stronger claim to whatever extra money there is. As one board member rightly put it: This library is going to have to start at the bottom and build up support in the community, so that another year it will have the backing needed to get more money from the crowd at City Hall.

In short, it looks like a big public relations job—and one that is going to take time to accomplish. At the present time, the Councilmen have no idea what goes on at the Library, and your average citizen is no better informed.

The opinion was then expressed that the Library will never get any more money as long as it is outside the city government. The city will have to own and control it before the council will feel inclined to allot it more funds. After some discussion, everyone seemed convinced of the truth of this argument. It is, of course, true that the private corporation-type library does not receive the financial support given the average public library. The explanation is probably two-fold; Most of these institutions are in the South where all libraries receive relatively poor support; and then there is the natural suspicion of the private corporation, remaining outside the rest of the city administration.

The President of the Board then asked each member whether he, or she, would be willing to turn over the property and control of the Library to the City. All answered in the affirmative. It then became a problem of getting the City to accept the gift. Apparently, the matter has been mentioned before to the city authorities and they have not been interested in taking over the Library. For one thing, it would mean extra expense to the City—in the form of pensions to retiring librarians who would then come under the City's retirement plan.

It was finally decided that individual members of the Board would approach the five Commissioners—"the five mayors"—separately and informally, to set the stage for a regular meeting with them at a later date. There is no question but what the Library should be a part of the city government. However, the Revised City Charter—now in preparation—will have to include a section providing for the deeding of the Carnegie Library to the City of Nashville and the continued operation of the Library as part of the city administration—but with a library board imposed between the Librarian and Mayor, to determine policy and appoint the Librarian. Under the present Charter, the Mayor would appoint the Librarian, and the only board possible would be one with *advisory* status.

■   ■   ■   ■   ■

June 11, 1946: Visited the branches again. I've yet to enter a Nashville Library branch and find more than one patron in the building. The one at East Branch the other night I almost chased out. I hate to see anyone reading in such poor light and endangering their eyesight. I am sure the light in that building would not register over 2 foot-candles; it should be at least 30 f.c.

One youngster came in there to get a book on fishes and snakes. Look as we did, we couldn't find anything on those two subjects—so important to young boys—in the library. That gives some indication of the state of the book collections in the branches. They are so weak from subsisting on allotments of only a few hundred dollars a year that it would take several thousand dollars to bring each branch back to even minimum strength.

It is unfortunate that two of the three branches are so poorly located. All three are in the northern half of Nashville, and all are fairly near the center of the City—leaving the greater part of the city without neighborhood library service. Only the East Branch, across the street from a junior and a senior high school, may be said to be adequately located. The North and Negro Branches are good examples of what can result when library sites are picked without sufficient study of the flow of population in large cities and careful analysis of building trends in the local community.

The books in the reading rooms of all the Nashville public library buildings are, for some reason or other, pretty much limited to biography and fiction. All the material in the system on sociology, philosophy, science, industry, business, technology, art, sports, and other practical subjects is shelved in the stacks.

As I was telling one of the branch librarians, books—to me—are like people. They must be interesting and attractive and readable to get a seat in the main reading room—the living room of the library. We should have all our best books out there where they can meet the public and be seen and utilized. Not just the best books in a few restricted fields, nor everything on a particular subject, but rather, the cream of the entire collection. For instance, suppose that all the books in the library were dumped in a pile on the reading-room floor, and one then went to work to sort out all the interesting books and those that he felt sure would be read. Well, those would be the books to put on the shelves of the main reading room. All the rest, regardless of subject, would be shelved in the open stacks.

In the main reading room of the Central Library, there are 46 sections of biography, 4 sections of collected biography, 6 sections of fiction, and 2 sections of short stories. That's all! The subject fields are completely unrepresented.

There are eight or ten times as many biographies in this room as there should be. No library can fill 50 sections—300 shelves—with biography, or any other subject, without getting into pretty weak material. Certainly no library can keep all its material on a particular subject in the main reading room. Some of these volumes have not circulated since they entered the Library. Many more have not been off the shelves in ten or fifteen years.

The physical appearance of these books is enough in itself to repel any possible readers, and there are no subject headings or signs to attract the visitor's attention. Just a solid mass of old dirty books.

The five magazine racks are in equally bad shape. Most of the magazines are hidden inside black covers, few of which have labels to indicate their contents. They present quite an unattractive, forbidding appearance. There are also too many different magazines, and too many that are seldom used. The assistant in the room is keeping a record of those that are being used, and her report should be very helpful when it comes time to renew subscriptions.

Every book, and every magazine as well, must justify its presence in our "living room". Later on, everything in the building will be required to justify its continued existence with us. This is not a storage warehouse or museum. Every person, every piece of printed matter, every piece of furniture and equipment, must serve a particular purpose—and that purpose must, in every case, be clearly understood. We can not have the place filled with material that is here simply because nobody knows what to do with it—and what library does not contain plenty of material in this category?

■   ■   ■   ■   ■

June 12, 1946: Spent most of the day preparing a big order for the Personal Bookshop. It should run to about 400 titles, but probably half of the books have not yet been published. Many of them will appear in August, September, and October. Meanwhile, this order will bring us up-to-date. I'll feel more comfortable when the Library at least owns a copy of the books being reviewed and talked about today. I am uneasy at the thought that someone in Nashville will read about an important new book and come to the Library only to find that we haven't yet got a copy. I never want the Library to be caught in that embarrassing position, and feel personally responsible when such things occur.

The two high school girls that are helping us out this week—since we now don't have a single typist or stenographer on the staff—are doing a good job for us and having a wonderful time, typing order cards and getting the list together.

Am streamlining our order file, having the girls omit the source and date of the review, and making only one card but keeping it in the file from four to six months after the book is received. This will give ample protection against duplicate orders and save having to check the public catalog as well—to catch books that have already come into the library. Most libraries waste time in extra checking to prevent the receipt of duplicate copies. Making *one* file for books on order and books received is a simple way to save time.

Am afraid I never have shared the fear that most librarians have of getting duplicates. I have always limited the checking of current titles to a single file and, while receiving a certain number of unwanted duplicates, have found that these extra copies can generally be put to some use in the library system, or returned to the dealer. Certain it is that any money wasted on these relatively few volumes is but a fraction of what it would cost in extra help to do the continuous job of searching that would be necessary to insure that no duplicates were received.

.   .   .   .   .

June 13, 1946: Had several candidates in today for a job at the Circulation Desk. Had previously called several employment agencies to see whether they had any bright young people who had the right personality for dealing with the public and who might fit into the library picture and quickly learn the fundamentals of circulation work. Figured that if we couldn't get any trained people, we might as well pick the basic human material we wanted and do our own training. Many a good circulation assistant never saw the inside of a library school, and I'd rather have the average charming Southern girl working for me here—even if she has never been inside a library before—than some library school graduates.

I realize "them's harsh words", but the human element is so very important at that point of contact with the public. Somebody who can smile and show a friendly interest in each person who comes in the door won't lose us any customers. Of course, she should be educated and refined, and have an interest in books, but not necessarily a professional librarian.

It has always been a matter of concern to me that banks, and department stores, and business offices should have more personable young women working for them than libraries. I'm speaking of non-professional positions, of course. They seem to get a good percentage of attractive, alert, human personalities who can sell and give life to their place of business. And yet these places do not offer any better salaries, in many cases, than libraries. I understand the leading department store of Nashville starts their sales clerks at $18 a week, and many bookstores have capable girls, who know their books, at this salary.

The salaries of professional librarians, of course, constitute another story. Most of our professional staff are operating on 1939 salaries, although the National Industrial

Conference Board's latest figures show the salary level to be 52 per cent over January, 1941 figures, and 73 per cent over 1939 figures. In other words, everyone from the Librarian down is operating with a severe cut in salary. He, or she, can in no way purchase what he could before.

However, to get back to our two candidates, the first one sent over was one of the most beautiful creatures ever to put foot inside a library. And not one of the "beautiful but dumb" variety, either. A college graduate, about 30 years old, she had all the poise and charm and intelligence that one could ask for. I showed her around the building, and she seemed very interested, but finally decided that the salary wasn't enough to make it worthwhile since she could get more money teaching. She certainly would have been something for the "customers" to talk about.

■   ■   ■   ■   ■

June 14, 1946: Visited the book mending and repairing room in the basement. Miss Wilkin, our Head Cataloger, had mentioned that, in her opinion, the basement people were "mutilating the books". They have certainly helped to darken our stacks by putting ugly, black book cloth on the spines of a great many books. Standing in a row on the shelves, with their white ink lettering generally worn half off, they present about as unappealing a picture as possible. Looking at them, it is difficult to keep from plucking them off the shelves and throwing hundreds of them away.

When asked about this, our part-time binding assistant explained that they had been told to stick pretty much to the black, although they had disliked doing so and would be very happy to change to some lighter and brighter colors. So I suggested that she sell the rolls of the black, dark green and dark brown material and use only the more appealing colors in the future.

While I was there I got to looking over the material awaiting attention. Much of it clearly should be discarded, rather than rebound. The mending people were of course delighted not to have to bother with this worn material, the discarding of which cut in half the pile of work confronting them. We also set aside a number of good novels that should go to the professional bindery. It is not economical to put a home-made and relatively unattractive rebinding job on a popular novel that has plenty of life ahead of it if re-issued in a strong, attractive binding. It may cost a dollar to give the book such a setting, but a rebound book may circulate three or four times as much as it did in the original publisher's binding, provided it received a fair break at the bindery. Many a good book has been relegated to the wallflower class by a drab new covering and a home-made lettering job that is soon unreadable.

　　■　　　　■　　　　■　　　　■　　　　■

June 17, 1946: Miss Johnson came aboard this morning. She's the new Librarian's Secretary that the employment agency sent over ten days ago. Offhand I would describe her as an attractive, pleasant, capable young lady. However, what I'm most interested in is her disposition—and this will take time to find out about.

A secretary is a very important personage anywhere, and I would place a Librarian's secretary well up on the list. She is a key person. She handles many important jobs herself and knows about everything else that is going on in the library. She is pretty much the liaison officer between the average Librarian and his staff, interpreting one to the other and helping to keep the ship on an even keel.

There are all kinds of secretaries. There are the dull ones, the inefficient ones, and those that are hard to handle.

And then there are the pleasant, alert, efficient, loyal ones about whom it is impossible to say too much. Work can be exceedingly unpleasant with one type, and a great joy with the other. Having had both types of secretary, at one time or another, I feel well qualified to speak on this point.

One secretary never smiled, another was always smiling or in a mood to smile at a moment's notice. One could never be corrected, or asked to type something over again, without showing her annoyance and making her boss feel like a dirty dog; the other could do a job over ten times without seeming to mind it in the least. As one supervisor remarked at United Aircraft: "It never seems to occur to my girl that she is being paid for so many days' work—and not by the number of different pages typed. And she seems to take every repeat assignment as a personal insult."

Yes, there are all kinds of secretaries—just as there are all kinds of librarians!

■   ■   ■   ■   ■

June 18, 1946: Had our first staff meeting at 8:15 this morning. It's a good idea to get the whole team together at not too infrequent intervals, even if the Librarian does do most of the talking. It's helpful to have everyone understand what the library's plans and problems are—what it's up against and what it's trying to do. Just as each person should be kept informed as to where he stands all the time, so he should know equally well where the library stands. His job is of the first importance to him, and if he is really a member of a professional team he certainly ought to be taken into the Librarian's confidence.

Every worker wants to be proud of his institution or company. He wants to know how it is going to meet current situations and what its plans for expansion are and whether its business is on the upgrade or not. Moreover, he wants to be consulted on matters that concern him and be asked for his opinion or suggestions on matters falling within his departmental or subject field. In short, he wants to be treated as an individual of some importance and shown the respect that is due him.

I started off the meeting by passing out a few bouquets to deserving members of the staff. The first one went to a circulation assistant who fills in for the branch librarians when they are away on vacation. Somehow or other she had been given the same vacation period as one of the branch librarians. It was then a matter of one of them giving way, or having to hire a substitute to take over the branch when both of them were on vacation.

When the branch librarian wouldn't budge at all, this girl moved her vacation ahead a month. I had thanked her over the phone and later visited her at one of the branches to thank her again, but it seemed to me the rest of the library team should know what she had done—since their organization, if not themselves, stood to benefit from the saving of the extra month's salary.

Then there was the new assistant who had come up with a good idea. And the children's librarian who had gone ahead and prepared an interesting display. And finally the head cataloger who had proved a pleasant surprise to the Librarian by demonstrating her readiness and ability to consider new ideas and give up inefficient routines of long standing.

A cataloger is no easy person to reason with. She is apt to be too wedded to the involved routines that she may have learned long years ago. Consequently, I had not looked forward to the eventual necessity of tangling with the Nashville cataloger, particularly so when I heard that she was well beyond the age of retirement. But, as I told the group, she turned out to be a pleasant, understanding person, ready to consider new methods and willing to give up wasteful little tasks despite the habit of years. That's certainly something to talk about.

I then pictured the Library's present weak condition, with its pitifully low appropriation and a circulation that has been on the decline for the last thirteen years and is now at its lowest level since 1912. I told the group that I felt sure that everyone wanted to reverse this downward trend and get the Library back on the upward track again—but that the future was up to them. Explained that we would go ahead just as fast as they wanted, and were willing to go. Told them that I had no intention of leading them any faster than they felt inclined to go—that life was too short to wear oneself out that way, and that I was more interested in seeing that everyone was happy in his work.

Went on to say that I was confident that we could increase the circulation 25 per cent by the end of the year, and double it in less than two years. Pointed out that this is the rate we *could* advance, but that to realize such progress everyone on the staff would have to be willing to look with an open mind at everything she did and be willing to give up any routine or record that was seen, or shown, to be unnecessary. Told them that if we all worked together to try to find out, and do in each case, what's best for the Library, nothing could stop us. However, if they would rather go more slowly, we would simply take longer to climb out of the cellar.

Tried to show them where they came into the picture, and how they were all working for themselves, after all. If one member of the staff finds a way to increase her efficiency, it means a saving of time—and hence, money—for the library. The money thus saved in the salary account can be returned to the staff in the form of small increases or be used to buy additional books or equipment to improve the service of the library. And the greater the progress that is made in building our business and winning new library users and friends, the greater the chance of our getting the additional funds that will mean real salary increases for all the hard-working members of the team. Explained how we had put into our 1946–47 recommended budget a request for a high cost-of-living increase for all of them, but that since the Library does not now carry much weight at City Hall it is extremely doubtful that these increases will be forthcoming this year.

In short, to get this extra money that they so well deserve, everyone will have to work together to do the best job of which each is capable, to build up the Library and gather the support of satisfied and informed library users to register with the men at City Hall. It is important that every member of the staff see the relationship between more business for the Library and more salary for himself. One big failing of business management is that this elemental relationship is not made clear to the working man.

I then tried to emphasize the point that we build business one person at a time. People come to the library one at a time, as individuals, and must be dealt with accordingly. In short, we must concentrate on each individual patron as if our only job was to sell that person on the desirability of continuing to use the library, and make the library as useful and productive to him as possible. And one can never let up when dealing with the public. You can't be pleasant and helpful with the first ten, or twenty-five, people that come to the desk, and then coast awhile, doing no more than is absolutely required. The point to remember is that there is no carry-over in this work. Each encounter is a distinct and important assignment, for everyone is interested only in his own problem and will judge the institution according to how well its representatives serve him alone.

When a patron comes in the front door he should be viewed as an individual of the first importance, and treated as such. We should jump to assist him and be pleasant and courteous to him. Nobody should ever be kept waiting while the desk assistants go ahead with their own work or engage in unnecessary conversation. The average person will resent such a situation—whether in library, post-office, or store—and never forget it. People may forget good service but they will remember what they consider discourteous treatment for years.

People at the circulation desk should always be busy. When not checking books in and out they should have their own little responsibilities and special assignments. However, if they are not busy they should get out of sight—behind the scenes somewhere. It annoys many library users to see librarians reading a book or magazine or simply doing nothing. The explanation for this attitude lies in the fact that we are public servants. And many taxpayers don't like to see those whom they consider their employees idle. As some have been heard to say: "Is that what we pay taxes for?" or, "So that's the way they waste our tax money." Hence, staff members who work out in front of the public must always consider their behavior from an observer's standpoint: 'how will this look from out there?'

I then went on to say that every customer should be called by his own name. Naturally it is not possible to recognize everyone and remember their names. However, when the attendant hands the customer his library card it is possible for her to glance at the name on the card and then, while returning it and terminating the contact, say to the person; "There you are, Mr. Jones" or "I hope you like that book, Mr. Jones". Anything to bring in the person's name and thus recognize him as an important individual.

I have used libraries and other institutions for years, in many cities, and have never been greeted by my name. I believe we are missing a great opportunity to make friends for the library when we treat the public as just so many borrowers, or numbers.

Toward the close of the meeting I introduced Mrs. Benson as the new Head of our Circulation Department, building her up for the job and making it clear to everyone that she would be the boss of this department and that I was confident of her ability to handle the whole thing. In personnel work I saw so many people promoted to new positions of authority without anything being said to the rest of their department—with the most unfortunate results—that I could never consider making any change without letting everyone in any way concerned know just how the change will affect him, and clarifying the new lines of authority and responsibility.

Mrs. Benson suggested this change to me on Saturday, and it seemed an excellent idea. She has been in charge of our government documents' collection and working part-time in the Reference Department. Necessary work, to be sure, but we need her much more on the first floor. Probably forty people visit the circulation desk for every one who finds his way upstairs to the Reference Department. And the Circulation Department has been floundering ever since Miss Cathey left on the 1st of June. It is our greatest trouble-spot at the moment.

Worked out a schedule for the Reference Department and find that we can get along fairly well up there with the two people left: Miss Bell and Mr. Lewis. With Mrs. Benson moving into the Circulation Department, the opening there that we had hitherto been unable to fill is neatly taken care of at no cost to the Library. We have thus saved ourselves another $1800 or more—which is a lot of money in this library—and avoided the dangers that always accompany the bringing in of a new department head from the outside.

Before closing the staff meeting I offered to work out a five-day-week schedule for everybody—if they were interested in the idea. However, it seems that nobody likes working until 6 o'clock in the evening, which a five-day schedule would require, so we will continue with our present hours.

II

Streamlining all Library Processes and Routines

June 19, 1946: Miss Johnson and I spent the day cleaning out the Librarian's office. The place was just cluttered with old dusty material: Hundreds of booksellers catalogs and second-hand book lists, shelves full of old annual reports from other libraries, stacks of 20-year-old book lists for distribution to the public, worthless gift material, piles of notes of titles to consider for future purchase, scrap paper and blotters in abundance, and much more.

It has been the policy of this library in the past to ''throw nothing away because you can never tell when you may want it''. Consequently, every book, every bill, every letter, every gift item, every card record, that came in the library simply stayed here and piled higher and higher. The place is bogged down with the accumulation of material that should have been discarded long ago. This situation is of course common to libraries; it would be difficult to find a library that couldn't do a more effective job if given a good house-cleaning.

A public library—at least one of this size—should be streamlined to do a service job. It shouldn't become a store-house of books, or a research library for the scholar. It should be run more like a department store than a university library. The people it is meant to serve are the people who regularly use the department store and are used to its brighter, livelier, more up-to-the-minute atmosphere. They are accustomed to finding the latest material, attractively displayed.

A department store can not keep old material on its shelves on the chance that someday, someone may be looking for a ten-year-old item. A public library can not afford to do so either. It costs money to keep a book on the shelves, and it costs money to keep material in a file behind the scenes. There is not only the cost of storage space, but also that of cleaning and maintaining, indexing and recording, and servicing the material. And then there is the psychological or morale cost—the greatest cost of all. It is depressing to see old, use-less material all around you, and it makes you feel less able and inclined to really get something done.

∎   ∎   ∎   ∎   ∎

June 20, 1946: Today it was the ''downstairs office's'' turn to be cleaned out. First came the files of old invoices and statements. Then the file of cards typed for every gift item ever received. Such files take a good deal of time in preparing and serve little purpose. The only need here is for a record of the important gifts of the year, to go in the Annual Report. When I told the office assistant that she need make cards only for the few important gifts we receive, and keep these records only to the end of the year, she was delighted. It is no fun for professional people to have to spend their time on such uninteresting clerical tasks, and the Librarian must try to make their work more satisfying by keeping such assignments to a minimum.

When the shelves and files were completely cleared of dead material, the room took on a new atmosphere. We then went over some of the jobs that Miss Johnson will be doing in her capacity of part-time Order Assistant. When we were through, her job had been cut in half.

For instance, the former Order Assistant had to write the source, the date, and the price in each new book, figuring the discount on each one. The price was later transferred to the Accession Book in the Catalog Department.

Miss Johnson will write nothing in the book, for the source, date and price serve no purpose there. She will, however, get a stamp to put the name ''Nashville Public Library'' on the end and sides of the book so that it can be readily seen. This will serve to advertise the library's service wherever our books are carried, and help to cut book losses as well.

The cataloger offered to save more time by discontinuing her accession book, although accession numbers will be stamped on the books and the corresponding shelf list cards, as before. The keeping of branch expenditure records will also be greatly simplified. The Order Assistant will simply take the Cataloger's figures for books sent to each branch and multiply by average-price figures—for (1) adult fiction, (2) adult non-fiction, and (3) juvenile books. This will give her acceptable figures to represent the total amount of book money charged to each branch during the month.

■   ■   ■   ■   ■

June 21, 1946: My attention was called today to an item in the paper giving the department breakdown of the proposed city budget for 1946–47. Was rather surprised and quite pleased to find the Library ticketed for $50,000. Even though we had asked for $84,000 and explained why we needed that amount, the general feeling was that we would be lucky to get another one or two thousand dollars above our present budget of $47,000. When I called Commissioner Cummings to express our appreciation for the increase, acknowledging that he had done all he could for us, he mentioned that we might even get more—but not less than the $50,000 for next year.

With this increase, I believe we can do a pretty fair job. I lay awake last night figuring our probable income and expenditures for next year (I suppose every Librarian does alot of that) and was excited to come up with a savings of almost $6,000 from the current budget. Approximately $5,000 will be saved by the streamlining of the staff. Where we had 20 people on the professional staff several months ago, we now have only 15. And with our work organized as it now is, not one of the five people who left in the Spring will have to be replaced.

Combining the $6,000 saved and the $3,000 addition, we should have enough to double our book budget and still make some needed salary adjustments. With a book budget to equal that of the good old days—in 1928 to 1932—we should be able to make quite a start on the way up again. But we have a *long* way to go! And it will take more than extra book money to get there!

■   ■   ■   ■   ■

June 24, 1946: Spent Sunday afternoon on the banks of the Cumberland River, checking titles in the Standard Catalog for 1941–45 that, in my opinion, ought to be in the Main Library and its three branches. Checked 110 titles as the most important published—in the last five years—in the fields of philosophy, psychology, and religion.

I expected to find practically all these well-known books already in the Library. Was disappointed to learn that only 40 of the 110 titles were in the Main Library and only 4 of them were in any of the branches. This is a good indication of the state of the Library's book collections. The Main Library, in the subject fields, is no stronger than the branches should be, and the branch libraries are completely inadequate.

This served to remind me that while a doubling of our book budget may enable us to keep up with current publications fairly well, it is not enough to permit any rebuilding of our various collections. If we only had another $10,000 with which to buy the best books of recent years to give some real strength to the four book collections! We have almost nothing to offer in a great many basic fields, particularly in science, technology, and the arts.

Later on, we will have to sell people with money on the idea of giving funds to buy books in individual fields. The subjects chosen can be as broad or as narrow as the individual desires, but it would be his particular assignment, or hobby, to build up that small collection. We would, of course, put a nameplate in each book so added, honoring the donor, or someone named by him. It should be possible to make these little memorials a rather popular thing.

■   ■   ■   ■   ■

June 25, 1946: The Catalog Department is quite proud of its recent housecleaning job. They spent most of last week cleaning out all the old books that have stood on their shelves for years because nobody could decide what to do with them. All the Nashville items—books published in Nashville before 1890—were simply moved into the stacks, near the Tennesseana collection, and are to remain uncataloged. Certain shelves were assigned for different purposes and different types of new books, so that one can tell at a glance what the situation is in the Catalog Department and what kind of books (and how many) are awaiting treatment.

Was delighted to find the Head Cataloger sympathetic with most of my views on cataloging. She has been cataloging in the old, illogical way—just as if this were a large university library—but she seems perfectly willing to simplify things.

All the old cataloging stupidities are to be seen here. For instance, a book by Faith Baldwin is to be found in the catalog, and on the shelves, under the name Cuthrell, and a book by Grace Livingston Hill under the name Lutz. In a hundred other cases, the catalogers have passed up the name on the title page and used a married name, or "real name", that is unknown to all but the catalogers. As a result, the public is perplexed and annoyed, and can not readily find the books they want, and hundreds of volumes are mutilated by having the author's name crossed out on the title page and on the back of the book, with the "right name" printed underneath.

In doing such silly and unnecessary things, catalogers show that they are cataloging more for other catalogers than they are for the public. They are simply not using their good heads. They are not keeping their mind on the public who will be using their work, and are forgetting why they are in the Catalog Department.

Catalogers spend far too much time checking entries for books. The author's name is shown on the title page, but they will check "Who's Whos", the "United States Catalog", the "A.L.A. Booklist", authority files, and everywhere else to find the name under which to enter the book. There should be no question about it: They should use the name the author gave himself on the title page. That is the name under which he is known, and the name under which the book will be advertised, discussed, and sought by the public.

Why should we waste time digging into the author's private life, checking pseudonyms and married names? Why should we go out of our way to make things hard for the public. It is time we were practical and looked at things from the standpoint of the library user. Let us put all our books under the name shown on the book,—and stop all this checking.

I hope eventually to persuade Miss Wilkin to simply use the title-page name and forget about what the Library of Congress does. Often tell her that the Library of Congress, in the case of each book, is simply one or two catalogers—no smarter than herself—and that I would put my money on her judgment because she is right here in Nashville, near the people for whom she is cataloging.

She spends considerable time running around the corner to check entries in the Authority Catalog—which contains author-cards for all books in the Library. With a little more selling I believe she can be persuaded to part with this extra, unnecessary, catalog. There might be some excuse for having it if it weren't for the fact that the public catalog is only 10 feet away.

I firmly believe that one good cataloger, having the assistance of a full-time typist or clerical worker, can handle all the books entering the small and medium-sized library. A cataloger would immediately shake her head at this statement. But let's analyze the situation. A library with a $6,000 book budget can not buy over 5,000 books a year. That means an average of about 18 books a day entering the library. Two-thirds of these volumes will be novels and duplicate copies. Most of this material can be handled by the clerical assistant, with hardly a look from the cataloger. This leaves perhaps half a dozen non-fiction titles for the professional librarian to handle, and these—for the most part—will be the sort that offers little pause to any cataloger.

The entries, and subject headings, for the type of books that enter this size library are pretty obvious. In my opinion, a cataloger that can not meet the demands of such a situation and get the work out quickly and easily is not efficient in her work. She is either wasting time reading the books, or wasting time in unnecessary tasks, or bogged down in poor organization.

Yet it would be difficult to find a library of this size that can boast a single cataloger. When I went to Brockton I found three people in the Catalog Department, and they were taking six weeks, on the average, to get the books into circulation after they had arrived in the library. So we sat down together and went over everything they did—making every step justify itself. Why did they put this information in the book? Why did they keep these records? Why did they check here, as well as over there? And so on down the line. The usual answer was simply that they had been doing things that way for twenty years. So then I would ask them to play along with me and just try eliminating certain steps. By the end of the month, we found that we needed only one cataloger, assisted by a typist, and that it was possible for this one person to get the books out in two days—except in the case of unusually large orders. The saving in salaries meant as much to the library as the improved service meant to the public.

. . . . .

June 26, 1946: Am starting to go through the stacks—weeding out old and unused material that is well past its retirement age. Working at it as I find the time, I hope to complete the Fiction section by the end of the summer. If today's thinning out is a fair sample, we should eliminate a third of the novels on the shelves.

Most of the authors represented here are the old well-known names: Willkie Collins, Hall Caine, F. M. Crawford,

Winston Churchill, Cooper, Conrad, etc. It is not easy to be hard-boiled with these authors and take their books off the shelves. It goes against all one's training. Yet, they are not being used. And when books stand on the open shelves for ten years or more without getting a single nod from the people continually circulating through the stacks, it is hard to make a case for letting them stay there.

To me, it is like a landlord continuing to put up with nice, refined tenants whose only fault is that they just don't pay their rent. He likes having them around, but sooner or later he is forced to admit that he can not afford to keep them there and must give their room to other people who may be less worthwhile, but, nevertheless, are able to pay their way.

I will agree with those people who are sure to say that a library of this size should have all the writings of such men. A library of this size should also have people interested in reading the works of these men. However, if such readers do not exist, the case for having these books in the library is equally non-existent. Every book should be in the library for a definite purpose. Those volumes that can no longer serve a useful function can not justify their retention.

Many of these old titles might find readers if we only had more appealing and readable editions. In a great many cases their print is so small that I feel no compunctions about retiring them. I don't want people endangering their eyesight by reading such poor editions—even if the author is James Fenimore Cooper or Joseph Conrad. One advantage of discarding such volumes is that it brings to light the need for readable editions of a great many titles. As long as the book is shown by the catalog to be in the library, one is not likely to feel the need for ordering a new copy—one that might be read.

It is a shame that so many of the classics are available only in impossible editions. If I were in the publishing business I would put out more of these important old books in editions that could meet the competition of current publications. Every library in the country has the same need for many of these titles.

     ■   ■   ■   ■   ■

June 27, 1946: Had an interior decorator in today to look over the reading room and give us the benefit of her ideas for brightening the place. She suggested painting the bookcases a dark green to blend in with the light green wall. We are interested in painting only the ends of the shelves, the pieces between sections, and the sides and base-boards—not the inside of the shelves, which will be fairly well covered by the books. In her opinion, such a paint job would help people entering the room to see the books where they now see only the dark shelves.

Several painters whom we have had in to give their opinions have suggested the same paint job. They have also given us a bid on the cost of varnishing the tables in the three sections of the reading room.

If I were asked to say, in one word, what I thought library buildings most needed, I believe I would be tempted to say "Paint" or "Color". Most of them are so dark and gloomy, so drab and unappealing, so tomb-like that the average person is glad to emerge from them into the bright sunlight. In many cases the architecture is too big a handicap to overcome. But nearly everywhere, the skillful application of paint—in bright colors—would do wonders. The psychological effect of such a move on librarians and readers alike would be considerable.

Where painting is not possible, a great deal can be accomplished with bright labels, signs and display boards. Even more effective than this is the free use of book jackets, both on display boards and on the books themselves. They help to circulate books faster than anything else, as well as adding considerable life and color to the circulation hall and reading rooms. In a library this size, jackets can well be kept on most of the new non-fiction books while they are in the library, being taken off and stored at the desk while the books are in circulation.

Incidentally, if I were an author I would give close attention to the way my books were bound. I would never allow my publisher to bind them in dark covers, always considering how they would look on the shelves without their covers. This is of no importance in the case of copies sold to private individuals, since such copies will stay in their wrappers, but the future of all library copies is in no small way dependent upon the appearance they present as they stand on the shelves. The exploring reader sees only the back of the book, and the book with a colorful and appealing appearance—with its author and title clearly legible—has a great advantage over the book with a dark book and lettering that is worn off. A number of times I have decided against ordering extra copies of a book for the branches because I could visualize the appearance of the unwrapped books on the shelf six months after their arrival.

■   ■   ■   ■   ■

June 28, 1946: Had a nice letter today from one of our new borrowers. A week ago we started sending every new borrower a personal letter from the Librarian, welcoming him to the Library, calling attention to the upstairs department, emphasizing the fact that it was his library—supported entirely by the taxpayers—and not Mr. Carnegie's, and asking him to let us know how we could make his library more useful to him.

It takes time to type a dozen extra letters a day, but if we can reach that number of people every working day we will have made a personal contact with over 3,000 Nashvillians in a year's time. And that would seem worth doing.

Later in the day, I happened across the typist in the Catalog Department putting a D on all her fiction cards. Asked her what the "D" was for. She didn't know. Asked other members of the staff. They didn't know. Finally reached the Head Cataloger who offered the information that the "D" had reference to the size of the book. I then asked her why she went to the trouble of putting the letter on the catalog cards when she was probably the only person in Davidson County who knew what the darn thing meant.

If only library schools would teach people to use their heads more, and not to continue doing things unless they know why they are doing them and can see a purpose thus served! This insignificant letter D is not the only notation that has no business on a public library catalog card.

After further discussion with the catalogers, we decided to leave the number of pages off the cards for fiction, along with the author's dates. People are satisfied to know the date the book was published, without having to know the date the author was born. A case of two novelists with the same name would be too unusual to warrant looking up dates on all novelists; dates can easily be added in such rare cases.

▪   ▪   ▪   ▪   ▪

July 1, 1946: Spent most of the day going over the books in the Business collection with Miss Bell. When we were through we had taken a third of her books off the shelf. Most of them were twenty-year-old books on finance, advertising, salesmanship, marketing, insurance and the like, that have been superseded in the collection by newer and better titles.

It is hard to know what to do with this collection. Ten years ago, the Library maintained a separate business branch in the Chamber of Commerce building down in the center of the business district. Here, the books were well used. When the books were brought back to the main library and shelved on the second floor in front of the Reference Department, their use fell off considerably. They are well out of the way of businessmen, and few of the people who climb up the hill to the Library continue up to the second floor. There has never been a sign calling attention to the departments upstairs and they have generally gone the way of all agencies located off the beaten path.

I believe that it would be better to move the circulating books in this collection down into the reading room— once we get most of the biography out of there and have room for other books. Many of these business books are first-rate and much needed, and I don't like to see them playing the wallflower upstairs when they could be used on the main floor.

The business reference books could be moved into the reference department with all the other reference volumes, and Miss Bell could continue on up there as the alternate reference librarian—one of the two required to ''cover'' the Reference Room. In short, the business books would be treated just like any other subject collection. No reason why they, unlike other circulating books, should require an assistant to help sell them.

■   ■   ■   ■   ■

July 2, 1946: Coming back to the Library last night (I guess I'll continue to practically live there until the family arrives in Nashville: There's so much to be done there, and so little to do elsewhere) I again ran across one of our steadiest customers shaving himself beside the Library, using our outside faucet. For him, and many like him, the Library is really a home.

Every library has its small group of regular customers. These are the "characters" that become so familiar to the staff. Some people ask why all libraries seem to attract the old, the homeless, the idle, and the peculiar. But there is nothing really hard to understand about that. The library is the one friendly environment that is always open to these people. It offers warmth and shelter, a place to sit down, something to do, and somewhere to go and get away from their other, one-room, home.

The library is the only place where these people can go and stay as long as they want to. It is also the one place where they can go and busy themselves and feel important and self-respecting. I have heard some of the staff mention that they were so sick of seeing the same old faces that they wished that this group of "regulars" would never return. They will be back, nevertheless. The Library is more a home to them than the place they sleep at night.

■   ■   ■   ■   ■

July 3, 1946: Went over to the offices of the Nashville "Banner" and "Tennessean". Was sorry to miss Mrs. Douglas who wrote such a nice letter in reply to mine telling how much I enjoyed her book page in "The Tennessean". Stopped by to thank Miss Freeman for her two-page spread in the Sunday Supplement about the Library and its new Librarian. Believe she did a good job in making people aware of the Library and its financial plight, but am sorry she gave such emphasis to my desire to add "glamor and excitement" to public library service. Am afraid the public will be expecting something that they have little chance of finding here.

Had the two editors put a notice in their papers about the Library being closed Sunday afternoons during July and August. The Main Library and the Negro Branch have always been open on Sunday from 2 to 6 P.M. I had my doubts about the necessity of such extra hours, particularly in view of the fact that most libraries close on Sundays during the summer months, and so had the girls check on Sunday attendance and circulation. Circulation ran from 0 to 25, and those in attendance were pretty much the same old crowd, so it seemed wise to close down and, at least, relieve the staff of the unpopular Sunday work.

Stopped to meet Editor Nye of the "Tennessean" and see if something couldn't be done about starting the microfilming of the two Nashville papers. The bound files of these valuable papers are gradually disintegrating in the basement of the library, and it is imperative that they be recorded on film as soon as possible. The publishers of the two papers have been considering the filming of current issues—but nothing has yet been done.

Mr. Nye took me in to talk further about this matter with Mr. McNicholas, Secretary to Publisher Silliman Evans. McNicholas prefers to concentrate first on the current issues, as he believes this angle can be more easily sold to the publishers, although he admits that the need is much greater in the case of back issues. He will send up a Mr. Andrews to go over probable costs with me. I suggested to him that the State Library, the Joint University Libraries, the University of Tennessee, and the Public Library, and perhaps others, would want prints and might be organized on a share-the-cost basis.

.   .   .   .   .

July 8, 1946: Took off the shelves for discarding many of the reference books overflowing from the Reference Department. Don't see any necessity for keeping all the back copies of "Who's Who" and "Who's Who in America" when we now have the use of "Who Was Who" which gives us sufficient coverage on the prominent people of former years. Likewise, I can see no need for keeping all the back issues of Patterson's "Educational Directory", the "Insurance Index", and all the other standard reference tools. In some cases we will keep every 5th, or every 10th, year to provide certain back-year information—statistics, biographical information, and facts presenting a picture of the thing in 1920, or 1930, etc.

Many cities are having to build additions on their libraries, or entirely new buildings, simply because they have blindly kept everything they have ever purchased or accepted as a gift. This may be all right in a university or research library, but small and medium-sized libraries must remember what they are and what they are operated to do. It all comes down to a matter of library objectives.

It is hard for a librarian to throw out standard reference works, but when one's thoughts are centered on library needs and purposes, and his decisions based on the matter of probable use, the picture is clarified and the right answer easily recognizable. The matter is comparatively simple here in Nashville where we have the Joint University Libraries to fall back on in the event that we should have need for one of these discarded volumes. The patron is assured of getting the information he wants either way—but the public library is spared the expense of duplicating the storage of a great many bulky volumes.

I believe it is important to remember that the public library is an agency for the dissemination of ideas and not a collection of complete sets of books and newspapers. It is more important that it be a source of enlightenment and provide the information and ideas needed in its community than it have certain standard works and a great many individual volumes. In short, a library should purchase books, and retain them, only for the ideas which they contain and which are thus added to the resources of the library to enable it to do a better job. If the information and ideas in a group of books becomes out-dated or is surpassed by that of other books, then these volumes become hollow shells that have nothing to contribute to the dynamic institution that a library is intended to be. They are then ready for retirement.

■   ■   ■   ■   ■

July 9, 1946: Spent a busy day going over the list of periodicals received in the Library. We now subscribe to some 250 magazines, and receive some 200 more as gifts. They cost us several thousand dollars when the cost of binding them is added to the subscription cost.

Upon my arrival here I was impressed with the number of different magazines that filled five racks in the main reading room and more upstairs. Many of them were titles that I felt sure could have only one or two readers. Some were well-known old publications—Blackwoods Magazine, Contemporary Review, Fortnightly, Hibberts Journal, etc. The Library has subscribed to them, and bound them, for years.

I started the reference librarians keeping a record of the use of these magazines back in May and so now had their reports against which to check my own feelings about some of these unappealing and little-used magazines. It is unfortunate that some of our most important magazines, from the standpoint of their idea-content, are issued in such unattractive and unreadable form. These are just the periodicals that should be made to appear the most colorful and appealing, to compensate for their more serious and specialized contents.

Upon completing my check of the 450-some titles, and getting the opinion of the reference librarians on all of them, I found that we had marked almost half of them for cancellation. We will allow the gifts to come into the library but will not necessarily display them as we have done in the past. Miss Porter was greatly relieved to hear that she need not continue to go to the considerable trouble of setting out every little gift publication that comes into the building. We are under no obligation to display this material and, in my opinion, if a magazine is not worth purchasing for the library it is probably not worth giving valuable space to in our reading rooms.

We also decided not to continue binding a great many magazines that have been almost unused, as far as back copies are concerned, and have no possible reference value. In most cases it is easy to estimate whether or not a magazine contains the sort of material that will be called for in the future. The contents of many periodicals are ephemeral, or fictional, and it would be hard to imagine a future call for back issues of such titles.

Binding and preserving back issues of periodicals is an item of considerable expense in any library and it is important for the matter to be considered very carefully by the librarian concerned. This is particularly the case with titles that have never before been bound. For once a periodical is bound, all the weight is on the side of continuing its binding. Every librarian is reluctant to break up or terminate a bound set, just as he is impelled, for some reason, to fill any gaps that may be found in a set of volumes. Librarians are allergic to gaps in such sets and will spend considerable money to fill them, even though they may not value the set particularly.

However, there is no point in throwing good money after bad, whether it is completing an unnecessary set or continuing the binding of a little-used one. Yet it is a problem to find the proper disposition of such uncompleted sets of periodicals where their future use is doubtful. Should they be given to the Joint Universities, or some other library, or should we attempt to sell them through the book trade? Or should we just keep these bound periodical sets, complete only to 1946?

■　　　■　　　■　　　■　　　■

July 23, 1946: Attended my first regular quarterly meeting of the Nashville Public Library Board this afternoon. It was all such a pleasant contrast to those New England [Brockton] board meetings, and I enjoyed every minute of it. The members of the Board are all of the highest type—which is, I believe, more generally the case among the private corporation-type libraries. Indeed it would be difficult to find a better trustee group, although one might perhaps point to more active boards.

There are no standing committees of the Library Board, which is a good thing. Board members should concern themselves only with policy matters and the broad problems of library interpretation and support, whereas standing committees can only busy themselves with library details that could better be left to the Librarian. Any matter that is important enough for trustee consideration is important enough to be presented to, and discussed by, the Board as a whole.

The Librarian's report opened with an enumeration of all the resignations, appointments and promotions of the last three months—all of which were quickly approved by a blanket resolution of the Board.

The Librarian then told of the old and unused material that is now being discarded from the Library and invited trustee opinion regarding the disposal of this material. He was immediately authorized to sell as much of it as he could.

I next mentioned our study of the use of individual periodicals and the consequent checking of almost 200 titles for cancellation. Explained that a few readers might be disappointed by the future absence of each cancelled title, but that by no longer taking or binding these seldom-used magazines we could save enough money to buy an additional 750 books a year that would contribute more to the strength and use of the Library. Left the matter to the decision of the Board, and they unanimously decided in favor of the books.

The next matter to come up was the urgent need for brightening the reading room. Presented some bids for painting the bookshelves and was quickly told to proceed as I thought best. The trustees' reaction was the same when I told of the serious lighting condition in the East branch and presented bids from electrical contractors who would put in twelve new fixtures for $475.

I then presented a proposed budget for the year starting August 1st, taking the figure of $50,000 which represents our expected appropriation from the city. Even after setting aside $2100 for a Salary Reserve, particularly handy these days, the amount budgeted for Salaries was less than it was last year when the staff was larger.

The amount allotted for books was increased from $5000 to $7500, and this figure was broken down to show the number of books that would be added, at a particular average cost, to each library unit. For instance, we will plan on 1,000 new volumes of fiction at the main library which, at an average cost of $1.45, will require an expenditure of $1450. A sum of $600 was then left for buying non-current titles to rebuild the branch collections.

The Board seemed to like this breakdown, and the use of unit-costs, and proceeded to approve the budget without change.

I then suggested that the Special Fund collections, hitherto included in the budget, be set aside to accumulate as a Retirement Fund. Explained how the average receipts of $2,000, from fines, lost books, fees, ets., would provide regular annual pensions of $500 to four of the older people who could be retired this year.

It was, of course, for the Board to decide whether these people would be retired in the order of their age or in the reverse order of their value to the Library, as well as how many should be retired now, and whether all pensionees should get the same amount or those with the greatest tenure be given more than the relatively later appointees.

After some discussion, President Ewing appointed two trustees to work with the Librarian in preparing a pension plan involving the continued use of the Special Fund money. Such a plan would call for retirement in order of the librarians' ages thus involving all six of our employees over 65—and a pension that would vary in amount in accordance with relative length of tenure.

Miss Porter is said to be receiving a good pension now from Watkins Institute, so the money will only be divided among the remaining five. The next oldest employee is only 48, so that once we take care of this group over 65 we should have a long breathing spell before anyone else is ready to retire.

The next item for consideration was my recommendation of a $25 raise for Mrs. Benson, to accompany her promotion and compensate her somewhat for taking over the headaches and responsibilities of heading the Circulation Department.

Upon approval of this salary increase, I proceeded to advise the Board of my negotiations with a possible successor to Miss Hightower in the Children's Department, pointing out that this experienced and very capable person would have to receive $2000 to come to work here. One of the trustees did not think it fair to bring in a new person at what would be the highest salary on the staff, and so recommended that her salary be recorded as $1800 for the position of Children's Librarian plus $200 for Extension work—supervising children's work in the branches.

All in all, it was a fine meeting with a good deal accomplished—and the meeting only lasted an hour and twenty minutes. Several trustees rose at the close of the meeting to express "appreciation for the Librarian's fine report" and I heard one mention to another that it was the best meeting of the Board that he had ever attended. Well, the first meeting with a new Librarian is always particularly interesting, with its expression of new viewpoints, and I believe library trustees welcome any meeting that sticks to policy matters and gives them an opportunity to pass on interesting matters well within the layman's comprehension.

■   ■   ■   ■   ■

July 24, 1946: Sent a copy of the detailed docket of yesterday's meeting to the trustees who were not there, and wrote one of them who was to thank her for her helpful suggestions at the meeting. As I mentioned to her, however, I don't think it will be long before we will have to add a new staff member at a salary above $1800—our present top figure, when Mrs. Benson's raise takes effect. We can't hold that lid on for long, even if the Memphis Public Library and the Joint University Libraries are still getting new people for $1500.

■   ■   ■   ■   ■

July 26, 1946: Dropped in at the J.U.L. to visit Dr. Kuhlman, taking along the list of periodicals we had tentatively marked for cancellation. He called me yesterday to say that he had heard we were discarding some volumes and thought the Head of his Order Department ought to have a look at them first—which was just the thought I had had about these books.

They will check the list of periodicals against the Union List for the Nashville area, and then we can decide what to do about the few titles that are not duplicated in another local library. They would also like to purchase the back files of magazines that we will not be continuing, to fill out their collection.

As for the books, they will buy any volume of biography, regardless of the subject, that is not already represented in their collection. Money seems to be no particular consideration to them here. They will also purchase some of the fiction, wanting to build up their collection of novels by well-known writers. They may even take our $750-Library of Congress Catalog of Printed Cards.

Dr. Kuhlman was very co-operative, and I am much pleased to hear that the university library will be taking all our discarded books of any value, so that they will be remaining in Nashville and still available to the public should someone ever call for a particular discarded title. And then, too, we can certainly use the money they will pay for these volumes.

Looking around this beautiful university library it is easy to understand why the majority of men librarians prefer the college and university field. For pleasant, attractive working conditions, in a beautiful campus setting, located out from the center of town—away from its noise, dirt, and traffic problems—and serving an interested and appreciative intellectual group, away from the pressures and strains of public service, the college librarian's job is hard to beat. Yet I still prefer to head a public library!

■   ■   ■   ■   ■

July 29, 1946: Stopped in at the City Hall to get better-acquainted with Mayor Cummings and Commissioner Luton. Dr. Kuhlman seemed to think that the Library would have received more money from the city in recent years if theLibrarian had visited the City Hall and had some contact with the men there. I fear most of us librarians fall down on this point.

My next stop was Gilberts clothing store where I introduced myself to Mr. Byram, City Councilman and Head of the Finance Committee. According to Byram, my letter offering the Library's services to the Councilmen—to assist them in their work at City Hall—was an approach never before made to them. The Library certainly should be made real, through service, to these busy men—but I am afraid that if we wait for *them* to call on *us* we will have a long wait.

Called on Mr. Wills, the Treasurer of the Library Board, at his insurance company office. If I am going to know the members of my Board, I am going to have to get out and call on them. These busy people, interested in their own problems, aren't going to find the time to visit the library.

Mr. Wills was one of the four members of the Library Committee that brought me to Nashville. Yet this is the first time that I have seen him in the twelve weeks I have been in Nashville—and only a block away from his office. This is no reflection on Mr. Wills, or any other Board member, however. There is no reason why they should visit the Library. The chief function of a library board is to appoint a good librarian, give him a free hand in running the library, and support him as long as he is doing a good job. This, the Nashville Library Board can do, and has done, very nicely without making trips to the library.

.   .   .   .   .

July 30, 1946: Had a librarian in from Memphis to see about a job. Seemed like a very attractive and capable young lady—but she required a salary of at least $2100. We need her, and want her, but I don't see how we can pay that salary—even though she is worth more than the amount asked.

We will probably have to go to that figure before we get the four new department heads we will be needing this winter. We might be able to get one or two local people for Nashville prices, but the odds are strongly against our being able to pick up four such "bargains". The break will therefore have to come sooner or later, but it will of course be less expensive if held off for four or five months.

I figure that it would cost us $7,500 to add a single new professional assistant at the beginning salary now recommended by the American Library Association. This large sum does not include the salary of the new appointee—another $2160. It is simply the total of all the salary increases that would then be required to get all our present staff members in line with the new person.

While library school graduates are demanding and getting $2100 to start with, we have experienced professional librarians working for $1320. We have nobody making more than $1800. So if we take aboard a youngster at $2100 we will have to add from $600 to $900 to the salary of every professional member of the staff. Department heads will have to be raised to at least $2400 to get them above the new starting salary of the people whose work they supervise. The salaries of the clerical and sub-professional people will also have to be raised to maintain proper salary relationships throughout the library.

Faced by this large-scale adjustment, and the present lack of funds to effect such a change, it is easier to pass up these new people, particularly when they come up one at a time, than it is to do anything about them.

Even if we can soon arrange to raise all salaries and bring in new people at $2100, some of the staff may find it difficult not to be troubled by the thought that they had to work ten or twenty years to attain the salary at which the new people will be starting. That is a very human reaction, but one that unfortunately can not be helped these days.

I don't believe the Nashville Library has ever employed any trained librarian at a salary above $100 a month. Even the people starting early this year came aboard at $100. From there to $175 a month is a tremendous jump in a period of less than a year. Because of these low salaries we are not now in a position to take on any new people, trained or untrained.

.   .   .   .   .

August 5, 1946: Am enjoying my teaching job at the Library School, even if I do have to get up early and race across town to get to my class by 8 o'clock. At the same time, I wish I had more than six students as it does seem rather wasteful to give a course for such a small group.

I've tried to make my "lectures" as practical and informal as possible, talking largely from my own experience and presenting a variety of "real-life" problems for the group to consider. A good part of the time has been devoted to the principles of administration and the fascinating subject of human relations—all of which is applicable to any business or profession and will be useful to them whatever library position they take.

The last two meetings have been devoted to the broad problem of human relations in the library, something that every library school should teach and none do. Every student is looking for practical advice on how to conduct himself on his first job so as to get along well with his fellow workers, please his supervisors and get ahead in his profession. Every experienced librarian can offer the newcomer helpful tips on things to do, and not to do, and much grief might be avoided if the young librarian did not have to learn everything the hard way.

I know I made my share of mistakes in my early years. And my three years' experience in the personnel field taught me a great deal more. I spent a good part of this time listening to the problems of both supervisors and employees and learning what each party disliked about the attitude or work habits of the other. After encountering hundreds of cases where young men and women were being held back for reasons other than a lack of sufficient technical knowledge or experience, one could easily compose a list of the five or ten most often violated rules. And these rules are equally applicable to library work, and just as frequently violated there, too.

In a nutshell, all the rules or advice that one can give these young people can be covered by the Golden Rule's admonishment to 'do unto others as you would have them do unto you.' A good supervisor makes his people feel comfortable and appreciated because that is the way he wants to feel. He talks things over with them, helping them to get ahead in their work and praising their better efforts because he is looking for the same co-operation and credit from his superiors. He treats them with fairness and consideration because he knows how important such treatment is to him.

In short, people are pretty much the same wherever and whoever they are. They react in much the same manner to particular treatment whether they are at work or at play, and whether they are top supervisors or day laborers. As a personnel man, I found department heads longing for the same attention and appreciation from their superiors that their people were looking for from them. As many of them remarked to me when I would try to get them to talk to certain of their people whom I knew were unhappy: ''Why should I bother to tell Jones how he is getting along, or tell Thompson that he is doing a good job, when nobody ever lets me know how *I* am doing?''

I spent one two-hour session talking to the class on human relations as it affects the supervisor—department head or chief librarian—and the other one telling them what they ought to do, and should not do, as a beginning assistant. There are so many unwritten laws that cover human relationships in any business organization. There are just as many, and they must be learned and obeyed just as carefully in a profession like engineering or librarianship as in business. They should be taught in all professional schools—but they aren't. Consequently, many young people step on the toes of others and get themselves into embarrassing positions that work to their disadvantage.

It was pleasant being able to talk to these young people as we had wanted to be talked to when we were in library school, and to tell them things that I knew would really benefit them. As I told them, what they would hear in these two sessions was more important than anything they would hear from me in the entire course, and if they remembered anything of what I told them in these six weeks I hoped they would remember this.

It was gratifying to see how intently they listened to these two lectures. Several of them came up afterwards to say that this was just what they had most wanted to hear and that they valued these lessons above anything that they had received in their year of library school. And as one put it, "All this is equally applicable regardless of what we do after graduation." I came away today thinking that this teaching business is not a bad one at all, provided one need only teach what one feels is important and really wants to get across to his students.

■   ■   ■   ■   ■

August 8, 1946: Had a rather disquieting letter this morning from the Iowa librarian who had been expected to head our Children's Department. It appears that her husband won't be coming to Vanderbilt to study, and she will be staying up north with him.

Faced with the prospect of having nobody in the Department a week from now—when Miss Hightower returns to Alabama—we had to do some fast thinking. We needed a good children's librarian, at a price we could afford, yet none was available from any professional source of supply. It appeared that the only thing to do was to look around Nashville for a capable young woman who could pick up the work on the job. Then I thought of Mrs. Moncrief—a charming young housewife, in whose home I had recently been a dinner guest—and decided that she was perhaps the best answer to our problem. Here was someone who loved children and got along perfectly with them, and had the common sense and enthusiasm—as well as the necessary time—to make a good children's librarian. I felt sure that she could progress more in a year's time than the majority of library school graduates.

So I called her, telling her about the job and asking her if she thought any of the girls in her group would be interested in taking it on. I was hoping that she would say "How about me? Why wouldn't I do?"—and, fortunately, that's just what happened. So now we have a children's librarian, and one who will, I believe, help to give the Department the life and personality that it now lacks.

■   ■   ■   ■   ■

August 14, 1946: Judge Ewing arranged for me to speak this noon to the Shriners—one of the city's leading businessmen's groups. I gave them a fast 20-minute talk on how the library can help them in their business, and had their attention all the way. I don't believe any of them had any idea what a library could do for them. By sticking to the highlights and the services most likely to open their eyes and be remembered, it was a simple matter to hold their interest and sell the library to them.

As in the case of all such talks, I don't expect to see any jump in the number of our reference calls as a result of it, yet I feel that the Library has been benefited by having its services made known to these influential citizens. Men do not have to make use of a public institution for it to benefit from their goodwill and supporting influence. The fact that an individual has never used the library himself does not keep him from thinking it a wonderful and necessary institution for other people. Most people, to be sure, consider the library a worthy and desirable institution, in somewhat the same manner that many value the churches that they never attend, yet their support of these churches and libraries and museums might take a more active form if they were given evidence of what these institutions were really doing for others, and could do for them.

The Judge called later to say that the talk was the best publicity that the Library had been given during his years on the Board, and that it should be repeated before similar groups in the city. I would of course like to have the opportunity of carrying the library message to all such groups, but don't imagine that the invitations to do this sort of thing will be as numerous here as they were in the smaller city of Brockton where I was before the war.

CHAPTER **III**

The First Budget
Increases & Raises
in 17 yrs.

August 16, 1946: Had a good staff meeting this morning. Before closing the discussion, I mentioned the fact that a number of raises had been given recently, and more would of course be granted from time to time, and I hoped that members of the staff would consider these matters confidential and not discuss them with one another. I explained that my only reason for saying this was to keep people from being made unhappy.

As a Salary Administrator in a large engineering company I had occasion to put through several thousand salary increases where I was in a position to note their effect on the recipients and their co-workers. I am convinced that few people enjoy hearing of increases received by others, even when the recipients are their good friends. The average person is likely to feel somewhat uneasy when he learns of raises going to some of his colleagues. He is likely to wonder whether or not he is slipping backwards in the competitive business world, and whether other men are being favored over him. It's a case of a person's being happier for what he doesn't know.

I feel certain that the girls on the staff, as nice as they are, are not going to be made happy by hearing of other people's raises. It makes little difference whether or not one has also been favored. There's a great deal more satisfaction to be had in feeling that you have been singled out for advancement—and are thus moving ahead in relation to the others. There's little pleasure to be had from a raise that you know to be merely part of a general increase in the salary level of the institution. In short, what one makes is generally of less concern that one's standing with relation to his fellow workers. And the pleasure derived from an increase in salary is in inverse proportion to the number of other people known to have been so favored.

Then too, many recipients of raises have had their happiness blasted by hearing that someone else received a greater increase. It often seemed that there were more cases of unhappiness than happiness among those receiving increases. Many a time we thought some young engineer would be pleasantly surprised to hear that he had received a $20-a-month raise, only to have him come into the office demanding to know "How come John Jones got a $25 raise—and I only got $20?" He would have been happy with a $15 increase if he felt that nobody around him had been favored over him, but as it was he was dissatisfied with $20.

We had to listen to a great many salary complaints in that position. Almost all the complainers would admit that they were well paid, and probably getting more than they were worth, but they still felt aggrieved at making less than someone else. All of them would point to someone making more than they were, and claim an injustice. But whenever attention was called to the fact that they made more than all the rest of their group, their reply was always, "I'm not concerned with what other men make." Most of the men compared their salary with those of their college classmates, or others who started with the Company at the same time, and whenever one of these salaries was discovered to be greater than theirs, there was sure to be a complaint. The fact that the individuals concerned were different human machines, doing different jobs in different departments under different supervisors, apparently made no difference to them; each still felt he should be making as much money as any of the rest.

In view of this experience, I thought it best to emphasize the fact that I considered a raise to be a very personal matter, involving only the Library and the recipient, and that I would be very sorry to hear that any member of the staff had suffered distress at the hands of a thoughtless colleague. I feel that raises should serve as instruments to build morale and inspire their recipients to even greater heights—not to destroy the morale of the group.

■   ■   ■   ■   ■

August 20, 1946: Visited the Chairman of the Finance Committee of the City Council at his place of business this morning and left him a copy of our proposed new salary schedule. He seemed impressed with my recent letter telling the Councilmen of the ways that the Library could be helpful to them and inviting them to call on it.

Feel like a big load has been lifted from my shoulders today with the conclusion of my summer teaching at Peabody Library School. Gave the students their final exam this morning and thought of that Biblical quotation, "It is more blessed to give than to receive." The three questions that I posed for them were more in the nature of problems that called for good common sense rather than the remembrance of facts and figures.

Agreed to talk to the delegates who will be coming here for the meeting of the State Federation of Music Clubs. Had to think awhile for a subject to talk about, but believe I have an adequate one now in the phonograph record collections that many libraries now boast. There is no better means for instilling a love of music in our young people, or for encouraging an interest in music in adults who can not afford to buy the records that they would like to listen to and have no other access to recorded music. It seems to me that these music club members would really go for the idea of these free circulating collections and be interested in furthering such a program in their local libraries.

.   .   .   .   .

August 22, 1946: Reading in this morning's paper that the Finance Committee of the City Council was going to meet in the War Memorial Auditorium at 10 o'clock to go over the budget requests of the various City Departments, I decided to pay a visit to these Councilmen. I remembered that the Library Board had emphasized the fact that the Library had not had a budget increase in the last 17 years, since 1929, and that no library staff member had had a raise since then either, and that there was no possibility of the Library receiving any more money this year. ''So don't even think about it.'' However, I felt that I just couldn't pass up this opportunity and so went to the Auditorium and knocked on the door of the meeting room.

The Councilmen were surprised to see me but immediately invited me to say what was on my mind. I started by asking them if they were aware that we didn't have a single clerk or typist in the Library making over $70 a month. The

Councilmen were astounded. They all knew that the clerk-typists in the other city departments, under Civil Service, are getting $175 a month. I was careful not to mention the librarians in any way as that would have simply muddied the water. City councilmen know what clerk-typists do, and what they should be paid; none of them, on the other hand know what a professional librarian does or what she should be getting in salary. To bring up the librarians would only have confused these men and made them feel unprepared to come to any decision in this matter.

Every one of the Councilmen was interested and sympathetic. One of them turned to me and asked how much I figured it would take to straighten out this situation and put my new salary schedule into effect. Reaching in my mind for a figure, I told him $5,900. He then moved that the Library be given an additional $6,000. All of the others quickly voted their approval of this resolution. I quickly thanked them and left the room. I don't believe I was there a full five minutes. And in that time I was able to secure a 12½ percent increase in our budget that was totally unexpected.

I floated all the way back to the Library and quickly called the President of the Library Board to give him the good news. He just couldn't believe it. He kept asking, ''Are you sure? Are you sure?'' He truly was as pleased as he was surprised.

I then gathered all the staff members who weren't busy with the public and told them of our good fortune. I told them we could do either of two things with this extra $6,000 and I would be guided by their feelings in this matter. We could of course spread the money around the staff, giving everyone a sizable and long-deserved increase in salary, or we could use the money to buy more library materials and brighten our library buildings, all to the end of increasing library use and securing a real boost in our library income next year. To me, it posed the same old question that farmers have to deal with: "Do you put your extra money into the farmhouse, which adds to your comfort but doesn't produce anything, or do you put it into improving your barn, which will make more money for you in the future?

Almost without hesitation, everyone present voted to go the second way. They felt the Library was now on the right track and if we continued to go forward and build library service with some of the new ideas I'd been talking to them about, we would all experience a 1947 that would be far greater than the present year, and individually and collectively we would all be better off. On the other hand, if the money just went to the staff, the service of the library and its future support would be deprived of its chance to bloom, which would have an adverse effect on all library workers and users. I couldn't have been more pleased and proud of my fellow staff members. With that spirit I'm sure we'll all experience that great future for the Library and for ourselves.

> ■   ■   ■   ■   ■

August 26, 1946: The painters arrived this morning to begin the long-awaited job of brightening up the main reading room. With three men wielding paint brushes, and having to do only the sides, molding, shelf-edges and partitions, the book shelves quickly took on their new green color. Fortunately, it was found possible to paint the shelves without removing the books. We couldn't afford to have the insides of the shelves painted, but—filled with books—the shelves look almost as good as if they had the complete paint job. The musty old books, on the other hand, look even more worn and drab in their bright new setting, and everyone will be relieved to see them replaced with some better-appearing volumes from the stacks. However, I am not sure that there are enough attractive and readable books in the entire library to fill this one big, three-section room.

■   ■   ■   ■   ■

August 27, 1946: Some of the staff members thought yesterday that the new green color was too bright and grassy and that a grayer green would be better. So this morning I had the painters experiment with a different shade of green and then called in the staff to kibitz and select the shade they wanted. Everyone seemed well pleased with the new softer shade of green, so the painters proceeded to use this color for the shelves' second coat.

Had two carpenters in this morning to put up three new sections of shelving where magazine racks had formerly stood against the wall. We have a good deal of extra shelving in the basement that is now holding the old, unwanted material that came to the library in the Victory Book Campaign. It is a simple matter to cut these shelves to the right heighth and width and set them in place upstairs so that they match the appearance of the rest of the shelving.

We are painting only two magazine racks and passing up the other six. These two racks will hold between 60 and 75 magazines—the number of popular titles that we want to keep in the main reading room. Many of the magazines now in this room are unimportant gift titles, many more are on the list to be cancelled as being little-used, and the remainder are technical, business and special-interest periodicals that we plan to remove to the room adjoining the Reference Department on the second floor.

I certainly wish we could do something about our newspapers. The papers left on the tables detract from the room's appearance, and the presence of the newspapers in the building attracts the loafers and fills up the chairs with the same old group of non-serious readers. We have considered putting the newspapers in every conceivable location in the building, and I trust that some solution to this problem can be found. Meanwhile, the painters are busy shellacking and varnishing the twelve long tables in the three connected reading rooms, and it is good to see everything looking so clean and bright.

.   .   .   .   .

September 3, 1946: Am proceeding with the weeding of our fiction collection, in the stacks, at the same time picking out the few fairly attractive novels for removal to the new shelving in the reading room. This is the start of the big book shift that may mean moving most of the books in the library but is absolutely necessary if we are going to achieve the best possible arrangement of our book resources. When we get all our most attractive, readable, and useful books—in all subjects—in the reading rooms, and move everything else into the stacks, I am sure that our circulation will take a jump upward.

The reading rooms are likely to be upset for several months until (1) the fiction in the stacks is completely weeded, (2) the novels remaining on the shelves are compressed into two-thirds of their present stack space, (3) the best of the biography now filling the reading rooms can be picked out, (4) the majority of the biographical material can be removed to the vacated fiction stack sections, and (5) the best books in all other subject fields can be brought out of the stacks and placed on the shelves in the reading rooms.

The job could be done in less time if we started with some reserve shelves onto which books could be moved. As it is, we can not move any books anywhere without first moving another group of books to make room on the shelves. For this reason, the first move in the above succession of steps must be the big weeding job now underway.

Am averaging six sections of fiction a day—which means the handling and consideration of over 700 volumes. Perhaps 40 percent of them are being carried into the Catalog Department for discarding. The shelves already look much better now that they are no longer filled to the floor and have been relieved of their oldest and dirtiest volumes. There are still many old books left on the shelves, but practically all those with very small type, dirty pages, weakened bindings, and those that have circulated only once or twice in the last ten years, have been removed.

■   ■   ■   ■   ■

September 9, 1946: Had a high school boy in this afternoon to help clean out the two basement storerooms that have been filled for years with old books that somebody hated to throw away completely. We are anxious now to get rid of these useless volumes, as well as all those that are piled on the floor and stacked on shelves in the basement hallway. The removal of these old books and the other discarded material lying around in cardboard boxes would certainly improve the entrance to the Children's Department.

Plans for improving this department are developing daily. It's the result of having two lively young ladies working and planning together. They are bound to stimulate each other's imagination and together build up the courage to strive for, and ask for, things that they might not individually seek. We were indeed fortunate in being able to get Mrs. Workman, a former children's librarian, back to show Mrs. Moncrief the ropes and work with her for a month or two.

It is good to have extra money so that when they ask if they can spend some money for this or that purpose it is only a question of asking how much money they want and then telling them to go ahead with their plans. I guess everybody likes to be able to say "Yes" to such requests, and I particularly want to encourage and keep happy these two members of the staff who have already breathed new life into the Children's Department.

This afternoon I gave them the keys to my car and sent them out to the Peabody Demonstration School to look at the library there which stands out in my mind for having the back of its bookshelves painted a bright red. As I expected, they came back planning to put Chinese red on the back of their shelves. They also plan to paint the walls, and I can see that they have no intention of stopping there.

.   .   .   .   .

September 12, 1946: Was pleased to receive complimentary letters from four members of the Library Board who were thrilled to learn that the City Council had just voted the Library an additional $6,000. They were all equally amazed by the Librarian's "single-handed effort" which gave the Library the largest appropriation it has ever had. My letter to them reporting on my interview with the Finance Committee and the subsequent action of the Council had come as a complete surprise to them.

.   .   .   .   .

September 17, 1946: Finished weeding the biography in the reading room. Hate to see all the little-used biographies that have been added in the last five years—people whose names are almost unknown, and whose biographies have consequently not been read. It does not seem right to remove from the collection so many books that have so recently been added to it, but one must be practical and consistent in judging the future use of each volume.

I suspect my predecessor was more of a scholar than I will ever be. He seems to have spent more time checking second-hand book dealers' catalogs than current lists. I am always running into groups of p-slips on which he wrote the necessary information for the future ordering of hundreds of these volumes. The Library's acquisitions of this period suggest the university library background of this fine bookman. I, on the other hand, must confess that I haven't even looked at one of the many booksellers' catalogs which come to us in a steady stream, and don't plan to give them any attention for a great many months. We will have to have more book money, and more readers, and do a much better job of supplying the current books of importance before I will feel that I can afford the time and money to check catalogs of older and more specialized titles.

> ■   ■   ■   ■   ■

September 18, 1946: The shelves in the Children's Department look great with their bright red backs. The rest of the staff appears quite impressed, and maybe a little envious. Miss Bell seems anxious to have the Reference Room similarly brightened.

Lorenzo—our janitor/handyman—has concocted a wonder-working liquid that is doing a rather effective job of lightening the dark woodwork in this room. He calls it "February 30th" and won't disclose its secret formula. The children's librarians are enthusiastic over the awakening of their Room and make much over Lorenzo. They believe that he should be taken off his janitorial job and assigned the job of applying paint and "February 30th" all over the building. Actually, his co-worker, Noel, is now doing most of the janitorial work, permitting Lorenzo to spend most of his time on the brightening of the building. We are indeed fortunate to have two such loyal, pleasant and helpful workers at the main library. Nobody knows their age, but they must be close to 70. The rejuvenation of the building seems to have given them new life, too, and new pride in their work. I expect Lorenzo is wondering what "Dr. Avareez" is planning to do next.

■   ■   ■   ■   ■

September 19, 1946: Was gratified to hear a visiting book salesman remark on the new atmosphere around the Library and the "more life and enthusiasm" of the staff members. A number of patrons have made the same comment recently.

Was also pleased to hear from one of the girls at the circulation desk that one of the trustees had come in and chanced to ask how the staff liked their new boss—and had then remarked that "the Trustees do too." Guess we all like to hear that others like us or are pleased with our work—and such news is particularly welcome to anyone starting out in a new job and in a new community.

Everyone has begun to watch the circulation these days to see whether we are beginning to move and to show gains over the record for the same period a year ago. For the past few months, the first thing I do in the morning is to go out to the circulation desk and ask the people there, "Well, how did we do yesterday?" By now, everyone knows what I'm interested in and going to ask, so they are prepared with the answer and give me the figures before I can ask for them. I'm a competitor and I care how we are doing, and I want my staff to care just as much. The more they are concerned about our progress, which is best measured now by our circulation figures, the better job they are going to do and the more enjoyment and satisfaction they will get from their work. It's my job to always set an example that will help my fellow workers derive some of the same benefits from their job that I do.

So far this month, we appear to be running a good 35 per cent ahead of last year's adult circulation at the main library. I don't check on the juvenile circulation every day but it's climbing at an even faster rate than the adult circ. What an interesting and delightful job! This place is like a three-ring circus!

■   ■   ■   ■   ■

September 20, 1946: Had a committee in to see me from the County P.T.A. They have long been interested in the idea of a county library and wanted to get my reactions to the thing. Their leader said she had heard from Judge Ewing that I was an ''expert money-getter'' and so was hopeful that I would be able to help them. They have asked Mr. Ewing, a member of the County Court, to bring up a resolution calling for a county-wide library service at the next meeting of the Court. Since this meeting is scheduled for October 1st, they are not allowing themselves any time for a publicity campaign.

What they have in mind is a simple request for $5,000—the same thing that Mr. D. and his predecessors have asked for year after year. They feel that the County Judge is the stumbling block: He apparently doesn't want to make an appropriation and jeopardize his present low tax rate, and he—along with some of the other magistrates—doesn't believe that the people in the county will read.

With Judge Hickman still feeling as he does, and with no time or ammunition to change his mind, it seemed to me that their chances of getting such an appropriation were almost non-existent. On the other hand, I did not want to throw a wet blanket on their enthusiasm; it's so seldom that one can get outside groups really interested in library goals. So I suggested an alternative request that seemed to offer more hope of the Judge's acceptance. All that would be called for would be a contract between the Nashville Public Library and the County Library Board, which the County Court could appoint as the other contracting party, whereby the municipal library would provide service to residents of the County and later be reimbursed by the County Court at the rate of 25¢ a volume borrowed. That is our present unit cost of service to Nashvillians.

It seemed to me that the members of the County Court would welcome such an arrangement as the easiest and most economical way of solving the "county library problem." Such a plan would not require a large appropriation on the part of the County Court, and county library service could be developed gradually and with the least effort on everyone's part. Furthermore, such an arrangement would give assurance to the county magistrates that county funds would be spent only for service to county residents, thus dispelling their fears that some of the money might be spent on the municipal library system. And if the Judge is right in thinking that the county people don't want to read, then the County is not out any money in discovering this fact. Another selling point would be the fact that all payments would be for "services rendered", rather than for "services expected."

The Nashville Library would immediately place its 130,000 volumes and its trained personnel at the service of all county residents, and would do everything it could to take books out into the County, by means of deposit stations and a bookmobile. The county service would, of course, be on a small scale until the library was in a position to carry the books to the people. Yet it would be a start—and better than things are now.

At present, the Library is receiving approximately $600 from county residents able to pay the non-resident fee. At the same time, it is turning away more county people who cannot afford to pay the $2.00 a year. Under the suggested contract, the Library would lose the $600 it now receives in non-resident fees, but should get this amount—and more—from the County through the circulation of books to all the county people interested in such service. It would immediately place county residents in the same class with city residents, as far as library service is concerned.

The committee seemed very much interested in this alternative plan, so I arranged to send them a letter explaining the contractual arrangement, which they could have copied and mailed to each of the 42 magistrates of the Court so that these men would be prepared to consider Mr. Ewing's resolution at their next meeting.

■   ■   ■   ■   ■

September 23, 1946: Mrs. Whitley left today—and the poor Circulation Department is really in a hole! She came in Friday to tell me that she had lined up a job as a high school librarian in the public school system. It wasn't too great a surprise, however, as I knew that she had long been wanting a job with better hours where she wouldn't have to work an evening a week and occasional Sundays.

Well, we can't compete with the high schools on the matter of working hours—any more than we can match them in salaries—so she is leaving us. The hard part about it is that she is giving us only two days' notice. The Supt. of Schools says she has got to be working for him by tomorrow. I am surprised at such a seemingly thoughtless and unreasonable demand, though I realize that he probably could not offer her more time. However, it seems to me that somebody might have called us to ask if we could arrange to let her go that soon. Still, I don't want to do anything to endanger her new position so will let her go and try somehow to replace her. But that does leave only two full-time people in the Circulation Department and they will be really up against it until we can find two more people.

.   .   .   .   .

September 25, 1946: Spent as much time as I could find today on a brochure setting forth the advantages of regional libraries and a state-wide library service. Mrs. McHorris, the President of the Tennessee Citizens' Library Association, wants something that she can hand out at the P.T.A. meetings which she attends as Chairman of the Library Committee of the State P.T.A.

.   .   .   .   .

September 27, 1946: Had Martha Parks call Miss Jones in the County Education Department to see if she had had a chance to talk to Judge Hickman. Miss Jones reported that the Judge was interested in my suggestion for free county library service and asked that I drop in and see him in November to tell him more about the idea. According to Hickman, it is too late to put the matter on the agenda for the October meeting of the County Court and he would rather wait until January. So I called the president of the County P.T.A. to call off the sending of letters to the 42 magistrates. We certainly want to play along with the Judge, at least until January.

Miss Parks seemed to feel that I had sold Miss Jones on the idea, so there is some hope that the Judge will finally go along on the matter of library service to the people living outside the City of Nashville. I was rather relieved to learn that the matter would be held up for three months since we are much too busy now to think about county service.

■   ■   ■   ■   ■

September 28, 1946: Mrs. D., one of the Library Trustees, was kind enough to drop in to say how pleased she was with the way things were going. While showing her the Children's Room with its brightened shelves, I half-jokingly remarked that we were going to advertise the Room to mothers as a wonderful place to leave their children while they were shopping. She was immediately interested and mentioned a Mrs. Douglas who was anxious to establish a nursery in the YWCA for this purpose. She called Mrs. Douglas who came over to see me after lunch and expressed delight at the thought of the Library taking care of children. I explained that we would like to handle children of all ages but just didn't have any space to take care of those too young to read. I told her we would be glad to call attention to this service to mothers, and that we meant to get a phonograph to provide stories on records, which would of course give the Room an added attraction.

Meanwhile, the painting goes on in the Children's Room. The persuasive pair of children's librarians have got Lorenzo going on the ceiling as well as the walls. It is really remarkable the job he has done in that room, in addition to his regular duties. Apparently, he never did anything like that before, and it is a pleasure to see him working so industriously and happily. He seems to be having a wonderful time, with Mrs. Moncrief, Mrs. Workman, and me providing abundant praise and appreciation. The girls seem to know that he likes to be kidded and fussed over, and are keeping him busy. He really has considerable ability, and if he continues to wield his paint brush throughout the building the place will be considerably improved at only the relatively small cost of so many gallons of paint.

*   *   *   *   *

October 7, 1946: Visited the editorial offices of Nashville's two daily newspapers in regard to the possibility of getting space for a weekly column that would introduce and evaluate the important new books. Such a column is an obvious necessity for any public library, particularly for one like ours which is faced with the problem of selling itself to thousands of people who have stopped using it or have yet to make its acquaintance.

I had originally planned to shoot for one good column in the Sunday *Tennessean,* since this would catch most of the readers of both daily papers. Several people, however, advised me to stick to the two dailies—each of which has roughly 80,000 circulation—so they were my objectives this morning.

My first appointment was with the editor of the book page of the *Banner.* I told her what we wanted and showed her several copies of "The Library Lookout" that I wrote regularly for the Brockton paper. There we generally had two full columns every week on the back page where it could be read without even opening the newspaper, and was readily distinguished by the cut of the Librarian at the top. I might add that their reader surveys showed that the column was one of the most widely read features of the paper, as I expect most library columns would be.

I had no thought of getting the same amount of space here—if for no other reason than because of the paper shortage which I know to be far from over—and hence was neither surprised nor disappointed when the editor said she could give us no more than half a column. It will be difficult to cover the important new books in this space, but we can still accomplish a lot with it, and if it appears to be well-received perhaps it will be allowed to expand.

Had to run out to Peabody later in the afternoon for a meeting of the Executive Committee of the Nashville Library Club. Plans call for five meetings during the year, instead of the old schedule of three. This means five issues of "Nashville Libraries," instead of three, which means more work for R.S.A. who will have to take Mr. D's place as its Editor.

■   ■   ■   ■   ■

October 8, 1946: Our ad for a new circulation assistant has now run its week's course, and we have certainly been surprised with the number of people who have come in to apply for the position. It seemed almost impossible this summer to find anyone with even the slightest library experience to work for us, and here we are now in the unusual position of being able to choose between several candidates. Six of them have had some library experience and all are quite capable of taking over the job here. Poor Mrs. Benson has had quite a time choosing between them. I have left the decision up to her since she is the Head of the Circulation Department now and has got to live and work with the new person.

She had planned to make her decision and clear the matter up on Monday, but after rating the five chief candidates on experience, personality, disposition, willingness to work evenings, and a few other points, several of the girls came out with the same total point score. So she took the list home to sleep on the matter, and came in this morning to find two new candidates waiting to see her. At 3 o'clock she had decided to take one of the girls who had just come in. She wanted to ask her to come in again to see me, but I told her to go ahead and offer the girl the salary she had in mind, and I would see her after she was hired. I have learned that I can rely on her judgment in such matters and, as I told her, even if I saw her and still preferred one of the other girls I would still want her to have the person she preferred.

Later in the afternoon I turned in my brochure on regional libraries to Martha Parks and was shown around the offices of the State Department of Education's large traveling library service. What they really need are several good people who could devote all their time to promoting the development of regional library service in Tennessee.

．　　　．　　　．　　　．　　　．

October 9, 1946: Started off the day by driving 16 miles to give a short pep talk on the Community Chest to the children in one of the county's elementary schools. It was interesting to see the youngsters in their various classrooms and later to talk to some of them in the auditorium before telling the group something about the Community Chest. Was in the Library by 9 o'clock—just in time to get a call from the Chest's Speakers Bureau assigning me several other schools to talk to.

My new secretary came in to see me before lunch to say that the Travelers Insurance Company had been calling her every day to get her to return to her old job there at a big increase in salary. She seemed to think that perhaps she ought to take the job, and because she isn't expert enough to warrant our matching the other offer I agreed with her that she would probably be better off at the insurance company and that we would do everything possible to facilitate her early departure. Keeping a secretary on a comparatively low salary is no easy matter these days.

Lorenzo has completed the job of painting the ceiling of the Children's Room and the improvement in the lighting and appearance of the Room is considerable. I found the two children's librarians rather worried because so many of the teachers had responded to their invitation to come in and get books for their classrooms that their shelves were already somewhat depleted—and more teachers were on the way in. One of them recalled that a number of their books were out in the Salvation Army's Red Shield Community Center on the East Side. Since this library station has been closed for several months it seemed a good idea to them to get some of these books back for the teachers. The three of us hopped in the car and were soon back with about 60 books that the librarians picked out.

We need many more stations and would like to open several of them this fall. However, I can't think of a new station without thinking of all the additional shelves that must be filled with good books. We certainly don't want to open a new station with old books and immediately kill the interest aroused in it, yet we don't have enough attractive, readable books to go around.

It is discouraging at times to think of all the books that are required to fill one section of shelving in a library, and to figure out how much it would cost to buy this many additional volumes. There's nothing like books for eating up money. We will have to spend five times as much money on children's books this year as in past years, and even then the difference will hardly be discernible. Just another case of a drop-in-the-bucket.

The widespread lending of books to the schools really presents quite a problem. If we continue to push the circulation of books through classroom collections and have many more teachers coming in to get 25 books apiece, we are not going to have enough books left in the Children's Room to build up a service at the main library. We are going to have to decide whether we want to retain our limited book resources for use in public library distribution centers or send a large percentage of our children's books out for use in the schools.

For myself, I want the books placed where they will receive the greatest use and do the most good—whether in school or library. However, I would like the children who use them, and their parents, to know that the books come from the public library. This is not a matter of wanting credit for services rendered. It is, rather, a matter of educating the children to library use and getting them into the library habit as early as possible. The idea is to reach as many children as possible who do not already use the public library and encourage them to read not only the books deposited in their classroom but a great many more books which they can get at the public library.

I want all the books going to the schools to be stamped "Nashville Public Library" on their three edges. This is not only to better remind the children of their source but, more, to suggest the library idea to their parents who are likely to run across these books in the home. We hope that it will occur to some parents that if their youngsters can get good books at the public library, perhaps they might be able to do likewise.

Later on, I want our pleasant children's librarians to visit as many as possible of the classrooms where there are library books to tell stories to the children—all to the end of better identifying the books with the library and stimulating more visits to the library.

Meanwhile, we will still have to keep enough attractive books at the main library and in the branches to enable us to satisfactorily meet the needs of all those who come there seeking readable material. After all, there would be no point in selling public library service in the schools unless we were able to follow through and give satisfaction to those who showed up at the library.

.   .   .   .   .

October 10, 1946: The Children's Room looks better every time I see it. What the room now needs, more than anything else, are some colorful drapes at the side of each group of windows. The black molding around the windows is particularly unattractive. No one would even think of having a home living room without curtains and drapes, or venetian blinds, yet most people seem to think it unnecessary or impractical to dress up the windows of a public building. As a result, the public is generally loath to stay in such a building any longer than is necessary.

Another little task that gave me a certain amount of satisfaction was the preparation by a local artist of several attractive signs directing people to the Reference Department upstairs. Apparently, in all the years the Reference and Business departments have been operating on the second floor, there has never been any sign directing people upstairs, or any printed notice indicating that the Library boasted such departments.

Had a long talk with the woman who heads the Children's Theatre here. She told me of their three productions: "The Indian's Captive", "Hansel and Gretel", and "Pinocchio." They certainly sounded like something the Library should be in on, so I immediately offered her a display of books in the lobby of the theatre, a list of books to go on the back of their programs, and displays in the library.

There is so much of this kind of thing we should be doing—tying in the Library with everything going on in town. And I have yet to see the event that didn't suggest some book connections. Our difficulty is that we don't have anybody on the staff with the time or special ability to handle this public relations work. For myself, I enjoy outlining such programs and never have any trouble thinking up plenty of things the Library should do, but that is as far as I like to go. I don't like to have to slave over the details, preparing the displays, hunting for material, and so forth. I want somebody to turn things over to, and to know that each little assignment will be taken care of.

·   ·   ·   ·   ·

October 11, 1946: Miss Welch came in to say that she had changed her mind about leaving and would like to stay on if I still wanted her. She had had a talk with the man who had enticed her with the higher secretarial salary and decided that the work wasn't nearly as interesting as her present position and that the extra money just wasn't worth it.

Was happy to be able to arrange with one of the Children's Theatre women for a series of story recordings to be put on in our Children's Room every Saturday morning for sixteen weeks beginning November 2nd. All we have to do is secure a phonograph and round up an audience of youngsters. Each program will last half an hour and feature phonograph recordings of favorite children's stories.

·   ·   ·   ·   ·

October 15, 1946: It is good to see Mr. D back again after his four months' trip to Denmark. He dropped in yesterday as I was leaving for the Community Chest luncheon, and then came around again today. Was glad to hear that he liked the painting downstairs and the changes in the reading room.

Had an invitation this morning from a minister to speak at his church on the 31st. Don't know why they scheduled an ordinary church dinner for Halloween. Would like to stay home and see the boys dressed up as Halloween characters, but accepted the date anyway. I always feel obliged to take on these speaking engagements. I never know, at the time, what I will talk about, but figure that if I commit myself I will just naturally have to find some suitable topic, and that there is plenty of time before the lunch or dinner to work out something.

Was very surprised and pleased to hear from the local Welcome Wagon Service that they will include the Public Library among their regular clients and sell library service throughout Nashville at absolutely no cost to us. The Welcome Ladies call on six categories of individuals, talking about and leaving some gift from each of the stores or other organizations that they represent. [They are very effective in making friends for their clients.]

I had contacted the Welcome Service several weeks ago relative to the possibility of including the Library in the visitors' sales talks. The thought of thus reaching such groups as (1) new Nashville residents, (2) new home owners, (3) returning veterans, (4) newlyweds, and (5) new parents, was indeed attractive. It was easy to picture a different approach to each of these groups. However when we learned that each visit would cost the Library 50¢ it seemed as if the whole thing was beyond our reach. And now we are told that we are going to be covered by every visit—not just in one category, but in all six. This of course means that we will have to prepare an attractive leaflet or introduction to the library, along with special booklists aimed at the different groups of potential readers.

This news was particularly welcome as I had been somewhat disappointed earlier in the day to learn that one of the radio stations could not give us fifteen minutes a day for a program in connection with the forthcoming Children's Book Week. We had a fine group of young players to put on a five-day series of fairy story dramatizations, but now it looks as if we will have to be content with short announcements of the occasion and news items regarding the Library's service to children.

The visit to the radio station may be productive of something, however. When the Program Manager started telling of a projected radio quiz program to match teams from local business firms during the winter, I suggested that he have the Library furnish the questions to be used. He seemed to like the idea. And certainly we want the public to get into the habit of associating our Reference Department with questions to be answered.

●   ●   ●   ●   ●

October 16, 1946: Took the afternoon off to visit some of our neighborhood branches and stations. They present a rather pathetic and discouraging picture. The branches appear particularly weak and neglected because they are so big for the little use made of them and look so empty most of the time. Equally depressing are the many shelves filled with ancient volumes that belong anywhere but on the open shelves of a neighborhood library.

My first stop was the station at Howard School. To be exact, the "library" occupies the second floor landing of one of the stairways in the Children's Museum on the Howard School grounds. It is open for service two afternoons a week, with two of the girls from the Main Library on hand to exchange the children's books.

As poorly located as this station is, it circulates between 100 and 150 books every three-hour period it is open. In six hours a week, with a book stock of under 500 volumes and a working area of 6 sq. yds., this station distributes as many books as the big Negro Branch which is open forty hours a week and boasts 6,000 volumes.

I next visited the South Street Community Center in the heart of the Negro section on the south side of Nashville. They have a front room given over to a library which the Public Library has just been asked to take over. We gave them several hundred old books last month but would, of course, have to do much better by them if the Library Board should decide in favor of this project.

I was disappointed to see how little use had been given to the relatively few good books they had. Before visiting the Center I had been inclined to favor the establishment of a library station there, but now I am not nearly as enthusiastic about the idea. The children in that neighborhood certainly need and deserve some good books to read—but of course that does not mean that they will read them if given the chance. Too often it is those who most need to read who do the least reading.

The Negro Public Library, the third of our Carnegie branches, was my next stop. I had a chance this trip to look over the shelves and was horrified to find them so largely filled with old and completely unusable volumes. Many titles I recognized as having discarded this summer from the Main Library. It is surprising to me that these books have so long escaped the hands of the weeder and that they were not removed years ago. Their continued presence there suggests that my predecessors probably spent no more time in this branch than I have been able to do so far. The Librarian would be the only person to discard these books, and rare is the Librarian who spends any appreciable amount of time in one of his branches.

It was indeed discouraging, too, to note only one or two circulations on the book cards of new volumes that are popular everywhere else. I couldn't help but feel that if the patrons of this branch won't read these books they can't be counted upon to read much of anything but light fiction. The total daily circulation averages about 30, which amounts to little more than two or three people an hour coming in to take out several books apiece.

The librarian there has been keeping a record for me of the number of people visiting the branch in the two evening hours, between six and eight o'clock. So far this month, the number has averaged 8, hardly enough to warrant keeping the place open in the evening.

The North Nashville Community Council (Negro) has asked the Library to operate a station in the Ford-Green School, to be open two days a week from 3 to 9. I suggested to the librarian of the Negro Branch that we might close the Branch on these two days and let her work out at the school station instead. This station is ideally located geographically to reach the greatest number of Negro readers, and everyone is anxious to see a successful library center there.

The Negro librarian was set against closing the Branch any day during the week, preferring to have the Library use her assistant at the school half the scheduled hours and employ a student from Fisk to cover the other six hours.

I explained that to do this would cost $250 a year that might otherwise be saved and spent for books to stock the new station. I suggested, furthermore, that we dispense with the services of her part-time assistant who now puts in nine hours a week at the branch. If the other two branches—with similar buildings, bookstock, and hours—can handle a larger circulation with only one attendant, I question the Negro Branch's needs for two attendants.

I tried to get across to her the thought that the Negro library building was simply a place of meeting between books and readers, and that its value was proportionate to the number of such meetings it facilitated. If we could circulate many more books from a wagon on the street corner, even that might be better than keeping open the branch building. In short, we wanted to see the greatest number of Negroes reading the greatest possible number of good books—and it was a matter of secondary concern how or where they secured these books. After a final look over the branch's reference collection, making a mental note to cancel standing orders of a number of expensive volumes never used there, I departed for our West side station. Located in the basement for a fire station, with some 400 books serviced two afternoons a week by one of the girls from the Main Library, this station staggers along with a circulation averaging only 36 books a week.

This is our only service agency on the west side of town. It is in the center of a populous residential area, and, if established in more accessible and attractive quarters, ought to do a fairly good business. Before coming back to town, I drove up and down Charlotte Avenue looking for such a possible new location, but without success.

■   ■   ■   ■   ■

October 18, 1946: Talked to a group of 60 high school librarians at the Maxwell House. Had a date to take the boys to the circus at 3 o'clock so, getting a late start, talked as fast as I could and ended by talking a good deal longer than my usual 20 minute limit.

The talk—on public relations and related matters— seemed to hold their interest, and I understand the library school students there enjoyed it very much. Sometimes I think people sit up and listen to my infrequent talks because I talk so fast and so enthusiastically and informally, and express so many surprising and unorthodox thoughts, that they just want to see what's coming next.

My chief interest in talking to such a group is to make them think, to question what they are doing, to consider new ideas, and to see the tremendous possibilities and amount of fun that a librarian can have in the enthusiastic and experimental conduct of his job.

■   ■   ■   ■   ■

October 21, 1946: Lorenzo has now tried five different shades of red on the floor of the reading room and it looks as if the Circulation girls finally have the color they want. The two end rooms have been shut off by magazine racks for five days already, and everyone will be glad when the floors are finished and the place can be opened up again.

Can't recall seeing any library with tile red floors, but they are certainly an improvement over the plain white concrete. The problem has been to find a red that would not look too Christmassy up against the green shelving. The final decision is up to Mrs. Benson, but any shade she picks will add a lot of warmth to the reading rooms.

Our little high school assistant, Miss Bennett, had a rather unusual experience Sunday afternoon. A colored man came in to ask for a $6 advance on his salary. Said he was one of our janitors, by the name of Albert, and that the Library often gave him his money in advance this way. The girl gave him the $6 from the fine box and then began to wonder whether she had done the right thing. She called the janitor on duty at the time, and found out that she had been tricked by a phony Albert.

Poor Miss Bennett was terribly upset, and determined to make good the $6. When I heard the story this morning I had Mrs. Benson try to reach her at the high school and tell her to stop worrying and to forget about the money. I was away in the afternoon so called her at home in the evening to be sure that she got the message. I told her that the thing could have happened to anyone on the staff, and that it just happened that she was the one on duty when the man walked in—yet I'm wondering if he didn't deliberately pick her to tell his story to, since she is probably the only member of the staff inexperienced enough to have been fooled. Anyone else would have known that the Library had no ''Albert'' on its payroll.

CHAPTER **IV**

A Long Needed Pension Plan

October 22, 1946: Was busy most of the morning getting ready for the Library Board meeting at 3 o'clock. Visited Mr. Whitmore, the Board's vice-president, at his bank office to give him the schedule of retirement allowances that I had worked out after talking to the Metropolitan Life Insurance people. They had agreed that the only way we could take care of the five people already beyond the retirement age would be to simply divide up our Special Fund money every year on the basis of their lengths of service. The five people have served a total of 163 years. Dividing $2,037.50 (our average annual Special Fund receipts from fines and fees) by 163, we get a figure of $12.50 a share. Then, multiplying each librarian's years of service by $12.50 we arrive at the amount of money each of them will receive every year in retirement. The amounts range from $325 to $537.50.

That may not seem like a lot of money, but when you consider that these retirement allowances will amount to al-

most 45 percent of the average amount of salary that these
people are now getting for working 40 hours a week, and until
this summer they had no chance or even the hope of getting
any retirement pay, it doesn't seem bad at all. And as our
circulation continues to increase at the rapid rate, our fine
money will go up at the same rate, which means that the
amount of money in our Special Fund which will provide the
retirement money, will increase from year to year. Our library
employees could end up with the biggest pensions in the city
government.

This whole thing is most gratifying to me. Before I
came to Nashville the Library Board told me they were faced
with two major problems that they had tried to solve for many
years but there seemed to be no answer to either one. The first
was the problem of their ''superannuated'' employees, refer-
ring to the six heads of their branches and departments who
were past retirement age but could not be let go because they
were not covered by the city's retirement plan and had no
financial support to look forward to in retirement. When I
suggested that the Library use its fine money (the only money
it could call its own) to provide the necessary retirement allowances, the Library Trustees and the older library employees were equally delighted. That seemed to be one of the
answers we needed. The other answer—which seems about to
solve the problem of providing free service to all county residents, which has tormented library officials for many
years—is my thought that we ought to stop asking the County
Court for $5,000, or $10,000, or any specific amount of
money, and simply offer to start giving service to county readers and have the County reimburse the Library at a later date
for whatever results, at the rate of 25¢ per volume borrowed.
In short, it appears that the Board's two biggest problems are
about to be solved at last. And the exciting part to me is that
neither of them calls for any more money for the Library. As I

told my library school students in July, most of the things that need doing in libraries don't require additional money nearly as much as they do new ideas. New ideas are the greatest need of any administrator.

Once our six older people are taken care of, it will be over 15 years before the next oldest staff member reaches retirement age. And by that time, some of the present retiring group will probably have passed from the retirement payroll. It does seem as if we might make out all right for a long time, but I do think we ought to consider a regular insurance plan for the younger two-thirds of the staff.

Discussion of this retirement schedule took up a full hour at the start of the Board meeting. It progressed from a suggestion that an exception be made in the case of one staff member who does not wish to retire, to a suggestion that all six staff members be told at the same time that they will be retired—but that, actually, each one will stay until she can be replaced—to the suggestion that everyone be retired at the same time, with the best ones re-hired on a month-to-month basis until they can be replaced with permanent employees. The matter was then turned over to a committee which was appointed to consider the whole question and bring to the next meeting its recommendations, together with the necessary resolutions to put these plans into effect.

The presentation of requests from the Salvation Army and the South Street Community Center that the public library share the cost of librarians to service their small book collections was met by a general expression of the opinion that the Library should definitely control the operation of any station in which it has a part. Everyone agreed that the Library should not pay to staff or support any library unless it has the right to determine policies, select the reading material, and manage the place as the Librarian thinks best.

The only other matter that the Board had time to consider was the request of the North Nashville Community Council for a library station in the Ford-Greene School. I suggested that we could have the Negro Branch librarian on duty at the School two days a week, and just as well close the Branch at six o'clock the other three week-days. Presented figures as to the average daily circulation and the number of evening visitors at the branch, upon which the Board agreed that it should be closed accordingly. Also suggested that the committee to sell the Negro Branch be re-activated, with another attempt made to find a buyer for the property.

In connection with this matter, I presented pictures and drawings of the one-room pre-fabricated libraries designed by TVA architects in 1944. The smallest-size library is designed to contain 2600 volumes, with a slightly larger building planned to hold 3000 volumes. They are divided into two rooms—for adults, and for children—by movable bookcases and a sliding curtain. They are extremely practical and I believe they are just what we want. As I told the board, if we could sell the Negro Branch we could use the money to build three or four of these little neighborhood libraries—to bring library service to the Negro communities in North, South, and East Nashville.

■   ■   ■   ■   ■

October 23, 1946: Things seem to be shaping up fairly well for Children's Book Week in November. The highlight of the program in the Children's Room at the main library is sure to be the two marionette shows put on by the very talented Tom Tichenor. Scheduled for Wednesday afternoon and Saturday morning during "the Week", they are sure to draw a big crowd as Tichenor's first performances since returning from the Army.

The big surprise is the fine schedule arranged by the Negro librarian for Sunday, November 10th, at the Negro Library. The program includes short talks by representatives of the city schools, county schools, and Girl Scouts, a main address by Arna Bontemps, the librarian-author of Fisk University, a group of singers from Meigs School, a choir from State College, remarks by the City Librarian, and the crowning of "Miss Book Week." Almost entirely a Negro program, and as fine a one as I have seen anywhere.

Mrs. Lockert has shown considerable ingenuity in planning the selection of a Book-Week Queen. The first step was the selection of five contestants—all high school Girl Scouts—from each of the five Negro districts in Nashville. Each contestant will be given 25 library application cards. They will line up votes by having these cards filled out by persons not already library borrowers. The applicant-voter will retain his card, signed on the back by the contestant, for presentation at the Negro Branch at 3 P.M. on November 10th. The contestant having the greatest number of cards turned in for her at that time will be crowned Queen of the Week. The Queen will also be the guest-of-honor at the Negro Library's weekly dance the following Sunday night. The Negro Teen-Town, like the one held every Friday and Saturday night at the East Branch, is a very popular event at the library.

．　　　　．　　　　．　　　　．　　　　．

October 24, 1946: Mrs. Brents was filing cards at the public catalog when I came in this morning. She stopped me and asked, "You really believe in having a public card catalog, don't you? It's silly, but someone suggested the other day that you weren't too interested in the catalog?"

I assured her that I was as strong a believer in a public catalog as any librarian, although, as a matter of fact, I couldn't remember having said two words about the use of the catalog since I'd been in Nashville. I went on to explain that my only feeling about the whole thing is that I would prefer to see less time spent in putting unnecessary and unintelligible information on the cards and more time spent on subject analytics and the addition of short descriptive annotations to make the catalog more useful to the reader.

She went back to the Catalog Department, saying that she would certainly set straight the person with the imaginative mind. It was nice of her to give me a chance to explain. Later in the morning, she came up to me to say "You're the easiest person to talk to . . . We all think you have the most wonderful disposition."

I feel the same way about her and all the other members of the staff. I've always heard how nicely dispositioned Southerners are, and it's been a real pleasure to find them every bit that way.

One of the trustees also commented on how happy the members of the staff seemed to be as they went about their work, and how enthusiastic they were in trying to improve the library in every way. It's just a great time for the Library, and I'm just lucky enough to be here as the new library director when everything seems to be opening up . . . with all new library supervisors, more money, increased business, new ideas and unlimited opportunities. No new administrator ever had it so good!

.   .   .   .   .

October 25, 1946: Called Major Arnold of the Salvation Army and Mr. Booker of the South Street Community Center to present the conditions set by the Library Board for the establishment of library stations in their community centers. Both gentlemen agreed that the Library should have complete charge of the libraries even though the major part of the salaries of the two librarians would be paid by their community agencies, and a majority of the books now in both centers belonged to them.

Called Chuck Nobis at the Western Reserve Library School in Cleveland to let him know that we are still thinking about him and have a lot of interesting work waiting for him to do when he finishes his library school course in February. Nobis remarked that they had just been talking about me and that most of the men at Western Reserve wanted to come to Nashville and work with me. It's probably cold up there today and who wouldn't want to exchange such conditions for sunny Nashville?

This all goes back to my visit to W.R. before leaving Cleveland. I had happened to read in one of our fraternity publications that there was a Phi Gam in the library school there so had dropped by to say hello. I mentioned to Dean Grant that I'd like to meet some of the men students and almost immediately found myself up in their lounge answering all kinds of questions about library jobs, different types of work, and the like. After talking for an hour with the seven veterans who happened to be on hand, I was asked downstairs to talk to about sixty of the students. Spoke very informally for some twenty minutes on the pleasant adventure of public library work. Miss Grant seemed to enjoy it as much as the students. She also mentioned afterward that Nobis was their top student, which matched my general opinion of him.

I told him over the phone that I'd like to start him out as an administrative assistant, to handle a great variety of little problems that I didn't have time for, and then see which way his interests led him. Later on, he might perhaps take over the extension activities that have never been organized under one

person. One of the girls seemed surprised that I had called
Cleveland instead of writing. To me, the extra cost is small
when one considers the much greater impression made by
calling, and the opportunity to sell oneself by talking directly
to the applicant. As Elmer Wheeler has advised millions:
"Don't write—Telegraph!"

.   .   .   .   .

October 26, 1946: Finally got myself a much-needed
desk lamp. Don't see how the two previous Librarians stood
the poor light in the upstairs office. The situation was particularly intolerable because the telephone company had fas-
tened their key box on the window side of the desk so that it
threw a long wide shadow over the desk's working surface.

Had a talk with Lorenzo Howse about his too-long
working hours. He works every day from 7 to 5, for a total of
some 70 hours a week. Finally had to insist that I didn't want
anybody in the building on Sunday before 9:30, at the earliest.
Certainly think he ought to be able to stay in bed one morning
out of the week.

We've got to re-arrange the time of the Negro Branch
janitor some way, now that we plan to close that building two
days a week. Told Lorenzo that I'd try and get Noel to work at
the main library one day so that we could give him a day off.
He admitted that he would like a day off, though he had no
idea what he would do with the time. The Library has always
kept him working 365 days of the year. That's a lot of work for
his money.

.   .   .   .   .

October 28, 1946: Called Miss Wilkin at the Library
and asked her to locate the three copies of Lindsay's "Time of

the Young'' that we purchased last month and discard them all. She had asked me to examine a copy when Mrs. Fleming returned her branch copy after reading only three pages.

I looked the book over last night and am amazed that a sensible publishing house would publish such a frightful novel. It is entirely without any virtue at all—an uninteresting, impossible to follow, story, with unpleasant characters and objectionable language. For the first time I felt the book reviewing and annotating fraternity had really failed us by not calling attention to the true character of this book.

Never before have I felt this way about a new title in the library. It is not easy for a librarian to throw away three new novels that would easily find readers if left on the shelves. They might stay in the collection and add 100 circulations to the annual total, but I'd feel that the Library owed an explanation and apology to 100 Nashvillians for wasting their good time and giving them the wrong impression of the kind of literature we are making available.

And, after all, what virtue is there in circulation per se? What difference does it make to anybody outside the library family whether the library circulates 300,000 or 200,000 volumes a year? Such figures mean nothing to the layman, except when compared with similar figures for other years, or other libraries. It's as if I were told that the Visiting Nurses made 923 calls last year, or that the Salvation Army gave service to 15,300 people; I would react just the same to reports of 1,721 calls and 11,914 people.

After lunch, I dropped over to see School Superintendent Bass about the projected library station in the Ford-Greene school. He will accept a six-months trial of a 3 to 8 o'clock schedule. Returned to the Library to find the circulation assistants upset over the presence in the stacks of another ''peeping Tom.'' It's a shame that libraries have to be infested with such mental and emotional delinquents. Besides making the members of the staff exceedingly nervous, they annoy feminine users of the library and give the institution a black eye with the public, many of whom are led to stay away from it.

All public libraries are faced with this problem, and it is such a difficult one to solve since nothing can be done about these people unless they are caught in an objectionable act. A detective might spend every afternoon or evening for several months in the building and never catch a "peeping Tom." All I could do this afternoon was to stay close to our suspect and make him feel that he was being watched and so might as well move elsewhere.

.   .   .   .   .

October 29, 1946: Came in this morning to find a number of foot-prints on our freshly painted reading room floor. Apparently some of the people couldn't wait to get at the light-romance shelves last night and had pushed their way through the barrier of magazine racks to cross the open floor when the girl at the desk was occupied elsewhere. It is mighty discouraging to see such evidence of the thoughtlessness of people you are trying to do something for. Everyone here is trying to make the reading rooms more pleasant and attractive for these people, many of whom visit there every day, and then a few of them knowingly mark up the floor so that it must be re-painted rather than wait one day to get a few more inconsequential books to read.

.   .   .   .   .

October 31, 1946: Always feel good the morning after a talk, or a Board meeting, or any other event that has been ahead on the calendar for some time. As enjoyable as they generally are, they loom as hurdles or markers that it is nice to pass and get out in the clear again.

The talk last night at the Vine Street Christian Church seemed to go over particularly well. A good percentage of the crowd of 100 came up afterward to say how interested they were to hear of the things the Library was doing, and how they had no idea that the Library offered so much to them. Many of them said they thought the talk would stimulate increased use of their church library, as well as the public library. Dr. Nooe was very appreciative and said that I should make the same sort of talk before every group in town.

A Librarian does not have to be a good speaker to give a successful talk. All he needs is enthusiasm and a taste for what will interest the public. Library work is so varied—it serves so many different people, in so many different ways, for so many different purposes—and what it offers, and does, is so little known by the public—that the library speaker has his pick of a tremendous amount of colorful and interesting material. He can talk about different kinds of books, he can call attention to little-known services of the library, he can cite cases of books being helpful in different situations, or he can let the people in on his plans and the problems that the library is trying to solve, and in everything he can be confident that what he says will be interesting news to his listeners.

Today was a big day for us as the waste paper men finally returned for the old books that have long cluttered the basement hallway. They got 2800 lbs. their first trip, but they must have taken a good bit more than that amount today. It's such a pleasure to have the entranceway cleared to the Children's Room.

Had Mrs. Moncrief out looking for a good phonograph for us this afternoon. Apparently, there is only one two-speed phonograph in town, and that can't handle large-size records.

It is essential that we have a machine that can play 16-inch records and operate at 33 ⅓ r.p.m. as well as at the usual 78 r.p.m. The faster speed is all right for ordinary phonograph recordings, but all transcriptions—children's stories, Shakespearean plays, Cavalcade of America dramatizations, etc.—are played at the slower speed.

I had planned to have one of the engineers at the radio station build a special speaker for us in the Children's Room, but I believe now that it would be better to get a smaller machine that can be moved around and taken out of the building. We ought to have a machine that we can take out to the branches and stations and anywhere else where children can be brought together.

■   ■   ■   ■   ■

November 4, 1946: Turned in all the copy for my first issue of "Nashville Libraries", and the girls proceeded to mimeograph a nice-looking six-page publication. The greater part of it is short news notes from the local libraries and, with staff turnover what it is these days, there is an unusual number of changes to be reported this time.

While the mimeographing was going on, I cornered a typewriter and knocked out library columns for the next two weeks. With so many interesting books coming in these days, and only a third of a column to fill every week, it is no problem at all to get off an interesting report.

When I see the long, high-class reviews of individual titles that stand next to my simple little library column on the book page I again wish I could write good literary criticism. I envy people who can write thoughtful, scholarly material, or who can write a great deal about a very little. I never can write or express myself except when I have some very definite thoughts on a subject—and then can't go beyond simple terms and garden-variety words. I realize that the simplest, most easy to understand writing is the best, and that people have liked my columns and read them because they have always been so childishly simple, but I often wish that I was capable of something more involved—even though I might never have the occasion to exercise such a talent.

For example, consider the column for Children's Book Week that I wrote this morning. It's almost too simple, yet I believe it will get across the point I want to make. At the same time, it should help to make the Librarian appear a real human being to the public. Those are the two things every column should try to do: Build up the columnist as a real personality of increasing interest to his readers, and get across one or two simple ideas in each issue.

People are most interested in individuals than in institutions. From the public relations standpoint, it is highly important that the Librarian be seen, heard, and known by as many people as possible. He represents, and *is,* the Library to the average citizen. If they think well of him, they are likely to think well of the Library. And it is perhaps only natural to assume that the Librarian's interests and personality will be reflected in the type of books added to the Library. A Librarian who appears interested in all the everyday things that most concern the average person ought to select books with greater readability and usefulness than one who seems scholarly and aloof.

Had a letter today from the Order Librarian at Vanderbilt, inquiring whether we would be interested in selling the Joint University Library our set of the American Quarterly Review, for $50. As the writer pointed out, the feasibility of their duplicating this title has come up for discussion many times in the past, with everyone agreeing that one file is sufficient for the City of Nashville. Up to now, nothing has been done about the matter. But with several Vanderbilt professors anxious to get their hands on these old journals, they feel they must purchase a set somewhere.

I rather hate to part with such material, but I called them back to say they could have our twenty volumes. As I explained to Miss Bell, I just can't argue with their logic: Certainly one set of this old title is enough for this locality, and if I were to have to pick the best location for this material I would have to specify the J.U.L. This is definitely research material, and it is never used at the public library.

Doubtless the same sort of question will arise in connection with other titles of interest to the university faculties. We have the best magazine collection in this part of the state, and—as the J.U.L. librarian points out—for years had a good deal more money to spend on books and periodicals than did the university libraries. For this reason we have many old books and magazines that they would like to get from us.

It will be a problem to decide just how far to go in turning over to them old material that is never used at the public library. It is not an easy thing to part with valuable items—things that give basic strength and prominence to the Library. Even though they are very rarely used, they give the collection a certain standing and contribute to its personality and historical interest. At the same time, the more scarce and valuable a title is, the more important it would seem to be to have it properly located. It should be made accessible to the greatest number of research students, or subject specialists, who might be expected to make use of it. If books are tools to be used, it is the obligation of all bookmen to do what they can to make them as available as possible.

This obligation would seem to call for the exercise of a broad and unselfish point of view. It would seem to require that the interests and needs of scholars everywhere be put ahead of the self-centered inclinations of individual institutions. In short, all questions should be decided on the basis of what's best for the greatest number of serious book users, and what will make for the greatest contribution to our general fund of knowledge.

I am a great believer in inter-library co-operation, and strong for joint efforts of librarians in such fields as book-buying, publicity, cataloging, and the elimination of duplication in all aspects of library work.

■   ■   ■   ■   ■

November 5, 1946: The Children's Room—for the first time in its history—now looks like a *children's* department. It has been transformed by more than a dozen figures of animals and book characters drawn, painted and cut out by Tom Tichenor and placed along the top of the bookshelves. They stand two feet high, on the average, and give the room wonderful atmosphere.

An expertly done poster announcing the marionette shows and a figure of two brown rabbits holding an attractive sign announcing the next story hour are not the least of Tichenor's contributions. They add considerable color to the charging desk and are a good example of the kind of work we so greatly need. However, as I told Tom, we have greater need for posters and other display material that can be shown outside the library. It seems almost wrong to set his work up in the library where comparatively few people will see it—and these already attracted to the building—when it really ought to be placed in a store window on Church Street for everybody to see.

In short, we are tickled to death to get any material that will brighten the interior of the building, but what we need much more is help in getting people to the library. We've got to reach out for the thousands who do not use the library now, and who never will use it unless special effort is made to sell them on the idea. Tichenor should be able to help us immensely along this line. I told him that we would like to put him on our staff—to work any number of hours that he could find time for—and he will try and plan such a schedule.

One visitor to the Room told the girls that the Children's Department had never looked so nice, and most of the people remark on the great transformation in the place. A book salesman who came in later in the morning said that the room now had more life and color than any he had seen in the public libraries he visited.

· The salesman brought in several suitcases full of books to show the children's librarians. I dropped in as he was adding the cost of their selections. To the girls' consternation, the bill came to $180. When one is ordering several copies of a book at a time, he is bound to be amazed at the speed with which his purchases mount in cost. At any rate, the girls wanted to know whether they ought to spend that much. I told them that they were the boss and would have to decide, but that they might consider the fact that they had already spent over half their annual allotment, with still nine months of the year to go. I left immediately after that, but expect that they will go ahead with the greater part of the order. They feel strongly that they need the books now.

The Children's Department really has a long way to go to recover the patronage it enjoyed before the war. Tom Tichenor was saying how, when he was in high school, he had to almost force his way in and out of the Room, through all the other children wanting books. Now, on an ordinary afternoon, it is unusual to see more than two or three children in the Room at one time. However, the same number of children are doubtless still available—and we'll get them back in here yet.

Our new, untrained Children's Librarian is working out nicely, but I have had to reassure her several times within the last month. She feels that the job is too big for her, and that

I ought to get a more capable librarian, under whom she would be glad to continue working as assistant Children's Librarian. I tell her that if I had wanted a trained librarian I would have hired one, but that I picked her because I felt she had certain qualities that seemed more important to me than professional training. As I explained, a year of library school does not automatically qualify one for doing an effective job of library work. If we were to send her to Peabody Library School now, she would become acquainted with some reference books, some cataloging routines, and a little bit of a number of other things, but would pick up surprisingly little that she does not already know to make things go better in the Children's Department.

My most convincing argument, however, is to point to the present appearance of the Children's Room, comparing it with what she saw on coming to work here several months ago. I admit that she didn't bring about the change herself, yet I give her enthusiasm credit for interesting others in the task of brightening up the room. In short, she is largely responsible for keeping Lorenzo interested in his painting, making Mrs. Workman want to come back to work, and encouraging Tom Tichenor to contribute to the Department. As I tell her, I want people who can interest others in working for the Library, and value the sort of enthusiasm that stimulates the best efforts of others ahead of professional knowledge.

■   ■   ■   ■   ■

November 6, 1946: The Reference Department, including the former Business Library, seems to be next on the improvement list, now that Lorenzo has finished with the reading room. Miss Bell has yet to decide on the color she wants for the floor, but meanwhile, Lorenzo can paint the window frames, clean the shelves and the walls behind them, and shellac the outside of the shelves.

The shelves on the south side of the front room will continue to house the Tennesseanna collection. The shelves on the north side, which recently housed the business collection, now stand empty and raise the question as to what material ought to be moved into this space. There seem to be three possibilities, and perhaps we can handle all three together.

There is just enough room to the left of the north windows to hold the 32 shelves of genealogy that have long been shelved in the Librarian's outer office. Moving these books into the old business library would permit supervision of their use and eliminate a poor situation in the office. Then, to the right of the windows, we will have sufficient shelving to hold all the specialized and little-used magazines that we want to get out of the main reading room. There is room here for 250 magazines of this type and, by displaying the magazines on open shelves, instead of on racks, it should be possible to stack half a dozen issues in each space, thus giving the reader ready access to the last six issues of each title.

A third possible addition to the room would be two turntables, with earphones, and all the phonograph records that would accompany them. We hope to have this equipment sometime this winter, and the old business library is one of two possible locations for it. The other possibility is the present P.T.A. room, adjoining the Children's Department. The upstairs room offers the advantage of constant supervision of the use of the record collection by the reference librarians. Use of the basement room, on the other hand, would require the employment of additional personnel since the Children's Department closes at 5 o'clock and there is nobody on duty in the basement after that hour to make the records available for evening use.

It would seem best to experiment for several months with the genealogical books and the magazines in the room with the Tennesseanna collection, and see how things work out. My only fear is that there will not be enough chairs and table space to take care of the people using all this material. However, by removing the steel stand containing the 167-volume "Library of Congress Catalog of Printed Cards"—in the center of the adjoining Reference Department—and replacing it with another long reading table, we should have enough seating space in the two rooms to handle all readers. As for the 167 little-used volumes, the chances for selling them to the J.U.L. are looking up these days.

Stopped at the East Branch on my way home and, as usual, flipped back the cover of most of the new books that were in sight, to examine their book cards and see how they have been circulating. Wherever I go, I like to study the turnover of individual titles, and different types of books.

It was disappointing to find that most of the important new books—best sellers elsewhere—have been taken out only two or three times in the three to six months they have been in the library. However, if the present clientele will read almost nothing but fiction, we certainly want to know about it so we won't waste money buying such books as Leland Stowe's latest, the one by Liebman, and other important titles, until we can build up the branch and stimulate its use by more and better readers. It might be thought that the purchase of these good books would bring the readers that the branch should have, but I am afraid that too few people even know that the library is there for them to use. What is needed the most is a broad advertising program on the East Side.

•   •   •   •   •

November 7, 1946: The waste-paper gang came back to get the last of the books in the basement hall, so the decks are now cleared for Book Week. Two professors from the Vanderbilt School of Religion also dropped by to go over some 350 discards from the upstairs stacks and picked out 33 volumes for transfer to the J.U.L. Now that they either have or don't want all the titles they passed over, I feel much better about disposing of them.

Later in the morning, a photographer took several shots of Tom Tichenor's figures, along with a story of children's department activities. Talking with him led me to think of the possibility of getting some of the high school art classes interested in our need for art work. It is quite possible that a few art students might be interested in working for us, getting credit for such work at school.

Another idea with possibilities is to have the newspapers print a copy of our library application card, along with an invitation to people to cut it out and mail it to the Library— properly filled out—and thus become a member of the library family. Many newspaper readers would doubtless be surprised to learn that they could so easily gain access to the library's great book resources.

In the afternoon, I drove over to the North Branch to see how things were progressing there. After my visit to the busier East Branch, I was not too surprised to find that the only adult non-fiction books circulated in the past week were a few collections of sports stories. These branches *really* need a shot in the arm!

I had previously asked Miss Schick to display the new books in the library—with their jackets on—but found no books on display, and learned that the jackets were being taken home on the books borrowed from the shelves. This quickly rendered most of the jackets unfit for further use, and deprived the reading room of a certain amount of color.

Just inside the front door of the branch are two long counters, which I soon had covered with fifty of the newest books in their bright jackets. I could see that Miss Schick didn't particularly care for my display-making so I kept up a rapid fire of explanation and flattery to sell her on the idea and keep her from thinking that my activity implied any criticism of her work as librarian.

When I left she seemed content about the whole thing and promised to call me a week from today to tell me how many of the displayed volumes had circulated. I told her that if only two books went out I'd be happy and that she could feel as if she had really accomplished something. After all, two non-fiction books are better than none on her circulation record.

She also promised to do another thing that I'd mentioned to her before—and that is stamping the circulation date on the book card, along with the borrower's registration number. It is impossible to tell the turnover of books when the card shows only a list of numbers, and no dates. One cannot tell whether the last circulation was the week before or several years ago. It is important to know how many times a book has circulated in the past five- or ten-years, when you are considering whether to discard it, or at least remove it from the reading room. Even though I can fairly well estimate the circulation of a particular volume, I feel rather at a loss when faced with the task of weeding a collection of books where I don't have the individual records of circulation dates to check my feeling regarding each title.

.   .   .   .   .

November 8, 1946: Happened to visit the staff room at coke time and was struck by the ragged appearance of the place. The walls, light fixtures, furniture, everything, is about as unattractive as it could be. Asked the three girls there why they didn't fix the place up. They replied that they would like nothing better—if they had a little money to spend on the job. So I appointed the three of them a committee to fix up the lounge and told them they could have $25 to spend any way they wanted. That's not much, but it ought to buy a lot of paint, at least.

Speaking of fixing things up, the children's librarians say they would like to do a job on my office. Well, it certainly needs some attention, and if Lorenzo keeps going with his paint brush he ought to get to me sooner or later. I don't seem to average more than two hours a day in the office these days so perhaps the need isn't as great now as it will be when things become more settled.

At the moment, I am interested in locating an electrically operated buffing wheel which can be covered with sandpaper and used to clean the exposed edge of all our old books. Such a gadget would remove the blackened ½0th of an inch and give the edges the same clean, white appearance that they have when returning from the bindery. If we can find such a machine we can put someone to work cleaning all the books that have been moved into the reading room.

■   ■   ■   ■   ■

November 10, 1946: Too bad it had to rain for the big doings at the Negro Branch. Only about 70 people turned up to register their votes for the five contestants for the title of ''Miss Book-Week'', and to hear the various speakers on the rather full program.

Arna Bontemps, the Librarian at Fisk—and a former student at the Graduate Library School—was the main speaker. All I had to do was make a few remarks at the close of the program, announcing the opening next week of the new library station in the Ford-Greene School.

Earlier in the day I spoke to the Couples Class at the First Presbyterian Church. Don't know why I agreed to ''lead

our Sunday School class'', and spent most of Saturday trying
to work up a talk that would be interesting to such a group. It
wasn't until 8 o'clock in the evening that I thought I had the
idea I wanted. After writing several pages, however, it
seemed too evangelistic—so I gave the thing up. Was getting
rather nervous with the time running out, and no organized
talk for the group the next morning. Then the thing seemed to
take shape—and I went to bed feeling quite comfortable
about the matter. The talk seemed to go over pretty well, and
I'm glad now that I accepted the invitation to speak—yet I
wonder whether it was worth all the stewing I went through.

I mention such incidents as this simply because they
appear to be part of a Librarian's experiences. Being head of
the public library does not qualify one for speaking to a Sunday School group, yet I know that I would never have been
asked to speak if I were just another newcomer to Nashville.
Neither would I have been visited by the half dozen church
leaders who have dropped by to invite me to one or another of
the city's churches.

Sometimes I wonder, however, what kind of salary people think a City Librarian makes. Since my arrival here, half a
dozen people have told me about houses that they thought I
might buy if I were not too particular. In every case, the price
of the house was eighteen or twenty thousand dollars.

Anyone entering library work is probably already
prepared to feel like a poor relation at times. This is perhaps inescapable, for any Librarian who tries to take an
active part in the life of his community is bound to come
together with leaders in other fields, and these people are
generally well above him—as far as wealth and social position are concerned.

This fact places the Librarian at a handicap. It would be
to the Library's advantage to have its chief executive on more
intimate terms with the leaders in the community, but mighty

few Librarians can afford to go where, or do what, these other men do. If they could afford to mix more with the influential people in their city, they might be more successful in obtaining additional financial support for their library, or in securing donations from wealthy people. As it is, most Librarians are obliged to refuse many of the infrequent invitations that come to them because they cannot afford to accept them, or to reciprocate.

■   ■   ■   ■   ■

November 11, 1946: Had a nice surprise this morning when I came to work. The two Children's Librarians had braved the rain to come to the library yesterday (Sunday) afternoon to set out all the new books that they had been storing up for Book Week. As several people remarked, the Children's Room just couldn't look any nicer.

It will take time to build back the circulation of children's books, but I am sure the girls can do it. For one thing, the Department has had more publicity in the last ten days than it had in the preceding two years. Both papers have been co-operative, printing half a dozen stories and a picture, too.

The reading room is gradually filling up with the best books from the stacks, and it looks as if the number of readable books on all subjects and the amount of shelf-space in the reading room (really three connected rooms) is going to match perfectly. If we have more room on the shelves I don't believe we would want to bring out any more books from the stacks. We want only books that we are proud to display and know can sell themselves and really satisfy the reader in the reading room—and it just happens that the number of these books in the library just fills the shelves in that room.

Miss Crocker tells me that they circulated 176 books at Howard Station the other afternoon. That is the record circulation for any of our library stations. She says they could do even better if they had some more "easy books". I told her that if West Station doesn't show any more life we probably ought to close it and move their books to Howard. The Children's Department is completely out of such books; they are anxious to get some back from Howard Station, rather than give them more.

Guess we will have to pour a few extra hundred dollars into "easy books."

·   ·   ·   ·   ·

November 12, 1946: The Children's Department played host this morning to 33 seventh-graders from David Lipscomb School. They poured into the Room with notebooks open and started writing down everything Mrs. Moncrief told them about the location of different groups of books. Practically all these children live outside the City and thus cannot borrow books without paying $1.50, yet we are glad of the chance to show any child our collection and teach him how to use the library. It's just unfortunate that we cannot bring in classes from schools within the city as I am sure that such group visits would greatly stimulate the use of the children's collection.

Later in the day I attended a small luncheon for Harnett Kane, the author of a very readable new novel entitled "The Woman from New Orleans". The party was given by the management of Zibarts Bookstore, and included two other local authors: Stanley Horn, author of "The Army of Tennessee", and Dr. Crabb, author of "Breakfast at the Hermitage", "Dinner at the Belmont", etc. The guest of honor proved to be a very cordial young man and, all in all, it was a very pleasant noon hour. Kane first became known for his "Louisiana Hayride", which he followed with "Plantation

Parade'' and several other books on the same region; his latest book should add considerably to his reputation.

■   ■   ■   ■   ■

November 13, 1946: Came home worn out from the Marionette Show that we staged for the Girl Scouts of Nashville. We must have had 200 girls packed into the basement hall—the only place in the building we can have such a show. Most of the girls sat on the floor, or stood on the stairs, while the children's librarians and I brought in chairs and tables for late-comers to stand on, and tried to keep the children up front from obstructing the view of those behind them.

Tom Tichenor did a wonderful job with ''Rumpelstiltskin'' and the children loved it—despite the noisy and uncomfortable setting. After the show, the Scouts poured into the Children's Room to look over the new books—and it was immediately apparent that the majority of the troops present were from the County. But even if these children can't have library cards—without paying $1.50—and are not likely to add to our business, the show definitely was not wasted on them. It provided some good library publicity and made friends of several hundred families who will be potential library users if a county library ever comes into being here.

We are all rather apprehensive about Saturday's performance. Being open to the general public, it is quite likely to draw so many youngsters that we will be swamped—even if we run two shows in a row—and it would be too bad to have to turn people away. The girls want to have some movable bleachers built for use in the basement—and it might not be a bad idea if we go ahead with our plan to have marionette shows every week. It might be a good idea, too, to limit attendance to children with library cards.

Earlier in the day, I went out to ''beg'' some money for our two phonograph projects. More precisely, I went over to the headquarters of the Lions Club to sell them on the idea of taking one of these library programs as their Club project. All they would have to do is put out $500 for a phonograph and records that would be available for use by anyone in Nashville.

The Secretary of the Club, and several other members present, seemed to think it a fine idea. The emphasis of my argument was, of course, on the wonderful publicity the project would bring the Club, and the amount of good will that would accrue to them through their provision of a service that many people in Nashville have long wanted. It appears that the Lions Club now has no project of any kind that they can point to—so we may truly be rendering them a service in giving them something attractive to get behind. I won't know their decision, however, until after I explain our program to their executive board next week.

■   ■   ■   ■   ■

November 15, 1946: Had another book salesman in today. It is nice to see some of these travelers from time to time, but one must exercise considerable caution in looking over their samples. It is too easy to spend money this year and find oneself purchasing a lot of attractive but unimportant titles that one would be just as well off without. It's poor business to buy books just because they are presented to one by a salesman, when a calm and careful consideration of the library's book needs would not lead to such purchases. It is generally safer, and a saving of considerable time, to decline the invitation to examine stocks of ''remainders'' and other miscellaneous material.

Later in the day I was called into the Reference Department by a very worried Miss Bell. After considerable worrying over possible color schemes for the two second-floor rooms, she had put Lorenzo to work painting the half-moon framework of the windows a Chinese red, planning to follow this up by having the floors painted gray. But, apparently, some of her patrons had questioned her choice. Their tactless remarks had unnerved her to such an extent that she could hardly sleep last night. She was still upset today and ready to give up the whole idea of brightening her department. Said she just didn't know how any particular color would look when applied to the whole room, and didn't dare try anything. I suggested that she call in an interior decorator if she wanted some more advice, but to remember that it isn't a matter of life and death and that while the colors could easily be changed at any time she'd never be able to make a selection that would seem right to everyone.

Had lunch with Mr. D. and returned to the Library to help pick from the stacks the best books of history and travel for the reading room. Found a great many readable volumes on the different sections of the United States, but almost nothing new or particularly interesting or attractive on Europe, Asia or Africa.

．　　　　．　　　　．　　　　．　　　　．

November 18, 1946: Was glad to hear that the Marionette Show turned out so nicely on Saturday afternoon. The audience was larger, but older and better behaved, and the girls did such a systematic job of seating them on the floor, by size, that everyone was able to see the whole show. Most of the audience had library cards and, after the show, took home most of the Children's Department's new books.

Tichenor is considering building a new stage for regular use in the main library. What would interest me more, however, is a portable stage that would enable him to put on marionette shows at the branches and anywhere else we could get children together. I am counting on such shows to help us get the youngsters back into the branch libraries.

Visited the Negro Branch in the afternoon to see how plans were coming for Thursday's opening of the station at Ford-Greene School. The librarian had expected to take only a hundred books to the new station but I suggested that she take a great many more of the new books that she had on hand at the Branch. I explained that the library will be visited by many new readers from North Nashville, most of them hoping or expecting to see a lot of good books, and that these people must not be disappointed on their initial visit. It would be better to pour in as many new books as she has room for there, to make the best possible impression. She can easily return a boxful to the Branch the next day, if they cannot be spared for the weekend.

CHAPTER V

Brightening the Main Library

November 20, 1946: Received a fine set of twelve large "stills" of the motion picture "Two Years Before the Mast" from some theatre agency in New York. Mrs. Benson immediately dug out a number of book jackets from other novels about the sea and put together a fine display centered around the pictures from the movie.

When we get more time, I hope to get together with the local theatre bigwigs and work out a continuous program for tying books up with the new movies coming to town. This is one of the best ways to sell books and benefits both the library and the theatres. So many of the big novels are sold to the movies nowadays, and almost every important picture is based on a book—or has some book connections.

Never could see why the bookstores haven't taken more advantage of the possibilities in this field. If I was starting a bookstore I would try and locate on the same street and near to a busy theatre and would center my window displays around the pictures currently showing there. In almost any crowd emerging from a theatre, one can hear people remarking that they would like to read the book on which the picture was based, or that they are going to re-read it, or that they would like to know whether or not the book actually turned out the same way as the movie. If it could be arranged, I believe I would try and sell copies of the book in the lobby, or from a wagon in front of the theatre.

Movie stills and book jackets make a very attractive combination that adds life to the circulation hall as well as stopping traffic and calling people's attention to a number of good books. We hope that we can have such displays in the library all the time.

We have also been experimenting this week with cellophane wrappers on the new books, covering the book jackets and keeping them clean and untorn. We have ordered 100 of them, at 7½¢ apiece, and will see how they work out. I've always been interested in seeing a library's shelves filled with the same sort of bright-colored, attractive, new-looking books that one finds in bookstores. I'll never be content with a library full of dark, dull-looking volumes, even if most of these books are old and worn, simply because the books are free, instead of having to be sold for several dollars apiece.

There is no comparison between the appearance of a bookstore and the average library. One looks alive and appealing, the other lifeless and unattractive. The big difference between them is due mainly to the presence of bright jackets on the store's books. It's these dust wrappers that sell the books in a great many cases. I daresay that a store that displayed its new books without their jackets would soon experience a real drop in its volume of business. The average book looks far more colorless and unattractive without its jacket than the average girl without her makeup on.

. . . . .

November 21, 1946: Several of the girls have spent most of this week painting the staff lounge. They simply put on old clothes and go to work. They have already finished the ceiling, the walls, and the woodwork and doors. At the moment, however, the entire floor and all the furniture in the room is splattered with paint. They have really wielded the paint brushes with abandon—as is clearly apparent from a glance at their faces and clothes.

The room is a mess now, but it should be quite attractive when they do the floor and the table and chairs, and get the new drapes and couch covering in place. They have been working hard at the job, and I trust they will enjoy the result of their efforts.

The painting of the floor in the reference rooms is progressing more smoothly. Lorenzo has finished the front room with a nice jungle green which is a great improvement over the plain concrete and goes well with the newly-painted windows.

Called the Negro librarian at our new station in Ford-Greene school to see how the new library was being received. She reported that she had already circulated all but five of the 150 books she had taken out there from the Negro Branch and was going to have to return to the Branch for more books to display to the people who would be visiting the new library in the evening. That certainly is good news from a branch librarian who is accustomed to circulating thirty books a day. However, I am afraid that with the public library station in the school, the children from that one school will keep most of the books in use and leave little material for the other children of North Nashville. Not that I mind that, for we will be only too glad to make any amount of additional books available to the Ford-Greene, or any other, station, as long as they will be used. It's such a pleasure to see books really used!

. . . . .

November 22, 1946: Finally sold our unused "Library of Congress Catalog of Printed Cards" to the J.U.L. Got $650 for the 168-volume set—almost more than I had hoped for. And when I think of what we can buy with that amount of money, it certainly seems like a good day for the Library. I told Mr. Clapp that they could take the books out to Vandervilt now, and wouldn't have to worry about paying us until next Fall, when they will have more money on hand. As a matter of fact, I would rather not be getting the money this budget year as we then would have to spend it now when we are as well-heeled as we ever will be. It will come in very handy next year when we won't have extra money as we do at present.

Mrs. Fleming called to say how much she liked the library column and how she wished she could write so clearly and concisely. I told her I had to write that way as I had so little space to play with, but was glad to hear that her people are using the column to get the books that interest them. Incidentally, I hope to prepare similar articles about the new books going regularly to the Negro Branch so that Mrs. Lockert can have them published in the Negro newspaper.

Having only a third of a column to fill, it is a simple matter to introduce from 10 to 30 new books. Not having time to read the books, I work from the bookjackets and "Retail Bookseller" annotations, together with what I know about the author and the general nature and importance of the book. Doesn't take a good writer or bookman to do the job. The trick is to pick interesting books and to talk about them in an informal and enthusiastic manner. Can't allow any rambling, or any high-brow stuff, or a single word that doesn't contribute something to the article.

To show how simple the job really is, here is the start of our introductory column:

"This is the first column in a weekly series that will try and keep you up-to-date on all the worthwhile new books. Every book mentioned in these columns will be in active service at the Nashville Public Library so that you can pick what you want to read and know where to go to find a free copy—sooner or later.

"We hope to introduce to you over 95 percent of the books that you will be hearing about and wanting to read, as soon after publication date as we can find space in this column. While we won't bother with juvenile books, mysteries, westerns, light romance, science fiction, teen-age books, or reference volumes— important as all this material is—we will present to you approximately 1200 titles a year of adult fiction and non-fiction. We follow books like some people follow the horses and we assure you that we won't miss many books of general interest that you will want to know about.

"However, since your public library can afford only a few copies of all these volumes we hope that you won't clip this column and rush to the library expecting to find copies of most of the titles on the shelves. You would be lucky to find more than one or two at any one time. Doubtless the best way of using these columns, in addition to just learning about the new books, is to tuck each one away in your desk drawer for six or nine months, then bring them out and start hunting for the titles you want. You will find so many more on the shelves, and the books will read just as well then. It is hard to convince people of that; they feel they must read only the latest books, as if reading matter somehow deteriorates in interest with each passing month. We see people scurrying to read some mediocre historical novel, just because it is new, who have never yet read *Gone With the Wind* or James Street's *Tap Roots*, or his *Oh, Promised Land* . . . "

∎   ∎   ∎   ∎   ∎

November 25, 1946: Mrs. Moncrief says she will need some help in the Children's Room on Saturdays—with her business picking up the way it has been lately. Last Saturday, she circulated perhaps four times as many books as used to go out. The morning story hours are responsible for some of the Saturday increase, and then last Saturday there was the judging of the entries in the Hansel and Gretel contest. The real explanation, however, is to be found in the large number of children who have been brought into the Room for the first time in the last few months. It's primarily a matter of drawing the youngsters into the library, letting them see what a nice place it is, and getting them into the habit of thinking of the Library and wanting to visit it.

The problem is much the same with the adult population, although I believe it is easier to work out in the case of the children. Children can be reached through Boy Scout and Girl Scout troops, through the schools, and through various other organizations, and they have the time and the inclination to respond to such activities as story hours, marionette shows, summer reading contests, and the like, whereas their parents are beyond the reach of such promotional instruments. Getting the grown-ups into the library is likely to be a much tougher proposition.

I believe we will save money and get better book service in the branches through a new scheme for distributing books that was inaugurated this morning. I've been ordering two copies of new adult books that sound particularly readable and that might be branch books if we could afford to put them in all the branches and had sufficient readers there to justify such purchase. These books are definitely better than one-copy titles, and it seems as if we ought to have an extra copy somewhere in the system.

As these books come in now, one copy of each title will be marked "B", instead of the letter of the main or an individual branch library. This will indicate to the catalogers that these books belong to a circulating branch collection—to be moved from branch to branch so as to take care of all units with a single copy of each title.

All "B" books will be held at the Main Library as long as there are reserves for them. When released by the Head of the Circulation Department, they will start their round of the three branches. They will stay at whichever branch happens to be their first stop until they appear to have stopped circulating there, and then proceed to another branch library. In this way, all three branches will have the use of many more books than would otherwise come to them. When we get our bookmobile, most of the ''B'' books that have completed their branch circuit will be put into this new mobile library unit. The letter ''B'' will then signify ''Bookmobile'' as well as ''Branches''.

■   ■   ■   ■   ■

November 27, 1946: Gave Lorenzo $10 as a bonus to show our appreciation of his fine work of painting this month and told him that these extra payments would continue as long as he was kept busy with his special painting assignment. That is little enough to pay for a much cleaner and more-attractive looking library. The work that he has done so far would have cost 30 times as much if assigned to professional painters.

One of the girls came in this afternoon with an idea for having a book-reviewing contest for adults, offering prizes for the best reviews. I hated to have to turn down the idea and show her why it might not be too good a thing to try. There's nothing that I like better than a new idea from some member of the staff. They don't have to be particularly good ideas. The important thing is that the people continue to use their heads and think how the efficiency of the library can be improved, and not leave all the planning to the Librarian.

In most cases, where the person's suggestion does not involve any great expense, I tell her to go ahead with the idea and see what she can do with it. I prefer to have her find out for herself why the thing won't work—if such is the case—than to throw cold water on the idea and send her away unbelieving and disinclined to do any more thinking for the library. Can't afford to take chances, however, with anything—like this book-reviewing contest—that falls within the field of the library's public relations. As I explained to the young lady, no institution that is dependent upon the good will of the public can afford to let itself get into the position of having to show a preference for one taxpayer over another. Every book reviewer would know very well that his review was the best one turned in and many of them might feel less kindly toward the Library for showing such poor judgment in picking the winners. Some individuals might be suspicious enough to brand the whole thing as "politics". In short, such a contest could make few friends for the Nashville Public Library—and might well leave us with fewer supporters than we now have.

Mrs. Baker left today to prepare for her forthcoming ocean voyage to join her husband in Austria. That leaves the Circulation Department in a hole until Mrs. Dale arrives on December 10th to take her place, but Mrs. Benson will try to persuade Miss Andrews, a former children's librarian, to come in and help out. We would very much like Miss Andrews to return to the Library as a full-time worker, and while she hasn't seemed at all interested so far, we are hopeful that if we can just get her in here for a few days, she will be so pleasantly surprised at seeing the "new" Children's Department, and will like working with Mrs. Moncrief so much, that she will want to come back for more.

．　　　．　　　．　　　．　　　．

November 30, 1946: Mrs. Moncrief called me at home to say that the phonograph they had borrowed for the "story-hour" this morning had worked particularly well and wanted to know what I thought about buying it. She said it had a better tone, and more volume than the others they had tried, and that this one was the only such machine in town. The store was asking for it back, so I told her to go ahead and get it if that was what she wanted. It is an attractive portable machine, and has a record-changing attachment that can keep the music going for half an hour at a time. We ought to be able to use it very nicely anywhere in the city.

She also mentioned that she had had the help of Miss Andrews all day and that life in the Children's Department was just a breeze with such expert help. It's been almost two months since Mrs. Workman left her to get back to her family. What really pleased me, however, was her saying that Miss A. was delighted with the Room and wanted to come back to work there. The two of them would make a wonderful team.

Before she hung up, she told me she wanted to give me some news that she knew would make me happy. The good news turned out to be her circulation figures for November. She reported that the Children's Department had circulated 3820 books last month—as against only 1680 in October. That's more than doubling the circulation!

Circulation figures aren't everything, of course, but they are probably as meaningful as anything else we librarians have to go by. Comparisons of circulation figures of different libraries must be taken with a grain of salt, since one library may be distributing more "rental library fiction" than another, and of course the communities served may be very different in their educational backgrounds, but even here they give a fairly good picture of the public service performed by the different institutions. Any librarian could, of course, double his circulation in short order by watering his stock with hundreds of volumes of light fiction, such as the publications of Gramercy, Arcadia, and other houses. There are a thousand potential readers for such stories to every reader of serious non-fiction.

The only comparison that interests us these days is of course the comparison of our circulation now with what it was in previous months and years. We simply want to know what progress we are making and whether the different steps we are taking to try and improve our service are meeting with any success. To be sure, the people at the circulation desk do not need any figures to tell them that they are busier than they used to be, but there's a good deal of satisfaction to be had by everyone on the team in seeing the circulation thermometer go up.

■   ■   ■   ■   ■

December 4, 1946: Have been home in bed with the flu all week. This has been my first absence from the library since my arrival here. The Library called several times every day this week, so I had some contact with most staff members. They have been so nice in telling me how much they missed me at the library that it made me appreciate again the smallness of our staff. Directing a small library like this one has the same advantages of closer contact with one's fellow workers that are offered in any small unit, whether it be a company, a city, or a school.

We really have a nice group of people at the Library now. I hope that our business grows so that we will be justified in taking on more staff, but one can be sure that we will always do without rather than hire someone not up to our standards. When a library starts appointing people simply to fill vacancies, it is headed for trouble. As long as it sticks to quality in its appointments it will have little difficulty in getting the good people it wants. But once it lets down the bars and accepts lower-grade people it will find it hard to recruit any high-class personnel thereafter. The wise job hunter considers the type of people with whom he will be working one of the most significant factors in determining his choice of position.

The thing that pleases me more than anything else these days is the evident pleasure with which the members of the staff go about their work. Everyone seems to be happy and enjoying what they are doing. And everyone seems to get along pretty well with everyone else.

Had a call Thursday from a young lady wanting to hold a social gathering of her church in the basement auditorium of the East Branch Library. The church doesn't afford the space required to handle the expected number of guests, and someone suggested the library to her. It sounded like a good enough idea to me so I called the President of the Library Board to get his reaction to the request. He asked me what I thought about it, and I told him simply that I always liked to see the library used and becoming more a recognized part of the community, and liked to be helpful whenever possible. If other churches pick up the idea and want similar service, all the better. The building is there to be used, and I'd much rather have it working every night than going to waste. He was good enough to agree with me, so the very appreciative young lady was told to go ahead with her party plans.

■   ■   ■   ■   ■

December 10, 1946: Finally got together with Judge Hickman to talk over the possibility of a county library service. Told him that I thought we had the answer to a problem that had been of concern to the County for over thirty years. Went on to explain how the proposed plan would require no immediate appropriation by the County Court, or any other special action to inaugurate such service, and that the County would pay the Library only for service given to county residents.

The Judge listened to the proposal, which is more than he is said to have done in past years, but seemed to feel that people really did not want to read. "If they did", he averred, "they would spend some of their money to buy books, instead of spending it all on the movies". My reply was that most city people wouldn't buy books either, if they were denied the use of free library books, but the fact is that they do have access to a public library and use it to the extent that the average borrower takes home more than $20 worth of books a year. And, as I reminded him, if he should be proved right in his belief that people don't want library service, then the County will not have to pay the Library anything.

I told the Judge that our circulation people were tired of explaining to County residents why they could not—without paying a $2 fee—borrow books from the library, and that our Children's Department had turned away several hundred children already this month because they lived outside the city. Also emphasized the amount of good will the County Court could gain by providing countywide book service, and hinted that the County administration could well use some favorable publicity after the recent unfortunate affair involving the question of salary raises for county teachers.

Hickman remarked that he favored the proposed cost-per-circulation contract over previous proposals which called for lump sum appropriations by the County Court, to be spent by the Library. He suggested that I see Ira Parker, the Chairman of the Ways and Means Committee of the County Court, and then check the feasibility of such a contract with the county attorney, after which Hickman, Parker and I could get together to talk the thing over further.

Am not permitting myself to get too optimistic about the final outcome of our proposal, but am happy to have a 'foot in the door' and hope to continue on through to a satisfactory conclusion. Mr. Parker isn't available this month, so it will be April before we can bring any concrete proposal before the County Court. Meanwhile, we shall keep our fingers crossed.

■   ■   ■   ■   ■

December 14, 1946: I can't help but feel uncomfortable having Tom Tichenor's beautiful Christmas Village on display this month in the Children's Department. With its perfectly made castle and many houses, its skating ponds, trees and fences, and its 50 well-dressed little people, it is the sort of masterpiece that ought to be in a store-window on Church Street where it would be admired by thousands instead of the relative handful that will see it in the library. It just doesn't seem right to tuck it away in the basement department, and it bothers me every time I see it with nobody around to enjoy the sight of the thing. We tried to get a picture of it in the paper to call attention to its presence in the building, but this is not possible since its picture has long been scheduled to appear on the front page of the Sunday Supplement in another connection.

Mrs. Benson has been doing a lot of moving of bookshelves, magazine racks, and tables behind the circulation desk, and has also broken up the oversize-book collection and filed these volumes in their proper places on the shelves in the stacks. Believe it is more practical to have all stack material on a particular subject together, but am not going to waste time considering the advisability of this move. I am happy to have someone in charge downstairs who is willing to try new things and get things done without waiting to ask for my opinion or approval. There's more satisfaction in seeing someone else on the staff do a real job than in doing it oneself. It's always good to be reminded that one has capable helpers around the place who can carry a good part of the load.

．　　　．　　　．　　　．　　　．

December 15, 1946: Got the final circulation returns for November and was delighted to find for the first time an increase in all three branches and the adult and juvenile departments of the main library. The month's total was a good 25 per cent above that for November 1945.

Miss Bell stopped by later in the day to see what I had in mind in the way of replacing Mr. Lewis who is soon to retire as Head of the Reference Department. She doesn't want anybody made the head of the department over her, chiefly because she doesn't want to get left with most of the detail work. I assured her that what I had in mind was a young person who would divide both the reference work and the "housekeeping work" with her. She seemed to like the idea of being head of the department but I told her that I couldn't help feeling that she would be unhappy carrying the responsibility of this position. Assured her that it was not a matter of ability, but more one of temperament. Most people don't want to be burdened with responsibility and would prefer to develop in their present positions rather than be promoted to supervisory posts where they would have to make decisions and tell other people what to do. Went on to say that I knew she _could_ plan a program for the department, supervise the work of an assistant, select reference books, decide the disposition of old material, and contact business leaders, but from what I knew of her I didn't think she would _enjoy_ having to do these things. Explained that if she were head of the department I would leave things pretty much up to her and count on her to make the place go and build up the reference service. With that responsibility she would have the department on her mind night and day, and might not be as lighthearted and happy as she is now.

I reminded her of her reaction to recent situations where she was called upon to make decisions and she admitted that they had upset her not a little. I think she could see that I was sincere in wanting to fit her into the spot where she would be most happy, and, after all, happiness is a pretty important objective. I was glad to have the opportunity of discussing this matter thoroughly with her. It had been giving me some concern lately.

■   ■   ■   ■   ■

December 16, 1946: Had a busy morning getting ready for the Board meeting that I'd called on rather short notice. When the two women on the Board called to say they did not believe they would be able to get to the meeting, I arranged to have a taxicab pick them up ten minutes before the scheduled hour. Was very thankful later that I was thus able to get them downtown as there were only three other members present, just making the quorum of five.

The first business to come up was the report of the committee working on the sale of the Negro Branch. Mr. Farris reported that several different groups had been interested but that all the deals had fallen through. The real estate business is not what it was a year ago and we can't get an offer now that is even half what the Board had once been asking.

Mrs. Miser pointed out that the leaders of the Negro community were getting anxious over the thought of losing their library and were wanting to know what they might be getting in its place. Even though they don't use the books in the library, to any great extent, they use the building for a variety of meetings and look upon it as a sort of recreational or community center.

The next matter up for consideration was the report of the committee on retirement and pensions. As accepted, the report calls for the almost immediate retirement of the six older staff members and the payment to five of them of annual pensions that will continue until their death. The amounts are small, to be sure, but they are better than nothing and will at least help to keep the people in food or give them something to pay relatives with whom they may be living.

It will be up to me to give the six people the sad news that they are retired, as of January 1, 1947. All have known for a long time that the evil day was approaching. But even with the assurance of a regular pension—which they had no hope of six months ago—I am sure that not more than one of the six people is interested in retiring.

To the other five, the Library means everything. It's their whole life. I don't know what they will do when they can no longer come to work every morning. This whole retirement business is certainly a very sad one. Of course, I can, and will have to, keep most of them on the staff—on a month-to-month basis—until replacements can be found for them. But even this is just putting off the final day and working under the shadow of the axe.

Next came the Librarian's Report which I telescoped to allow more time for discussion of the four recommendations that I wanted to bring before the group. The first one of these called for turning the P.T.A. room into an attractive Young People's Room. The room is now used only for infrequent meetings, and the P.T.A. seems to like the idea of making better use of the room and moving their books on child care and parent education upstairs where they will reach more people. The youngsters who have heard our plans seem quite enthusiastic, which spurs us on since we are well aware that the young people do not now use the library. I've never known a public library that had so few patrons of high school and college age. There certainly is a real need for action in this field.

What we want to do first is to have the room painted—ceiling white, walls light blue, and floor tile red—and then cut up the extremely high bookshelves and put low shelves around three sides of the room, leaving the fourth wall free for furniture. Want to get some more comfortable and cheerful furniture in the room and give it a better atmosphere.

Particularly want to get the young people "into the act" so that they will take a real interest in the room and feel that it belongs to them. What I have in mind is a sort of Junior Library Board, with representatives from every high school in the city, that will share in the management of the Young People's Room. Will have to discuss the thing with the school people and see if we can't have some Junior Trustees elected or appointed.

Believe it would be well to let the young people select the magazines that interest them—after examining a wide range of possible titles—and share also in the selection of the books that go into the room. I would like to see them reading reviews and really getting into the spirit of the place—tho that may be asking the impossible.

The Room's real drawing card will be our new phonograph and the collection of popular records that we plan to have. Every library record collection that I've heard about seems to stick to the classical music, but it seems a shame not to give the young people the sort of music they want to hear. We won't have any boogie woogie or anything else that is too noisy or objectionable, but we do want to have good popular music.

The music is deserving in itself, but it is perhaps even more important to us as a device to attract young people into the library and put them into close proximity with bright, readable books. It would also be a tremendous public relations asset and help to keep the library talked about and appearing more modern and vital than most people now believe it to be.

My second recommendation called for the customary type of phonograph record collection. What we have in mind here is getting two victrola turntables, four sets of earphones, and 100 albums of the best operas and symphonies, and putting them in the old Business Library upstairs. We have had a number of requests for such a service and are anxious to make these wonderful records available. We don't have any money or space to construct sound-proof listening rooms, so will have to confine ourselves to the use of earphones which will permit the playing of records within a few feet of the people reading books in the room.

The phonographs and record collections, together, should cost about $1,000. We have the money to purchase this material tomorrow, but I want to wait six weeks and try in that time to find somebody who will give us at least one collection. I hate to spend library money for something that offers a good possibility of attracting an interested donor. A memorial gift, furthermore, generally provides better publicity, gives the collection more prestige, and helps to make a strong friend for the library.

The third recommendation was that we consider the acquisition of a bookmobile to serve the outer sections of the city. Two-thirds of Nashville has no library branch or station, and it is this area that contains most of the library's potential users. Here are the three universities with their many students and faculty members, to name only one large group.

I feel sure that we could do as much business with a bookmobile, making twenty or thirty stops a week, as we now do from all three of our branches put together. And the bookmobile would be a wonderful library advertiser that would stimulate the use of the main library and all branches. A traveling library carries the appeal of anything on wheels; it is something that everyone can understand and appreciate. It should make the Nashville Public Library come alive to many thousands of people, and help educate them to the fact that the library belongs to them, and wants to serve them, that its service is free, and that a great many others are already using it.

While at Baltimore I gathered a considerable amount of material on bookmobiles and trailer branches, including letters from librarians operating such service in other cities. I presented this material to the Board this afternoon, inviting the President to appoint a committee to study this material and see what type of machine they thought best for Nashville. They seemed to prefer to leave the whole matter up to me.

Before spending any library money on the bookmobile I am going to try and find somebody who might be interested in giving us the money for it. Don't believe it will be too hard to sell. But if we can't find the necessary angel, we will have to push the project so as to get the job done and the money spent before the end of July. This is probably the only year that we will have money to spend for such special projects, and if we don't spend the money this year it will revert to the City and we may never get some of the things we need.

I believe it is important—on the rare occasions when one has a little extra money—to put this money into projects that are productive and that will build business and help the library obtain larger appropriations in the future. One has to take advantage of his good years to strengthen his business and do everything possible to insure that there will be many other good years to come. Here in Nashville where circulation is so far below what it should, and could, be, it is particularly important that our money be spent for things that will attract new readers and make friends for the Library. Always in the back of my mind is the next appropriation time when we will have to make our case for another increase.

My fourth "recommendation" was that we give Mrs. Benson another salary increase to get her nearer where she belongs and above the new department heads who will soon be joining us. That will mean two increases of $300 or more for her within a period of five months, which is rather unusual for libraries, but she has been working herself to death as our new Circulation Chief and well deserves her raises.

All four recommendations were given quick and unanimous approval by the five members present. This may not seem so remarkable to the average librarian, but I couldn't help contrasting the co-operative and progressive attitude of this group with the customary reaction of that other library board of my experience. They would have fussed and found fault with all four proposals simply because such things had never been done before and it was the new librarian who was suggesting that they be done now.

As this was the last Board meeting of the year, I took a few minutes to summarize the progress that we had made in recent months. When I arrived here in May there were five things that we particularly wanted and needed. These needs, or objectives, I outlined as follows:

1. The need to provide for the retirement of the six staff members who have passed the normal retirement age.

2. The need for more money—to increase our book budget and raise our salary level.

3. The need to attract more readers and increase the circulation in all library units.

4. The need to brighten up the interior of the main library and make it a more attractive place for all concerned.

5. The need to get a county library to serve the thousands of potential readers living outside the city limits.

Well, our batting average is rather good on these five points. The retirement situation is being taken care of, we have a great deal more money and have already used it to raise salaries and double our book expenditures, our circulation is already going up, and the appearance of the library's reading rooms is greatly improved. As for the fifth objective, we are nearer to having a county wide library service than we have been at any time in the past.

The members of the Board seem quite heartened by the progress that has been made this year. This is particularly true of the minority of them who have been inside the library in recent months. If they continue to tell the others about the building's improved appearance and atmosphere, perhaps we may yet see some of the other six trustees come in for a look around.

Before departing, the five members present voted the Librarian a generous "Christmas bonus" amounting to $80 for each month he's been on the job. That means a check tomorrow for $600, and another month's check in January, which will carry up to the next regular meeting in January at which time the matter of an adjustment in the Librarian's salary will be considered by the full Board.

■   ■   ■   ■   ■

December 19, 1946: Had one of the finest of staff meetings this morning. Planned to run from 8:15 to 9:00, it lasted until 10:00, with everyone taking an active and enthusiastic part in the discussion. I started off by reviewing the accomplishments of the last six months and pointing out the distance that we have come since our first meeting. I then gave the highlights of yesterday's Board meeting, reporting that everything was now all set to go ahead with our phonograph record collection, our Young People's Room, and our bookmobile.

I think most everyone had the feeling that we were really beginning to move, and that we could do almost anything if we wanted to enough. The only unhappy thing about the meeting, to me, was the sight of one of the older people looking sad and forlorn and having little to say. It was the first time I had seen her that way, and when I asked her closest friend if there was anything troubling Miss W. she said she thought she was just beginning to realize that her days with the library were numbered and that she would not be here to have a part in the interesting things now planned.

Several members of the staff made the remark that most Nashvillians do not even know where the Library is and that many do not realize that anyone can come in and borrow books from us. This is only too true. We will definitely have to publicize the location of the main building and make people more aware of the availability of free library service to them. We will have to prepare a series of spot announcements for the radio stations to broadcast for us. And it might not be a bad idea to erect a colorful signboard on the front lawn, inviting people to use their library. I'm afraid many passersby do not notice the ''Carnegie Library'' across the front of the building. The two soldiers who came up to the loan desk last week to ask for their room reservations apparently associated the library with the neighboring sign that points up the street to the ''Hermitage Hotel''.

        .   .   .   .   .

December 23, 1946: Got a call from Red O'Donnell, the town's leading newspaper columnist, thanking me for my letter and saying he wanted to come up and see me about running the whole thing in his column. It all started with a chance remark in a recent column of his to the effect that the average Nashvillian read less than three library books a year. I had taken advantage of this opening to write him a long letter about the library, saying that his remark was a lot like stating that the population of Nashville is ''less than half a million.'' Actually, as I pointed out, the average Nashvillian reads less than *one* library book a year. Went on to explain why The Athens of the South made such a poor showing on public library use, as compared with Memphis, Chattanooga and

Knoxville, giving the two reasons of continuously poor financial support and the lack of a county library service that the other cities have had for over thirty years.

I then proceeded to give him some catchy library statistics that always seem to go over well, and that would fit nicely into his column. For example: The average N.P.L. user borrows over $20 worth of books a year, making public library service—costing 27¢ per capita—the greatest bargain one can buy. No.2: If all the books borrowed from the N.P.L. last year were stacked on top of each other they would make a pile 28 times as high as the Woolworth Building. If laid end to end, they would stretch from Nashville to Madison—nine miles away—and back to Nashville and then out to Madison again. It would take six hours to walk from one end of the continuous line of books to the other.

Since most everyone seems to read his personal column, we are thrilled at the possibility of getting our story into this channel. Incidentally, it would be the first time that he has devoted the greater portion of his column to any one subject. Many of his readers would doubtless be surprised to find him going all out on such a topic as the public library.

Lorenzo has been doing an excellent job of adding new shelves halfway between the old bookshelves in the front reference room upstairs. The stage is now set for bringing up the 125 little-used magazines, relieving the situation in the reading room and making a substantial and attractive concentration of current periodicals.

After the shelves have been painted, the magazines will be spread out on them—two or three different titles to each shelf. With the magazines piled on shelves, instead of displayed in racks, it is possible to save on magazine covers and display four of five back issues of each publication together with the current copy. This should be a popular change since most people don't get in to see their favorite magazines every

week and hence want to see more than the current numbers
when they do come to the library.

.   .   .   .   .

December 24, 1946: Except for our regular patrons
who wouldn't desert us for even a circus parade or a three-
alarm fire down the street, the library seems deserted today.
I'm afraid the poor people who keep our daily newspapers in
constant use have no family or money to buy Christmas presents for or with, and all our book readers are doing their
browsing today in bookstores.

The girls at the loan desk kept the air filled with Christmas carols, from our nice new portable, but even so the atmosphere was definitely last-day-of-schoolish. Several people
suggested that we close at one o'clock, but since Mrs. Benson
had informed a telephone inquirer that the library would be
open until 6 o'clock, we had committed ourselves to working
until then.

It was possible, however, to let everyone go at noon
except one person in the Reference Department and one at the
loan desk. I sent Lorenzo home with the rest of the people and
he was delighted to get an afternoon off—even though he
doesn't have any Christmas shopping to do. The poor man can
count on his fingers the number of afternoons he has away
from the library during the year.

I left at four o'clock, carrying an interesting looking
package that the staff had planted on my desk when I was out
for lunch. The bottom fell out of the wrappings on the way
home, and I found myself holding a beautiful electric clock.

CHAPTER VI

Building Staff Morale

December 26, 1946: Rounded up Mrs. Benson and the two children's librarians for a raid on the bookstores. Several of them had hinted that they were desirous of getting rid of the stock that had failed to sell itself as Christmas gifts at rather high discounts, so it seemed as if we ought to look over the situation a bit. One store proved a false alarm but the other offered good pickings, and the girls—particularly the children's librarians—had a wonderful time. I told them to go ahead and get as many books as they wanted, but I'm afraid they were too unused to buying books where they didn't have to watch their pennies, and didn't get as many volumes as they needed.

It was good to be able to turn the girls loose in the bookstores and let them select what they felt they needed. I wish every librarian could be given this opportunity, particularly when they are young and new to the profession. Almost any librarian would rather buy books than do any other library task, and the sad thing about it is that few of them get the chance to engage in this popular pastime. What is more fun than visiting a bookstore and picking out all the books that look interesting to one—saying "I'll take this one, and this one, and two of these, and you can also send along all those I've piled on the counter there." It's really very enjoyable, when one is playing on library time and with library money.

I like to give the young people a taste of this sort of living, because I know no better morale builder. It's not the acquiring of books that carries the punch, but the feeling of importance that it gives one to be spending the company's money, together with the comforting evidence that the boss has sufficient confidence in one's judgment to send him on such an assignment. There's no better way to build up one's staff, in any line of work, than to let them represent their department, or their institution, away from it. It's too bad that libraries don't have the same occasion, or amount of money, to send their young people on trips that business concerns do. I believe I went on some pleasant trips for the engineering company that weren't absolutely necessary—but they were good for my morale and doubtless paid off when I returned to the office. I wish now that it were possible to send some of our staff members to study other progressive libraries around the country and bring back new ideas that could be put to work here. Even if they picked up nothing of value, they would return with greater interest and enthusiasm for their work.

■   ■   ■   ■   ■

January 2, 1947: I believe we have finally found the signs that we need for the reading rooms. The various sections of shelving have never been identified in any way so that the newcomer must follow the shelves all the way around to learn where the books in different subject fields may be found. A good set of signs and shelf labels was one of the first things I wanted to get for the reading room, but I had been holding out for wooden letters—which are more attractive and durable than painted signs—and they were nowhere to be found in Nashville.

We had asked one of the department stores for help and this resulted, today, in the arrival at the library of a salesman from an Ohio concern which supplies most of the fancy signs in the nation's leading department stores. His samples immediately rang the bell with us, even though they did seem a bit expensive. We tried a number of them on the shelves for size and picked Gothic type letters 1½ inches high. All the signs will have maple letters on a walnut board. We will have to go over the shelves, listing the important subjects and noting the amount of space that each covers so that we will know where the signs will be placed and what the room will look like with all of them in place. We figure that it will cost us about $100 to cover the place with the necessary subject headings. But it will be well worth the expense to have the reading rooms properly labeled—and in a thoroughly professional manner. Most libraries are sadly lacking in this respect. It would be difficult to find more than two or three public libraries that can rank with the department stores when it comes to labeling their shelves.

While looking over the reading rooms this afternoon we got to thinking how much better the place would look with a fresh coat of paint on the walls. The re-painted walls in the front room upstairs look so nice that I am afraid we won't be happy until the whole place is brought in step with them. However, the job on the walls has shown the ceiling up so dirty, by contrast, that it looks now as if we will have to paint the walls and ceilings in both reference rooms and the three reading rooms downstairs.

I told Lorenzo that the painting of each of the five
rooms would bring him an extra $5 bonus. I'm anxious to get
the building in shape, and the more work he does the more
jobs that come to mind for future attention. In addition to
these five main rooms, there is the P.T.A. room to be painted
from floor to ceiling, the Librarian's office which is the dirtiest room in the building, and the basement hallway which
leads from the lower entrance to the children's room. I told
Lorenzo that we'd have to have an ''open house'' in April to
show everyone the new library he'd given them, and that
eventually we would probably change the name of the building to ''The Lorenzo Howse Memorial Library''. It's certainly a break for us to have such a useful Jack-of-all-trades on
the janitorial staff.

＊　　　＊　　　＊　　　＊　　　＊

January 3, 1947: The Library received a good bit of
publicity in this morning's TENNESSEAN. Red O'Donnell
gave most of his column to my recent letter to him, starting
each paragraph with a ''Did you know that . . . '' I had pur-
posefully written the letter so that he could use it in his column
almost without change. My only regret was that he didn't start
the column with the paragraphs about the great number of
books borrowed from the library, instead of beginning with
the part about how low our circulation is in comparison with
the Tennessee cities. However, the column does get across the
needs of the local library situation, and presents facts that are
true and well worth publicizing.

＊　　　＊　　　＊　　　＊　　　＊

January 6, 1947: All six of the older staff members
have now been informed of their retirement on January 1st and

the amount of the pension that they will be receiving. I'm glad that the unhappy assignment of breaking the sad and final news to them is over, even though all of them were as calm and pleasant about it as could be and there was none of the strain or sadness that one might have expected.

All of them had been told that the thing was coming, so there was no surprise—but only a desire to know the amount of their retirement income and the actual date of their departure. I explained that they were now on a month-to-month basis, for as long as it takes us to find adequate replacements for them, but that I was not making any particular effort to find new people and hoped that they would be with us for some time.

It was important that the retiring librarians be made to feel that they had served the Library well and that their services were still valued. I believe that they could see that we were sincere in wanting them to continue working for us, if for no other reason than it would cost the Library $1,000 a year to replace them. They are a mighty nice group and we will greatly miss them. It is equally certain that we will have to pay their replacements an average of $600 a year more than they are now getting, which—when added to the $400 average pension—makes the additional thousand dollars per person that could otherwise be spent for a variety of important purposes.

The pensions, admittedly, are small, yet—as one of the people pointed out—they provide as much money as they would be getting if they had put $10 a month into a retirement program for the last twenty-five years. They all seem glad to have this small amount to add to their meagre savings and I got the happy impression from each one that he or she will now be able to make out some way.

■   ■   ■   ■   ■

January 7, 1947: Spent the morning looking for the fluorescent lighting fixtures that we want to put into the reference rooms. Have long been concerned about the poor light which I deem partly responsible for the slight use made of this department. I know I wouldn't want to do any work in light that registers only 3 foot-candles.

We had a lighting engineer in last week to see what it would take to provide adequate light for these two upstairs rooms. He returned Friday with a blueprint calling for the installation of solid banks of fixtures down each side of both rooms. When I learned what they would cost I started cutting them down until the 16 four-foot (4 tube) fixtures in the main reference room had been reduced to 6, and the 10 in the front room had been cut down to 4. The engineer tells me that these ten fixtures should still give us 30 f.c. on the reading tables, which is probably as good light as any public library in the country can boast—though admittedly below illuminating society standards.

With a 40 per cent discount on the fixtures, they will cost us only $231. The tubes, at a dollar apiece, will run another $40. I believe we are going to get them installed for around $25, which is very reasonable, so that the entire job will come to around $300.

This matter of library lighting is an extremely important one. I have never been in a library yet where the light was strong enough for me to stay and read in comfort. The idea everywhere seems to be to provide enough light for the people to find the books they want on the shelves but don't worry about the comparatively few people who may want to study in the building. Some libraries have goose-neck lamps on the tables, but besides being unattractive they don't throw their light more than a foot or two and the reader has to lean over the table and keep his book within the narrow range of the beam. It is a rare library where one can sit and read a book with anywhere near the intensity of light that he is accustomed to in his home. Good light is expensive, yet we owe it to the public to provide it. And I feel sure that better lighted libraries would mean better used libraries, in the same way that better lighting means more customers and bigger sales for any retail store.

We were fortunate to be able to borrow two ladders and a plank from the painter who did the bookshelves in the reading room. He also introduced us to a wallpaper cleaner that is a wonder-worker. Miss Welch and I cleaned a few walls in the office in a matter of minutes, and then turned the cleaner over to Lorenzo to whom it represented a great improvement over other and more drippy ways of cleaning his ceilings. The old way of cleaning walls and ceilings seemed like such a long, unpleasant assignment that he had almost decided to give them two coats of paint instead. Well, this wallpaper cleaner works as easily and quickly as a paintbrush, and saves expensive gallons of paint. And with the walls and ceilings thus cleaned, he should be able to get by with one coat.

The only trouble with this cleaner is that it does not take off finger marks, and all such marks show up more conspicuously when the soot and dirt have been removed. As a result, one can not use the cleaner on any surface without becoming convinced of the urgent need for painting. It does an excellent job above the 7-foot level—where the surface is relatively free from marks—but probably should not be recommended for use below that height.

■   ■   ■   ■   ■

January 8, 1947: Dropped into the Catalog Department for my regular morning's chat, but this time it developed into a discussion of our method of ordering Library of Congress cards. We order all our non-fiction cards from Washington, and apparently some of them do not get into our public catalog for six weeks or more after the arrival of the book in the library. In other words, books may circulate four or five times before there is any public record of their being in the library, and people may be looking for them in the catalog and going away thinking that the library doesn't have a copy.

Miss Wilkin sees a copy of all our order letters but of course has no way of picking out all the adult non-fiction titles. She looks up all those that she is sure of, in the Cumulated Book Index and The Booklist, to find their L.C. order number—that is, if she has time. Otherwise, she waits until the books arrive in the library and then searches for their order numbers. All the cards are ordered by their order number.

When I found out what she was doing, I suggested that she order these cards by author and title, which only costs a cent and a half more per title than ordering by number. This would eliminate all the searching for order numbers and enable her to place her orders for cards at the same time that the books are ordered, which is generally well in advance of publication date. This way, we should get our cards at the earliest possible date and no longer have them arriving a month after the books.

This change will only cost us about $20 a year, and as I told Miss Wilkin, her time is worth a great deal more than that. Particularly so, when most of her searching is fruitless, since a good percentage of her numbers can not be found. The Cumulative Book Index and the Booklist are about six weeks ''late'' in listing the new books, and even when the books are found listed in the C.B.I., the L.C. order numbers are frequently omitted. The difficulty is simply that we must have our catalog cards ordered well in advance of the time their order numbers are revealed.

Miss Wilkin seems interested in trying the author and title method of ordering the cards, so we will have to help her by letting her know what orders are for non-fiction and by providing her with the full information as to each book's author, title, publisher, and publication date, so that she can adequately fill out her card order forms. I'll have to be careful to indicate all adult non-fiction orders by adding a distinctive tail to the checks by which I mark the books to be purchased. Then, whenever Miss Welch comes to this special kind of a check, she can take down the added information regarding the publisher and date, and when Miss Wilkin gets a copy of the order letter and comes across a title with the full bibliographic information, she will recognize it as a non-fiction book for which the Library of Congress catalog cards should immediately be ordered.

Visited the Methodist Publishing House this morning for the first time and found a very attractive and well-stocked bookstore. They have all the new books from all the publishers, as well as a complete stock of Abingdon-Cokesbury Press books in the field of religion.

I dropped in there for two reasons—to take advantage of their after-Christmas sale and to look over the religious books. Spent an hour examining books and taking down authors and titles that I could check against our catalog and include in a later order. Don't like to order religious books without being able to first look them over and see how readable they are. Often can't tell from reviews whether a particular book is clear-cut and understandable or just a mess of words.

People who look for ''religious books'' are looking for help. The great majority of them are looking for something practical—and not the sort of thing that might appeal to a student of theology. The books that we carry in this field must qualify as capable tools that can be expected to 'do a job' and leave the reader better off than they found him. I believe books in this field have a special appeal for the lonely, the unhappy, the unadjusted, and those with more than their share of troubles and worries. These people are looking for comfort, and for help in meeting their problems and getting more happiness out of life.

There are many books available today that offer real help to such readers. E. Stanley Jones' ''Abundant Living'' is just one example. However, there are a great many more that are wordy and lacking in idea content or just too theoretical or hard to understand. There are too many religious books being published that should never have been accepted for publication, although the output in this field is much better than it used to be. And it is the librarian's job to see that his readers get the type of book that will really give them something to think about and apply in their daily living.

■   ■   ■   ■   ■

January 9, 1947: I must remember to get hold of a locksmith tomorrow to fix the lock on the front door of the library. Stayed down tonight to get some work done and when I came to let myself out of the building at ten o'clock I couldn't get the door open. Had to climb out the office window.

Finally caught the head of the County Ways and Means Committee in his office at the paper company and had a chance to talk county library service to him. He was friendly but, unfortunately, he seems to feel that there are many things more important than adult education these days. In his opinion, too many silly women read too many love stories when they ought to be taking care of their children and their homes, and he thinks that this may be one explanation of the high divorce rate. He also feels that with the demand for higher teachers' salaries, there just isn't going to be any money for such luxuries as libraries, and seems to be afraid that while county library service may cost little to start with, it might soon grow to such proportions that it would require an annual expenditure of $15,000 or more.

Tried to get him to see that if it did develop as he feared, it would only be because it was meeting a need and serving a great many people, and that an expenditure of $15,000 to serve thousands of people is certainly a small amount when compared with the much greater expenditures designed to benefit smaller groups. Also explained that the State was preparing to spend $100,000 on a regional library service that might leave Davidson County the only county in the state without rural library service. But, as I told him, he is a mighty hard man to sell.

When I got back to the Library I had calls from several of the trustees who were concerned about the case of Miss Porter, the oldest member of the staff and the only one of the six to be retired this month without any pension from the Library. She was passed over because she is already receiving nearly twice as much, in a pension from Watkins Institute, as the others will get from the Library. Still, $750 a year is not much to live on, and the little lady is frightened.

I had suggested that she come to our next meeting and tell her story to the Board, but she preferred to write several of the members a letter instead. She also rallied the support of a cousin who is the city tax assessor and a man who carries some weight politically. This Mr. Steger has guaranteed to get money from the city to take care of Miss Porter in future years if we will keep her on the payroll throughout the present fiscal year. He, of course, is interested only in his cousin, and he already has the support of several members of the Board who take particular interest in her as a member of one of the oldest and most respected families in Nashville's history.

As much as I would like to see Miss Porter get a greater retirement income, I can not help but feel—along with at least one member of the Board—that we should not appear to be favoring one member of the retiring group. We should take advantage of the interest of Mr. Steger in the fate of one member of the group to win from the city an adequate retirement allowance for all six. If he had to exert his influence in behalf of the whole group to get the favored one taken care of, perhaps all six people would come out ahead.

We had a good bit more excitement today over the young war veteran who has been acting and talking strangely around the library and giving the girls some uneasy moments. He comes into the Children's Department and stands and stares at the girls, all the time grinning and dancing on one foot or the other. He pops out with the silliest questions, and frequently remarks about how peculiar he feels. Says he has seen a number of doctors at the Veteran's Hospital but he certainly hasn't seen as much of them as he should.

I called the Detective Bureau to see what help they could give us, giving them the boy's name and address. Was disappointed to hear that all they would do would be to send over a few plainclothesmen, as I felt sure that they would never be in the library at the right moment. Five minutes later, however, the circulation desk called to say that the chap had just entered the building, and I went downstairs to see him. Several of us were talking to him when the detectives came in and took him away.

Things really happen around this library. So many things pop up every day that I never can get done all the things that I want to do. At the moment I'm faced with the problem of finding the time to advertise our weekly marionette show, get some "bleachers" built to seat the children for our first show on Saturday, prepare a set of questions for a radio quiz show, write some spot announcements to publicize the library over the radio, prepare some material that we can give the Welcome Wagon Service to transmit to the housewives that they visit, do some work on a radio program to promote a greater use of our reference department, contact some moneyed people with regard to the possibility of their giving us our phonograph record collections, promote the organization of a Junior Library Board to help us develop our Young People's collection, locate a chassis for our bookmobile and get this project underway, prepare an annual report for the next Board meeting, and take care of a multitude of other extracurricular matters.

But it's wonderful to be so busy and have so many things ahead to look forward to. So much better than never knowing what you may have to do when going to work, and then waiting for somebody to throw you something to work on, and never being able to plan ahead or enjoy the satisfaction of seeing something grow. This is truly the kind of work for me! The only thing more that I could ask for would be to have my salary tied in closer with the amount of business that I might build for the Library and with the significance of whatever things I accomplished for, and with, the institution. I believe the job would take on still more zest if everything I succeeded in doing, or failed to do, would be reflected in my current income. One of the few unhappy aspects of work in this field is the limitation on one's income which makes one feel somewhat held down and unable to keep up with his associates in business who can fly as high, salarywise, as their ability and efforts will take them.

·   ·   ·   ·   ·

January 10, 1947: Things were rather disorganized today at the library on account of the excitement over the case of the young fellow who was scheduled to appear before the city court at 2 o'clock. The library girls were so uneasy over the prospect of his being set free again this afternoon—particularly after learning that he had remarked to the people at the Travelers Aid station that the case of the murdered Ohio librarian was preying on his mind—that I called the detective bureau again to see if it wouldn't help at all if some of us appeared at court to tell the judge something about the fellow. They seemed to feel that we might persuade the judge to have the young man confined under a doctor's care. So six of us trooped into the courtroom at 2 o'clock and, within a few minutes, everything was all arranged to have him sent home to a hospital in Ohio.

From time to time during the day, I'd slip into the reference rooms to see how much difference the new fluorescent lights were going to make in the appearance and lighting of the upstairs rooms. What a joy it is to see the dark, gloomy area come to life! When the fixtures in the front room were installed, the main reference room—with its weak old lighting—looked like another world, in contrast. The Department's habitués seem to like the change, though few would think to say as much. Nevertheless, they had it coming, after being forced to strain their eyes for years. We will be interested to see how great an increase good lighting will mean in the use of these rooms.

.   .   .   .   .

January 11, 1947: It was a rather busy day today in the Children's Department. Started early in the morning when a scoutmaster brought in her whole Girl Scout troop for a look around—while the staff were trying to prepare for the marionette show at 2:30. All the youngsters wanted to stay right through and see the marionettes perform, but they compromised by staying only for the regular Saturday morning "story hour".

The marionette show this afternoon was the first of a series of weekly performances by Tom Tichenor and his Marionettes. Tom is now a regular member of the staff, scheduled for about eighteen hours a week, and we are lucky to have the benefit of his many talents.

These shows are being given for the school children of Nashville. The idea is to get as many children as possible into the library so that they can see how nice the room is, and how nice the librarians are, and start the habit of using the library. We are glad to present these shows simply because the children love them so, but they are chiefly a means to an end—a pleasant and effective way of drawing to the library hundreds of children who have never been inside the building before.

We have multigraphed 6000 tickets to the first show— ''Cinderella''—and will present it every Saturday afternoon until all the children of Nashville have had a chance to see it. We are distributing the tickets in all the elementary schools, visiting each one several days before its scheduled performance. The idea of the tickets is to secure the widest possible coverage and to insure that every section of the city is represented in the different weekly audiences. We were afraid that if we didn't have tickets with which we could select and limit our audiences, the children's department would be swamped every Saturday afternoon with the same children.

We figured that we would be able to take care of three schools a week, thus making each show last for three months. However, when Mrs. Moncrief and Miss Andrews took a batch of tickets to the first school, along with two puppets that Tom had given them, they were mobbed by the children. The principal and the teachers were exceedingly hospitable and let the girls say a few words in each classroom and pass out tickets to the children who wanted to see the show. Almost every child asked for a ticket and many wanted them for younger brothers and sisters, as well. At this rate, it will take almost nine months to complete one circuit of the elementary schools.

All these shows will be held inside the children's room, rather than in the hall where the November performances were given. Most of the children will still have to sit on the floor, but they ought to be able to see all right now that Tom has built a new stage several feet off the ground. The girls also wanted some "bleachers" for the children in the back of the room to sit on, so we had some carpenters rush us eight long sturdy planks, each supported at the ends and in the middle by blocks. The first row's blocks are 6" high, and each succeeding row is 2" higher. The "bleachers" can easily be stacked in the storeroom between performances.

■   ■   ■   ■   ■

January 13, 1947: Our most enthusiastic library user and supporter was bubbling over this morning with another idea to build up the library. In a nutshell, she wants to make it famous as the "White Spot of Nashville." She would have the outside of the building sandblasted twice a year, cleaning off all the dirt and making the library the one really white spot in the smoggy city of Nashville. We would then light the front of the building at night, and speak of it everywhere and designate it on our stationery as "The White Spot of Nashville."

That's really not a bad idea. It's the kind of stunt that can make an institution known all over the land. It would certainly make the library known in Nashville, which would be accomplishing a great deal. I believe we will have the place cleaned in the Spring and see how white it can get—and then we can decide whether the "White Spot" idea is practical.

Every time I run into this library fan we get to tossing back and forth our big promotional ideas. Most of them are creations of the moment, and they are apt to snowball into something pretty fancy. Five minutes after we had sand-blasted the library we had the local Garden Club taking over the beautification of the library grounds as their pet project, planting flowers and sowing bluegrass in the lawns, had set up signboards to advertise the library to passersby on both streets, had torn up one lawn to make a parking lot for our readers, and had gone into business with a filling station in front of the East Branch to provide a good source of additional income for the Library.

That's about the way our sessions go. Some ideas are good, some are impossible—but its stimulating to toss them around. That filling station idea is really not too bad. The East Branch occupies one of the best locations in the city. Someone once called at the branch to offer the Library $150,000 for a twenty-year lease on the property for use as a service station.

I believe, however, that it might be possible to put a station on the big triangular lot and leave the library standing. It's unfortunate that the building is in the center of the triangle, since any construction would have to come almost up to it. If we did have a filling station, however, we could either lease the land to a private concern or build and operate the station ourselves. I'm sure we could make it yield a good profit for the Library.

If it isn't possible to have a filling station there, it might be a good idea to build a booth at the apex of the triangle—in front of the library—with a driveway cutting across in front of it, from one street to the other. With several hundred books on shelves in this "booth", we would have the makings of a fine "curb service" that might attract many readers from the thousands of motorists driving by there on their way to and from work.

Didn't get any lunch today as I was just able to get away from the library in time for a 2:30 meeting with Mr. Gale, one

of our trustees, and Mr. Steger. The latter started off by saying
that he had secured a list of library salaries from the city
finance office—and "they are terrible; they can't compare in
any way with salaries of the other city departments". Moreover, he pointed out, the library is the only department that
doesn't provide pensions for its employees.

Mr. Steger then stated that he planned to contact all
nine of the Nashville men recently elected to the State Legislature to seek their support for a paragraph on library pensions
that Mr. Hume could write into the new 1947 Charter. This
would stipulate that all library employees receive the same
pension benefits as are provided by the Charter for all other
city employees. He is going to ask, however, that the library
employees remain outside Civil Service, which may throw
out the whole thing.

He is anxious that we retain all six of the older people in
service until July 31, during which time he will try to secure
pensions for the group through the new Charter, or—failing
that—by getting a larger appropriation for the Library in August. It's up to the Library Board to decide whether or not they
will go along with Mr. Steger in this plan. As far as I am
concerned, I would like to let him see what he can do to get the
pensions that our people should have. And, as I pointed out,
the Library would save money by retaining the six people
until August 1st—and might have to keep some of them that
long, anyway, through inability to find suitable replacements
for them.

.   .   .   .   .

January 14, 1947: Followed up on the Steger proposal
by calling on Mr. Hume, the chief architect of the new Charter
who is also a library trustee, and asking him how he felt about
inserting in the Charter a clause bringing the librarians under

the same pension provisions that are in the Charter to take care of all other city employees.

Mr. Hume, and library trustee Mr. Whitmore, who happened to be with him at the time of my visit, seemed to feel that the legislators would not approve a request for pensions for people who had already passed the normal retirement age, and were of the opinion, moreover, that the Library's employees simply do not belong under the city's retirement program inasmuch as they are definitely not employees of the city.

It appears, therefore, that any pension money coming from the City will have to be secured in the form of an addition to our next year's appropriation. I would be happy to see the pensions come through in any form, but if I had a choice I would prefer to have this money kept separate from our annual appropriation for library service. I don't want the Councilmen to feel that they are doing well by the Library in giving us an additional $4,800 when that money will go entirely to our retired librarians and will not contribute anything to our operating budget.

All of us at the library are still amazed at the difference the new fluorescent lights make in the appearance and usability of the reference rooms. It's such a thrill to come into the bright rooms from the relatively dark hallway. The Reference Department looks so much bigger—probably for the reason that the dark corners have been lighted so completely. As one patron remarked, ''The place now seems *alive*, where before it was dead.''

I don't believe we will ever spend $300 to better advantage. The place *does* seem alive now. It attracts, now, instead of repelling the visitor. Never saw so many people reading in the room as were in there today.

I've always hated the dark, drab appearance of libraries. It is this cheerless, depressing atmosphere that characterizes them in the minds of so many people and does as much to keep them away from books as anything else. If businessmen do not feel that they can economize on lighting, how can—or why should—libraries? The reader certainly requires better light than the shopper.

We are finding, however, that putting good light in only one or two rooms is like painting only part of the building. The well-lighted rooms make all the others appear so dark that we find ourselves contemplating putting fluorescent lights in even the few small rooms that had been considered fairly well lighted before with incandescent light. And as for the reading rooms with their large hanging fixtures and their gooseneck lamps, we feel almost compelled to tear them out and put in the fluorescent fixtures. Even when all the table lamps are on at night, the overall appearance of the room is dark.

I believe I'll go ahead and order 17 more four-tube fixtures for the three connecting reading rooms, with an additional fixture thrown in for the basement hallway. At a cost of $23.10 per fixture (wholesale), 75¢ per tube, and $2 for installing each fixture, the whole job will run slightly more than $500. That isn't too much, and I believe we can get something for our old fixtures to help reduce that amount. When I think of the check we got today from Vanderbilt for the "Library of Congress Catalog of Printed Cards" that we sold them for $650, I can't help feeling that we can afford anything. It's hard for me to believe that that one little-used set could have been thought worth more to the library than a relighting job, or a phonograph record collection, or any other project that would really contribute something to the use of the library and would cost no more than the catalog volumes.

.   .   .   .   .

January 15, 1947: Prepared a set of forty questions for the program manager of Station WSIX to use on his new

"Quiz Biz" program, and took them over there. He seemed to like them and promises to give the Library a number of "plugs" on the show, as a result.

Also took over several possible spot announcements—40 words long—that I would like to try out for the Library, and he says he can use them a few times a day. I want to get them on all four local stations. Nothing particularly good about them but I know they will help us a great deal. For example, one says:

> "The Nashville Public Library is *your* library. Thousands of Nashvillians pay taxes to support it. Thousands of Nashvillians borrow books from it. The average borrower took home over $20 worth of free books last year. Are you getting your share?"

The other one reads:

> "Keep up with the new books by borrowing from your free public library at 8th & Union. All the newest best sellers are there, along with books on every conceivable subject. It's smart to *be* smart!"

■   ■   ■   ■   ■

January 17, 1947: We were all disappointed this morning to find that we can't have venetian blinds in the front office. Miss Welch had ordered some new shades to replace our tattered old green ones that don't reach down far enough to keep the winter sunlight off the desks, but when I went outside and got a look at the shabby appearance of the library from the street it seemed wise to spend more money and get the office windows covered with the more attractive venetian blinds.

However, when the windows came to be measured for the blinds, someone woke up to the fact that the high windows go right up to the ceiling, and that the blinds can not be pulled up above them. And, since the windows open into the room, it would be impossible to open the windows in the summer with the venetian blinds in place. We could, of course, cut off the top sections of the long windows to make stationary transoms, and pull the blinds over the shorter windows, but this would add too much to the cost of the thing. So—we will have to be content with new shades.

The downstairs hall—in front of the loan desk—has now been lighted with two twenty-foot strips of fluorescent light, one down each side. This greatly improves the light over the public catalog and the display cases and gives a more pleasing introduction to the library. The two feeble, though glary, fixtures that hung behind the loan desk have been replaced with four-tube fluorescent fixtures that chase the darkness from behind the desk.

Two other much-needed improvements were made by replacing the single exposed bulb in the basement hall with a four-foot four-tube fluorescent fixture, and putting two two-tube fixtures in the Librarian's office. Don't see how the previous occupants of this office made out with the old ceiling lights that provided no more than 5 foot-candles of light. I had had to install a desk lamp which wasn't at all satisfactory because of the variation in the intensity of the light at the top, the middle, and the edge of my desk, and in the corners of the room.

By the end of next week, we should have the building almost completely relighted. All public reading rooms and all offices will then have adequate light. I am extremely anxious to see the main reading room decked out with the new bright light. Then, when that is taken care of, the Catalog Department, and the front office will have their turn. By the end of the week we should be able to invite the public to ''come in and read under the new fluorescent lights—in the best-lighted public library in the South''. I'll have to check that last statement, tho, just to be sure.

Meanwhile, Tom Tichenor and his uncle are busy building a new and more substantial stage in the Children's Department. The wings on this one will fold back to take up less room, and the whole thing will be much less subject to damage from the children crowding up to it during the weekly marionette show.

■   ■   ■   ■   ■

January 20, 1947: Had another unpleasant experience with the mentally unbalanced in the library yesterday. A young fellow grabbed a girl at the front door of the building. She screamed and managed to escape out the door. Her husband was waiting below in his car and, upon hearing her scream, came dashing up the front steps. Some of the men came out to the door from the reading room to see what was up. Behind them came the young fellow, who had apparently circled around behind the stairway. The girl pointed him out as her attacker. He denied her accusation. However, when the librarian asked everyone to step inside to get to the bottom of the matter, he refused—and departed on his way.

Incidents of this type are as infuriating as they are disgusting. And they are the worst possible publicity for the library, as well as a source of uneasiness among all the girls on the staff. Public knowledge of such goings-on at the library can keep more people away from the building than we can attract with the best public relations efforts. And it is so difficult to wipe out this threat because the people involved are rarely willing to go to court to identify the trouble-makers.

The building cleaners sent in their estimate of the cost of steam-cleaning the outside of the library—$1,000. That seems an awful lot for a few weeks' work. I figured out that they ought to be able to do the thing for $500 and, when they called about the matter, told them we couldn't pay more than that amount for cleaning the building. Don't know whether they will come down to that level, but they are planning to bring over their steam equipment and put on a demonstration for us.

We've got to work out some better way of handling the children at the weekly marionette show. Almost 300 of them turned up for the last performance, and that is too many for the Children's Room. Believe we will have to limit the crowd to the children from the particular school visited during the week, most of whom bring their tickets with them.

Meanwhile, Mrs. Benson is busy brightening up our magazine racks in the reading room. I never could stand the black, and dark green binders that make most magazine rooms look so drab. Don't see why the library supply houses don't produce these binders in lighter colors, with more attractive lettering on their covers.

We ordered five binders of the lock type for the pocket-size magazines that have hitherto been kept at the loan desk for safe-keeping. They were found to disappear when put in the reading room, but they aren't asked for enough at the desk to permit this sort of treatment. So the only answer seems to be to put them out in binders which can be opened only with a special key kept at the desk and hope that the public doesn't run off with both binder and magazine.

The rest of the magazines, except for a few extra-heavy ones, will be transferred to transparent cellophane covers which make them far more recognizable and add considerable color to the magazine racks. They won't last as long as the buckram binders, but they cost less—and, even so, it is worth money to have the room more cheerful and ''alive''.

.   .   .   .   .

January 21, 1947: A man came in to see us today about building the bookmobile that he'd heard we were planning to have. He can supply a Reo chassis and have one of his men build a body on to fit any specifications we want to give him. And he can turn the whole job out in less than a month, for under $5,000. That is good to know, as we would like to have the machine on the road this Spring.

His idea is to build the bookmobile and lease it to us at a rate of approximately $3 an hour—which would cover the cost of a driver, gas and oil, storage and cleaning, insurance, maintenance, etc. At such a rate, however, we could buy the machine for less than what it would cost to lease it for two years. And, as I explained to the man, we are more concernced with operating costs than the initial cost since we hope to have the bookmobile given to us as a memorial or as an advertising stunt.

We didn't have much time to gover the material that I've gathered on bookmobiles, or work out any specifications, but we could see that the interior of the bookmobile would measure about 18′ in length, 6¼′ in heighth, and 6½′ in width. The Springfield, Ohio, bookmobile is designed to carry 3100 volumes, but I'll be content with 2000 volumes in ours. We could do a very good job with that many attractive books, and a somewhat smaller bookmobile, and smaller bookstock, would be easier to handle in every way.

He took most of the material back to his body-builder to study, and from this he will try to arrive at an estimated cost that I can pass on to the Library Board at next week's meeting. I am afraid, though, that our bookmobile will cost twice as much now as it would have in 1939.

Mrs. Moncrief and Tom Tichenor were out visiting another school this afternoon and ran off a little puppet demonstration before 600 children in the school auditorium. The children had stayed after school to see the "show" and were delighted with the brief performance. Mrs. Moncrief left 300 tickets with the Principal to distribute, but that's going to leave many children without a chance to see next Saturday's performance. I wish we could handle more than 200 children at these marionette shows. It looks like we could present "Cinderella" a hundred times and not run out of an audience.

VII

Self-Service Collections in Supermarkets

January 22, 1947: Ran across an interesting article by Stewart Smith in a recent issue of the "Library Journal", telling about the "booketeria" that the Lincoln, Nebraska, P.L. had established in one of that city's supermarkets. They installed a section of five-foot shelves in the front of the market, and filled them with 750 jacketed books. The customers serve themselves, just as they do with their groceries, and take their books past the cashier to be checked and the book cards marked with the date due. Books are returned by dropping them in a bin.

It's a wonderful idea—as I wrote and told Stewart— and we hope to have half a dozen "booketerias" in operation here before long. They are extremely economical to operate, as the usual costs for heat, light, rent, personnel, etc. are saved by having the library unit in a store—and operated by the readers themselves. In Lincoln, it is necessary only to have a staff member visit the supermarket for a half hour every morning to count the circulation and straighten things up a bit.

It should not be very hard to sell a businessman on the idea of installing a "booketeria". He ought to be able to see how it would give his store or market a new drawing card that should attract many customers away from his less fortunate competitors. It would, at least, get his store talked about and help give him a reputation for progressiveness—all of which is worth much more to him than any time or money that he would have to put into the project. I'm anxious to get out—after the first of the month—and pick some likely locations for booketerias and learn how local businessmen react to the idea. What a thrill there is to be had in a good new idea!

    ■   ■   ■   ■   ■

January 23, 1947: Had a good day today. Two good ideas were thrown at me this morning, and it was an exciting time until we followed them up and found that little could be done with them.

The first one came with the information that the Hume-Fogg Technical High School had an excellent bindery that did all the rebinding work on public school textbooks. They were said to do a very professional job for only 25¢ a volume. Well, since we have to go to considerable trouble to get our books to a professional bindery and pay over $1 a volume for rebinding, we naturally jumped at the thought of getting our work done by the high school bindery. Immediately called the Superintendent of Schools about this possibility, only to find that they already have more work than they can handle. Mr. Bass remarked that the bindery saves the schools a good $12,000 a year.

The second suggestion—from our No. 1 patron—was that the library buy a spray gun and paint the outside of the building white. She felt that this would be cheaper than cleaning it. The idea certainly was worth checking on, and by that time I was visualizing Lorenzo using the spray gun on the interior of the building, too, painting every wall and ceiling in the place in short order. On calling the supply houses, we found that a commercial spray gun would cost several hundred dollars—and that none are now available. We will try, however, to borrow or rent one. I am anxious to see what its possibilities are.

The Coca Cola man was in today, to see about the possibility of selling us a Coca Cola vending machine for $180. The staff now drinks three cases a week, having to go to the trouble of buying and keeping ice on hand in the staff room. I would prefer to lease one of these machines, if it is possible for them to put one in here. We would then pay 15¢ a case for the use of the machine, but would make 40¢ on each case used. In short, by leasing, we would have the convenience of the machine and make 25¢ a case, besides.

On the other hand, we could probably pay for the $180 vending machine in one year—if we made it available to the public. Under those conditions, we would probably use ten cases a week, or more than 500 a year. At 40¢ a case profit, we would clear $200 a year. I have no objection to this plan, though I wouldn't want the machine on the main floor where all the unsightly empty bottles would be in everyone's view. We would have to set it in the basement.

■   ■   ■   ■   ■

January 24, 1947: Believe we will start charging 5¢ for reserving a book, provided the change is satisfactory with the Library Board next week. We have never been very satisfied with the system of free reserves. Too many people have been reserving "all the best sellers", and too many books are continually tied up awaiting their readers. A book can circulate three times from the open shelves in the same time that it will take to circulate twice from the reserve shelves. Four days are lost in contacting the reader and waiting for him to claim the book, and it doesn't seem right to have these popular books sitting on the shelves for even two days.

When there is no charge for reserving books, many readers are tempted to reserve books that they really don't need. With a 5¢ charge, they will be more selective. And this will mean less work for our small circulation staff, and more popular new books available to the majority of our readers.

．　　■　　■　　■　　■

January 27, 1947: Spent most of the day on my Annual Report for 1946. Tried to make it as short as possible and to limit it to matters understandable to the average layman, but there was so much to write about that it still ran to seven pages. However, that is still quite a cut from the usual sixteen to twenty pages. I could see little point in filling pages with the number of books added to particular collections during the year, the number of catalog cards filed and withdrawn, the number of people entering this department and the number of telephone calls in that one, and all the other customary bits of statistics. I don't expect more than fifteen people in the United States will read any part of the Report, regardless of how many copies are distributed, and they will be interested only in the highlights.

The Children's Librarians want Tom Tichenor's carpenter-uncle to make them a new circulation desk. So I sent down a copy of Wheeler and Githens' book on public library buildings, which is one of my favorite books despite all the evenings I spent editing chapters of it, and told them to pick out the sort of thing they wanted and go ahead with the job. Will be interested to see what it looks like. Incidentally, Tom has made an attractive ''Children's Department'' sign that is supported over the doorway by a number of bright colored birds.

■   ■   ■   ■   ■

January 28, 1947: Had a good Board meeting today. It is encouraging to see the attendance at these meetings running higher than has been the case in recent years. As the Library becomes more active and talked-about, I believe the Trustees will take more interest in it—and more pride in their membership on the Board.

Judge Ewing asked to be relieved of the Chairmanship of the Board, having served in that capacity for a good ten years. Banker Whitmore was elected to succeed him. The three members of the Board whose terms expire in 1947 were voted back for another 3-year term.

Mr. Hume read a strong statement that he had been persuaded to incorporate into the new City Charter, calling for the placement of all library employees under Civil Service—the minute the Charter goes into effect—and the making available of pensions to all our people of retirement age. He said he felt sure that the thing would go through as written, since many of the important politicians were in favor of the proposal. Mr. Steger expressed the same opinion to me this morning.

It's too bad, in a way, that we have to give up our independent position and move into the civil service group. However, I am perfectly willing to give up my complete freedom in making appointments if it will mean $800 pensions for our six older people, and possibly more money for all members of the staff. If the Civil Service examiner classifies our clerical positions with similar ones in other city departments, some of our girls should be in line for large salary increases.

After summarizing my Annual Report for them, I told them about the marionette shows, the fluorescent lights, our radio program, and the other things now underway, but the thing that most interested them was my recommendation that we try and install self-service "bookaterias" in supermarkets. Explained that we needed more book outlets away from the center of the city. They liked the idea and immediately authorized me to go to work on it.

Just as quickly, they approved my recommendation that we start charging 5¢ for reserves, and told me to go ahead and purchase the Coca Cola machine that the staff wanted. I've certainly got the nicest library board any librarian ever dreamed about. Funny how you can go from one extreme to another.

Judge Ewing said it was the best board meeting he had ever attended. He explained that they had been working for twenty years to get pensions for the Library's employees—and now, at his last meeting as President, they had finally obtained their objective. I marvel at my good fortune to have come here at what appears to have been just the right time. So many things seem to be falling into place. And we are doing, and getting, so many things that have been wanted for years. Of course, many of them actually could have been done before—if one had wanted to spend his money differently—but, regardless of that, there is real satisfaction in accomplishing things that others have desired for a period of years.

．　　　．　　　．　　　．　　　．

January 29, 1947: Both papers carried a story today about the "bookaterias" that the Library is going to install in strategically located supermarkets. That must have been interesting news to the grocerymen. They also reported that we would have a bookmobile on the road this Spring. Looks like they have really committed us to something. Not that we mind. It's often mighty helpful to get into such a position because one generally produces better when he is committed to a certain deadline.

One of our patrons was telling today how she came in on the bus behind two women who were talking about the big improvement at the Library. One of them remarked that "We apparently have to have a damn Yankee come down here to put our library in good shape". At which, our friend leaned forward and said "Pardon me, but he's a Californian—not a damn Yankee". That's keeping the record straight, all right.

The steam-cleaning people gave us a nice demonstration today of what they can do to the outside of the building. A small section at the back now looks mighty white in contrast to the blackened area around it. I still feel that a cleaning job will be worth more than $500 in publicity for the library, and will get the job done this Spring if the cleaner will give us a reasonable offer. A white library building would be seen and talked about by thousands of people, and would get across the location of the public library better than anything else we might do. With lights on the front of the building at night, we could really make a good thing out of the cleaning job.

■   ■   ■   ■   ■

January 30, 1947: The head of the Youth Rehabilitation office called on us yesterday to see if we had any work that one of her charges—a 19-year old spastic—could do. She had been all over the city trying to find work for the girl but hadn't had any luck. The poor girl can't use her hands and talks with difficulty, so there is little that she can do. It is important, however, that she have a job and feel that she is helping to earn her living. Apparently, she is not at all sensitive, and would be the first one to admit that she couldn't handle a particular assignment.

I arranged to have her come in a few hours today to get the feel of the place, after talking it over with the people with whom she will be working. Everyone felt that she ought to work entirely behind-the-scenes, where the public would not be throwing questions at her, and someone came up with the suggestion that she help out with the government documents. She can look them up in the indexes to find the proper code numbers, and then scrawl the number on a piece of paper and place it in the document for the reference librarian to copy on the front cover.

We don't expect her to be able to handle many documents in her three hours a day, but every one she does will save the reference librarian just that much time. The Rehabilitation people are willing to provide the money to pay her, at least during an ample training period, and we are glad to give her a chance to discover what she can do and help maintain her morale.

■   ■   ■   ■   ■

January 31, 1947: Had a fine time imparting my enthusiasm for public library work to the assembled students at the Peabody Library School. I believe it's a fine idea to have different speakers in to talk about their particular field of library work—to help the students pick their second semester course of study.

Miss Cundiff wants me to teach the course in Public Library Administration again this summer. It will be an easier job this year, but it does come at a rather bad time, inasmuch as it prevents one from taking a vacation in the best part of the summer. She had scheduled me for 10 to 12 o'clock, four days a week, but that would break up the whole morning and take too much time away from the library. The 8 to 10 shift is much better as it cuts only an hour out of my usual library day. And now that she has changed her schedule around to give me those hours, I feel as if I ought to take the job on again. I would like to interest a few people I saw there in the Nashville situation. The big thing to the students these days, however, is the Veterans Administration library service. Mr. St. John is offering a starting salary that is quite out of this world. The tough part about it is that while few people get these jobs, all of them are given big salary ideas which are likely to make them dissatisfied with their other offers.

When I got back to the library, the electricians had finished installing the 19 additional fluorescent lighting fixtures. The three reading rooms, the catalog department and the front office are now completely taken care of, giving us practically a clean sweep of the building—except for the Children's Department and the stacks. The Children's Room probably does not need fluorescent lights since its many windows give it adequate light during the day and it isn't open after 5 o'clock.

.　　■　　■　　■　　■

February 3, 1947: Dropped in at City Hall this morning to talk to the Civil Service director. I wanted to get a clearer understanding of how our probable new status would affect the handling of library personnel. In short, I was anxious to learn just what we are getting ourselves in for—in trading our independent status for civil service pensions.

I don't doubt but what most librarians would think me very foolish to deliberately seek to place the Library's personnel management under civil service restrictions. And frankly, I am not too happy about the prospective change—even though I feel it is the right thing to do, considering the benefits that will accrue to the members of the staff. I know I'm not going to like having someone on the outside determine the salaries that will be paid everyone on the staff, and require that I grant stated salary increases at stated times, regardless of whether or not I believe them to be merited by the individuals concerned. Neither am I going to like having to require new appointees to take civil service examinations and then wait for 90 days to know exactly where we stand, and perhaps have to appoint someone I don't want because all three people certified by the Commission are undesirable.

No, I'm not looking forward to the change. Nobody ever appreciated his freedom to appoint, transfer and promote the members of his staff more than I do. Nobody ever placed a higher value on staff morale, and the use of salary increases to stimulate and reward individual growth on the job. Every executive should be in a position to grant or withhold a raise at any time, and his employees should feel that he is free to reward them for any increase in their efficiency or production. People can't be expected to work with the same energy and enthusiasm after they learn that their supervisor has little control over their salary advancement and that everybody is going to get a raise anyway, whether they work their heads off or do just enough to get by. Such conditions are as deadly as the seniority principle in their effect on staff initiative and morale.

I felt a little better about the whole matter after meeting the Civil Service officer. He appears to be an able personnel man, with an open mind and a firm belief that the important thing is to effect the appointment of the best person for each position. I believe, as he does, that we can work things out together so that the Library will be handicapped as little as possible in the appointment and handling of new people.

Examinations will, of course, be required in every case—after June 3rd—and I only hope that they don't frighten away many of the people who might otherwise be interested in working for us. Many people are afraid of examinations and others just don't want to be bothered with having to take them. In times like these, when every good library school graduate has her pick of a dozen jobs, I am afraid that most of the young people will give little thought to a library that requires them to take an entrance examination.

I don't believe that we can count on the offer of a pension 40 years away to help us in competing for graduate librarians, either. The type of young people we are interested in are not going to expect to be here at age 65. Consequently, a pension plan will mean nothing more to them than a regular deduction in salary which they stand to lose upon their separation from the service. I might add that I wouldn't employ anybody I didn't think capable of ultimately attracting either a husband or a better job elsewhere, so would not be inclined to mention the pension provision anyway.

Mr. Worke seems to believe that it will be possible for us to get together and write up the specifications of the various library jobs we want to classify, before we actually come under Civil Service. I am anxious to get the librarians' jobs taken care of as soon as possible, so that they will not be left behind when our clerical and secretarial people are automatically classified with the clerks and secretaries of other city departments. It just wouldn't do to have our untrained people making more than our professional librarians—even for a month or two.

I am particularly concerned at the moment with what would happen to the Librarian's Secretary. According to Mr. Worke, she would automatically be classified as a Steno Clerk II, which would increase her salary from $125 a month to a minimum $185. That would, of course, make her the highest paid member of the staff, ahead of department heads with five years of college training and ten years of library experience. The fact that she is also the youngest member of the staff would make it even harder for the rest of the people to accept such an impossible salary situation.

So, as soon as the new Charter is approved, I expect to waste little time in (1) preparing "write-ups" of our professional positions, and (2) finding a secretary who is more nearly worth the $185 that she will receive. For that kind of money, we ought to be able to get a really efficient sort of person who could take care of more of the detail work around the place.

I was glad to learn that I will be on the examining board and will have an important hand in preparing the examinations for our applicants. That means that I will be able to set as high a value as I want on the important factor of personality. And as long as I can get the people who appear to rank high on judgment, tact and enthusiasm, I believe I will be quite content.

There appears to be some delay these days in holding the necessary examinations and getting the eligible lists posted. We can, of course, make temporary appointments, but these will surely lead to trouble unless our appointees can be examined and permanently classified within a 90-day period.

The chief complaint against the civil service concerns the difficulty of getting rid of people you no longer want, for one reason or another. To be sure, it is extremely difficult to remove a civil service employee, but then it's no easy matter to drop one of your people in *any* kind of organization. However, this disadvantage doesn't worry me, as long as it is possible to let an undesirable person go during her six months probationary period—quietly and without complications. I'm quite satisfied with all the people now on the staff, and feel comfortably sure that should an unsatisfactory worker ever slip into a library position, we will be able to detect his or her deficiencies in time to get rid of this weak link.

On the way back to the library I estimated the salary increases that are likely to be called for to bring our salaries up to any respectable set of salary ranges, and figured that it will take an additional $7,000 a year to implement such a revised salary structure. There is, of course, no assurance that the City Council will come through with the necessary increase in next year's appropriation for the Library, but I believe that they can be persuaded to provide the required funds.

■   ■   ■   ■   ■

February 5, 1947: The Children's Department held its first mid-week Marionette Show this afternoon. One of the girls suggested on Monday that they schedule two shows each week so as to bring more children to the Library and facilitate a quicker coverage of the city's elementary schools. As things have been working out, they have not only been unable to handle more than one school a week, but have had to hold two shows—on successive Saturdays—to accomodate all the children of a single school. They plan to continue having these Wednesday afternoon performances.

The big event upstairs was the displaying of all the reading room magazines in their transparent binders. With all the bright covers shining forth for the first time, it was as if a dark woods should suddenly blossom into a colorful array of roses, tulips, and other bright flowers. The public responded to the display by taking almost every magazine from the racks. For the first time, they could tell what was inside the various binders and quickly find the magazines they wanted. Such an improvement over the dark-colored buckram covers!

■   ■   ■   ■   ■

February 6, 1947: Miss Cundiff called up from the Library School to say that she had caught one of our spot announcements over the radio this morning and thought it sounded very good. Nobody had heard them when I asked the people at the meeting Monday night, and Miss Cundiff's report was our first real assurance that our advertising was going out over the air. Later in the day we received a postcard from one of our reading-room characters taking us to task for advertising our free service. "Free?" he asks. "How about fines?" Anyway, we were glad to get his card and learn that someone else heard one of the library announcements.

Speaking of queer characters, it seems that the library is haunted every evening by a rather uninhibited and unconventional individual who consistently takes off his shoes and socks and props his bare feet on the shelves in the stacks. He seems to take particular pleasure in shocking everyone around him and daring the girls to say anything to him. Last night he conceived the idea of taking off his socks and washing them in the drinking fountain inside the front door. When he had finished with his washing, he hanged the socks neatly over the radiator and retired to the reading room, returning for his socks at the closing hour.

Something has got to be done about people like that. Their brazen antics make a strong impression on the other patrons and give the library a black eye that is difficult to eradicate. One of these undesirable characters can steer more people away from the library in a day than we can attract in several months of concentrated effort. An institution just can't afford to be talked about as the hangout of the wrong kind of people.

I was glad to learn today, however, that the peeping Toms have been giving the library the go-by since Mrs. Benson covered the openings between the two stack levels and so shut off their view. She saw one of them wandering around in the reading room "like a lost chicken". With all the best books in the stacks now out in the reading room, there are few people to be peeped at in the stacks these days, anyway. Almost everyone has now discovered the new location of these books, and the reading rooms have come alive with readers. People seem to like the more accessible and attractive location, and the books are going out at a much faster clip.

■　　　■　　　■　　　■　　　■

February 7, 1947: Had a call from Mr. Manier of the Watkins Forum regarding the possibility of devoting one of the Tuesday night forums to the subject of the Library. I had mentioned the idea to him once at a dinner party and apparently several of our Board members had made the same suggestion to him. He was thinking of discussing our plans for taking books to the readers—by bookmobile, bookaterias, etc. but I suggested that it might be more helpful to discuss the matter of a countywide library service for Davidson County.

Mr. Manier is now willing to devote a forum to the subject of a county library provided we can give him some assurance that there will be enough people there to provide a suitable audience for the members of the panel. He is sincerely interested in the subject but is afraid that it lacks the appeal of some of the other forum topics and doesn't want to be embarrassed by having the speakers that he has invited arrive at Watkins Institute and find only a handful of people in the audience. And, while the first half-hour of the program is broadcast, the remaining hour is confined to two-way discussion among the people in the room, and a good-sized audience is certainly helpful.

I told him that I thought that I could get the County P.T.A., the Nashville Library Club, the Business & Professional Women's Club, the A.A.U.W., and other such organizations to sponsor the county library forum and urge their members to attend, and that we would be glad to send announcement cards to all our non-resident borrowers. The 300 county residents who now have to pay a $2 annual fee to use the library ought to be interested in a discussion of ways to eliminate such fees.

Meanwhile, I am delighted to hear how well our young spastic is coming along in her work with the government documents. Miss Bell said this morning that Jean seemed mighty happy in her new job, and later in the day the head of the Youth Rehabilitation office called to say that she had never seen anyone so happy. It is good to know that our efforts to help this handicapped girl are proving so successful. It is easy to imagine what it means to her to have a self-respecting job at last— one that she can really handle, and one that is interesting to her.

Miss Bell seems to feel that she will soon be able to do as much work with the documents as would any normal person her age. She appears to be very alert and intelligent and is already talking about the various government bureaus like a veteran documents assistant. Furthermore, where she was thought incapable of writing the index numbers on the documents, and filling the documents themselves, she is actually doing both these things now. On the basis of Miss Bell's report, I have assured the Rehabilitation people that the Library will be glad to assume her small part-time salary after her training period is over, I pointed out again, however, that we only have enough work of this type to keep her busy 15 hours a week—three 5-hour days—but they feel that those hours will be quite adequate as far as Jean is concerned.

．　　　．　　　．　　　．　　　．

February 17, 1947: Everyone felt very fortunate and happy to be able to come to work this morning. The stoker broke down Saturday afternoon and the building got rather cold before nine o'clock came around. We decided to close the library on Sunday, rather than try to get through the day by hand-firing the boiler. There are regulations against that sort of thing, and we didn't want to make a lot of smoke and get the Smoke Inspector after us—even if it was Sunday and few people would be downtown to be affected by our smoke.

It looked Saturday as if the building might have to be closed for a week or more, until the necessary parts could be obtained from outside the city, but the repairmen managed to get the stoker back in running order yesterday. We were lucky to have the accident occur on the weekend so that we didn't have to lose a good day's business.

The Circulation Department was mighty proud today of the amount of business they did on Saturday. They circulated 452 books—topping the 400 mark for the first time in a number of years. They haven't had many days over 300 in the last six years, so that a circulation of 452 is really something for them to talk about.

We are all getting a kick out of seeing the circulation go up at the main library, particularly the adult circulation. Five days ago, the girls compared the figures for the first ten days of this month with those for the same period a year ago, and found that they had a 40 per cent increase. Today, they totaled the circulation for February 11 thru 15, and again compared with February 1946. The increase for these last five days had risen to 47 per cent. As one of the girls laughingly pointed out, it's too bad we all don't get a commission or bonus for the increased business we're doing.

.   .   .   .   .

February 18, 1947: Lorenzo has now moved into the
reading rooms and has already given the front room a very
light green ceiling. We had planned to paint the ceilings in
these rooms white, but the interior decorator had pointed out
that the ceilings were too high to be painted white and had
suggested that we mix in some green to bring the ceiling down
and reduce the amount of contrast with the green walls. Everyone seems to approve of the new ceiling, so Lorenzo has
been given the go ahead to complete the main floor ceilings.

We will all be glad when the redecorating is completed.
None of us likes to have rooms closed off from public use and
I know that some of our steady customers will feel more comfortable when the painting is all over. On the other hand, it is
good to hear so many people remark on how the library has
been improved in recent months. I helped out at the loan desk
for a few minutes this afternoon and had three or four people
comment along this line.

.   .   .   .   .

February 19, 1947: Looks like we are going to have a
pretty nice Bookmobile on the road in May. I've talked to five
truck builders this week and have worked out a new interior
design that appears to have a great many advantages over any
bookmobile that I have ever read about. As far as I know, all
existing machines have their interior walls lined with bookshelves. Consequently, most of them require artificial light,
and present a rather bare appearance on the outside since the
solid rows of shelves permit only a minimum of window space
in the side of the truck.

It always seemed to me that bookmobiles would be
brighter and more attractive, and would draw more attention

and use, if they could have more windows to break up the solid shell and permit people to see into the machine. The only way to get 2500 books into a bookmobile and have some windows in it is to get the shelves away from the sides. If the shelves are brought into the center of the machine and faced outward— back to back—we can then have our windows all the way around the body of the truck. The windows offer the double advantage of providing plenty of natural light throughout the machine and letting all passersby look in to see what's going on inside. The sight of the bookshelves, and other people picking out their books, should draw more people into the bookmobile than a solid outside panel with nothing to appeal to the imagination or suggest the availability of books but the name of the library painted on the side.

At first, I thought we could get a bus body—with windows already all the way around it—and build an island of bookshelves, 18 ft. long, down the middle. That would allow ample room for walking around it, with over three feet between the shelves and either side of the body. Several other advantages of having the shelves in the middle of the body were soon apparent. In the first place, with bus ceilings higher in the center than at the sides we could easily have seven shelves there, thus compensating for the greater length of the shelving that is six shelves high around the shell of most bookmobiles. In the second place, I believe the books will receive closer attention when arranged so that all books are directly in front of the reader as he moves through the machine, rather than overwhelming him with a row of books both in front of and behind him.

I was determined to have shelf space for at lease 2250 volumes. The book island did not have quite enough capacity—even with shelving along the back of the bus, under the windows—so we decided to add some shelving at intervals along the sides. These shelves would only come up to the windows, and would be low enough for people to sit on. However, even though the shelves would only come up to one's waist, leaving room to swing one's arms above them, it seemed too close a squeeze for people to pass each other on either side of the center island.

Our next step then was to eliminate the low shelves on the street side and move the center shelves some six inches over. Looking for additional inches to add width to the passageways, we measured books in the reading room and found we could reduce the width of the shelves from the standard 8″ to 6½″. That gave us an extra 4½″ across the body of the truck. As it stands now, we will have 36″ between the low shelving on the sidewalk side and the center shelves, and 33½″ on the other side. We have allowed more room to pass between the two sections of shelving since there will be more readers and more stooping down for books on that side.

One of the truck men says he can get us a Chevrolet chassis and a Thomas school bus body. Both chassis and bus bodies are extremely hard to get these days, so it looks as if we will be doing business with him, particularly since his price for a bookmobile ready to roll is $1,000 less than that of the other dealers and the price of the school-bus bookmobile recently acquired by the Evanston Public Library. He suggested this afternoon that we drive over to the factory and have a look at one of the school bus bodies. I got up to go along with him, but it turned out that "the factory" is some 600 miles away— in North Carolina. We won't go that far to see a school bus, but it's good to have one of these truck builders so interested in our business. Most of the businessmen I've encountered recently seemed to have little of that aggressive initiative and interest in going after the business.

I expect to have all the information and cost estimates available for presentation to the bookmobile committee of the Library Board on Friday. Meanwhile, we are trying to find time to check lists and do a careful job of selecting the books that will go into the bookmobile collection. We are anxious to have nearly all new books to give the bookmobile a proper start in life, and that means purchasing about 4,000 books. We hope to circulate 400 books a day, which means an ample reserve supply of books to keep the machine well stocked.

Seems like every time I go through the Children's Room I ask the girls to see what they can do about getting us some more books. However, I don't believe that they have yet gotten used to the idea that they can buy all the books that they want to get. Right now, they are anxiously awaiting the arrival of the new edition of The Children's Catalog. When they start checking that volume—the easiest and quickest way I know to spend money—I'm sure that they will come up with all the new books that we need and can afford.

I mentioned to them a week ago that they were going to have to give me 2500 new books for the bookmobile—to say nothing of the new books that they need themselves. That's a big order around these parts, and they want to do a thorough job. What I want to do in ordering all the bookmobile books is find a few dealers who are having big sales or who will give us big discounts for quantity orders. I don't want the bookmobile books—both adult and juvenile—to average much over $1.25 a volume.

Our big problem regarding these books is where to store them. There is not an empty square of space in the main library in which to store and handle these special volumes. I believe that we will have to utilize one of the spare rooms in our North or East branches. The space is there, yet there are many disadvantages in having the bookmobile collection so far away from the main book resources of the library. Another thing, it will mean that one of the girls will have to spend one day a week out at the branch.

.   .   .   .   .

February 20, 1947: Stopped in at one of the big supermarkets on Gallatin Road this morning to talk to the Manager
about the possibility of installing a bookateria there. The market is across the street from the city line, but this fact only
makes the location more interesting to me. A great many
Nashvillians shop there, and if we had a service unit there I
would hope that the shoppers from outside the City would
become aroused at seeing their neighbors taking home books
that were not available, without payment of a fee, to them, and
that they would then make a noise that the poky County Court
couldn't fail to understand.

The manager was interested but will have to wait until
his partner returns from Florida to give us his answer on the
matter. Meanwhile, I believe I will look into the possibility of
putting a bookateria into a bank or department store downtown. Such units could be operated equally well on a self-
service basis, but the disadvantage here is that there is no
controlled exit and no cashier who can stamp the book cards
and see that the books are properly charged out. However,
there is no reason why something couldn't be worked out in
one of these downtown locations, even if it meant having one
of our girls on duty there all the time. We should be able to do
enough business there to warrant this extra expense.

I'm convinced that it is not going to be an easy matter to
find somebody who will give us the money for either the
bookmobile or the phonograph record collection. Even
though we already have the money for these projects I'm determined to try every possible avenue to get them given to the
Library so that we will be able to use our extra money for more
books, instead. Called on the publisher of the ''BANNER''
this afternoon and came away with the names of some people

to try to sell on the bookmobile, and then made a call on the head of the Nashville Community Concert Association to see if I couldn't get a lead on somebody who would respond to the idea of a record collection memorial at the Library.

I realize that it is getting harder and harder to raise money these days. But here I am on a committee to raise a big new endowment fund for Sewanee University—a grand little school in the Cumberland Mountains that I would have liked to have attended—and will soon be calling on ten of its alumni to try and drain off money to Sewanee that we could use so nicely at the library. But the contacts that I make in this campaign may be of help to us at some later date.

My secretary's new husband called today to say that he believes she ought to give up her job at the library. She has been home all week and apparently doesn't have the constitution to enable to her to handle the twin jobs of wife and office secretary. I was afraid we would have to replace her but couldn't very well do anything about it until I knew for certain that the Library was going under Civil Service and what the future salary range for my secretary would be.

Talked to C.S. Director Bob Worke this afternoon and learned that his job—called Steno Clerk II—has the extremely awkward and narrow salary range of $185–$200 a month. This means that my secretary will have to be making $185 at the time the transfer to civil service status takes effect—June 3, 1947. In view of the fact that such a salary would be the highest of anyone now on the staff, I want to hold off paying that amount as long as I can. I believe I will try and get a $175-a-month girl but start her at $160 or $165, with the promise of a jump to $185 on the 1st of June. If she works out satisfactorily, I believe she will be worth that amount; if she doesn't prove satisfactory, we will have time to discover this fact and find a more suitable replacement before June. We've got to be sure of all our people by then because once they are civil service employees it will be almost impossible to remove them.

The joy of the thing, however, is that there is nobody on the staff now that I would want to see go. In August we will have probably the youngest staff of any library in the country. The average age will be approximately 30, and the median age will be less than that. Don't believe we will have anyone on the staff over 48. This is an extremely unusual situation and I expect to enjoy it to the full, knowing that I'll probably never again have such a pleasant, hand-picked group of people to work with. I like experienced people, but more than that I want to be surrounded with personable, enthusiastic, fast-moving assistants.

I want people who are responsive—who can respond to my enthusiasms, get fired up over what the library is trying to do, and make the public feel their interest in serving them. A number of library users have commented recently on "the tremendous improvement in the attitude of the girls at the circulation desk. They never seemed to care about things before or have much interest in what they were doing. But now they seem so enthusiastic. You can tell the difference the minute you step in the door." Such remarks mean more to me than the frequent comments about the many new books or the improvement in the appearance of the place.

.   .   .   .   .

February 21, 1947: Had a fine meeting with the three-man committee of the Library Board that called me down to the Bank to talk over the salary increase that they had decided to give me. Since these members also constituted a along majority of the Board's Bookmobile Committee, I took the material on the bookmobile that looked the most promising to me, together with the bids of the various truck body builders.

The committee was mighty interested in the project and impressed with the amount of business the bookmobile is expected to do. They agreed that the price of $3750 is quite reasonable for a complete bookmobile, ready to roll. That covers a Ford chassis, a school bus body 24' long, shelves for 2350 books, and all the heating, lighting, ventilating, and other equipment needed.

After some discussion of my plans for selling someone on the idea of supplying the money for the fully equipped machine, the discussion was brought around to the matter of the Librarian's salary. The President reported that the Committee had been authorized to express the unanimous approval of Board members regarding the accomplishments of the new Librarian, and that they had decided to express their appreciation by increasing the Librarian's salary to $6,000. That is a 50 per cent increase from my starting salary last year and $1,000 beyond the temporary increase granted me in December. And, just as that first $1,000 increase was retroactive to last May, this increase is made retroactive to January 1, 1947.

There's nothing like a good raise to bolster one's morale—particularly when it is accompanied by such expressions of appreciation and satisfaction with the work that one has been trying to do. Where could one find a nicer group to work for and with, and a happier atmosphere in which to apply himself?

∎   ∎   ∎   ∎   ∎

February 24, 1947: Took three members of the staff to the big book sale at the Methodist Book Store. When the four of us had finished picking out all the books we wanted, we had

200 volumes to carry home in the car. Most of them were from the 39¢ table—an inexpensive way to fill some of the shelves on the bookmobile.

Before we left the library, I found an opportunity to tell Mrs. Moncrief that we thought that she had worked out so nicely as the Children's Librarian that we were raising her salary $15 a month. It occurred to me on the way to work this morning that she had now been with us six months and, since we liked her work and had often told her so, we ought to do something tangible about it. Then, too, I am not always going to be able to give merit increases in this free and easy manner, and I mean to take advantage of this opportunity before I lose it in June. I know that the members of the staff would much rather receive this type of recognition than an automatic civil service increase that everyone else is due to get.

VIII

The Quickest Way to Stock a Library

February 25, 1947: Finally got Mrs. L. back to the library for a day's work. It's no fun being without a secretary, and the work has really piled up in the week that she has been away. She tells me that she is willing to come in and train her successor but doesn't want to do any more work than that.

However, after seeing the state of her books, I'm not so sure that I want her in even long enough to train the new girl. Just discovered today that she had not made an entry in several of her books since the middle of November. I have been content to check her monthly report of expenditures from the city fund, and to look over the list of bills that she has regularly sent to the City Hall for payment. This has always seemed in order so that I never bothered to investigate to see whether her books of receipts and expenditures were being properly kept. Mrs. L. had been properly trained by her predecessor and I had never had the time or inclination to learn or supervise the details of her bookkeeping assignments.

I confess I have been rather concerned about the bookkeeping end of the business since the recent shortage in the books that led me to have the combination of the safe changed so that responsibility for the library's money would be more strictly defined. I have also been wanting to go over the books with Mrs. L. to find out why our Special Fund isn't growing any faster than it is. She has been away so much lately that we haven't had a chance to get things straightened out.

Right now, I am deeply concerned about the money situation. Before I left yesterday afternoon, I counted $103 in the safe. This noon, there was only $71 in the safe, and Mrs. L. says that she has paid out only $9 during the day. In view of the terrible shape of the books, I must admit to a certain suspicion of Mrs. L. Doubtless I'd be more suspicious of her if I hadn't discovered how careless and negligent she is about keeping track of the money. Any kind of mistakes are possible with such a rattle-brained youngster. All I can say is that she resigned just in time.

.   .   .   .   .

February 26, 1947: Mrs. L. stayed home again today. When I called her at home, she said she wasn't coming in any more because she didn't want to be "fussed at" about the condition of the books. Before she left the office yesterday I had had a chance to compare the fine money book at the loan desk with her office record of the money taken in and paid out of the safe. Found that only half of her collections at the desk were being recorded in her office book. In many cases there was no record of the money recorded as "collected" at the desk ever getting into the safe in the office.

She could have been putting the money into the safe and forgetting to record the matter—or she could have been pocketing this money.

Because she has always seemed to be such a nice person, and such a sloppy worker, I gave her the benefit of the doubt yesterday and didn't accuse her of taking any library money. I did, however, have plenty of questions to ask her about the records—and apparently she didn't welcome all this "fussing", as she calls it. When I got this reaction of hers over the telephone, I lost all my patience with her and hastened to remark that she apparently did not realize what a serious spot she was in and that she had jolly well better come down and show us where the rest of the money had disappeared to. Went on to explain that we couldn't turn the books over to a new bookkeeper-secretary in the shape they were in and that we simply had to have her in to straighten things out. However, she said that she was upset and was in no condition to come to work and didn't think that she would be able to get back at all.

Meanwhile, I have been busy interviewing the two candidates who appeared to be the best of the group that applied for her job. Couldn't decide between the two girls yesterday so had them both come in again today to meet the rest of the staff and learn more about the work that they would be doing. Wanted them to know the type of people they would be working with, the kind of atmosphere in which they would be living and working eight hours a day, and really understand just what their job here would be like. After the short stay of the last two girls, I want to make doubly sure that the new secretary knows what she is getting into and feels sure that she will like the work and want to stay with us. A library is so different from the average business office with which these girls are familiar that it is important that the newcomer realize the difference and come to us with the proper attitude. I want the new secretary to be happy here, because if she is happy she will stay with us.

After both girls had been in, met the people, learned what they would be doing, and expressed a real interest in the position, I gave myself an hour to decide between them and call them back to let them know my decision. It was a mighty tough decision to make, but I finally decided in favor of the one who seemed to have more animation and spark than the other and who had had more experience with keeping track of money.

That matter decided, I turned back to my study of the bills that were paid this month and came across one that seemed rather odd to me. It was from Sears Roebuck and covered a "Cellarette" purchased by Mrs. L. Couldn't imagine why the Library would want a cellarette, and asked several of the girls who happened to be in the office what a "cellarette" was. They didn't know, so I decided to call Sears Roebuck to find out if the Library had really purchased what I believed to be a cabinet for holding bottles. When I asked the store people about the purchase, they said, "Why yes, we remember it very well. The young lady from the Library came in and got the cellarette; she explained that the Library was giving it to her as a wedding present."

Well, that did it! The whole picture then became perfectly clear. No longer was there any question as to what happened to our money. The only thing to do now was to do a complete job on the books and find out how much money she had gotten away with.

.   .   .   .   .

February 27, 1947: Called up Mrs. L. to try and get her down to the office but her husband reported that she was too nervous and upset to leave the house. Meanwhile, I had rounded up Mrs. Benson and started her on the big job of finding out how much money the Library had actually taken in during the last six months. This means adding up all the fine money, the money received for lost books and nonresident cards, and the money that has come in from the sale of old books and other library equipment.

The main difficulty in bringing order out of chaos and learning exactly where we stand is getting down to bedrock— figures that are understandable and clearly reliable. So many of the records stem from earlier figures that are either incomplete or incorrect. It looks as if the job may take a week to do, but it must be given priority over every other assignment.

The one bright spot of the day is the fine work that is now being done in the old P.T.A. room by the carpenter that I ran into on the way to work this morning. He mentioned that the job he had expected to have today had fallen through, so I suggested that he come on up to the library with me and look over the job we needed done, particularly as I learned that his hourly rate was only about half that charged by the contractor who had given us an estimate on the job of cutting up the old high shelves and setting four-foot shelves around three sides of the P.T.A. room. He has done a fine job there today and the girls are quite pleased over the new appearance of the room.

■　　　■　　　■　　　■　　　■

February 28, 1947: Finally got Mrs. L.'s husband in to see me about the situation she had created. He was understandably shaken to hear what his bride of two months had done, but fortunately took the sensible attitude that the only thing to do was to straighten the whole matter out and pay back what she had taken. I stressed the necessity for quick action, to get the matter cleared up before somebody on the outside started asking questions and let the cat out of the bag.

Told him that I didn't want to cause any trouble or public embarrassment for them, and said that I felt sure that we could keep the matter from becoming public knowledge if we got the money back right away.

He mentioned that his wife has been hysterical and had to be taken to the hospital last night. In view of this, I told him that I thought that it was absolutely essential for him to tell the story to her mother and then go to her and tell her very simply and lovingly that "Everything's going to be all right. Your mother and I know all about it, and we're going to do all we can to straighten things out for you." She is in a serious condition now, and it is worry and fear that is eating her up. She will never get out of bed again until she can unburden her mind of these fears. Doubtless, she is scared stiff that her husband and mother will learn what she has done. But her health is more important than what anyone may think of her. And, I feel sure, that when she discovers that these two loved ones already know the whole story, a great weight will fall from her mind. Now that they know, there is no longer any cause for worry or fear that they will find out.

■　　　■　　　■　　　■　　　■

March 1, 1947: Spent all Saturday at the Library, trying to make some sense out of the Special Fund books that had been left in a very incomplete shape. I believe that we are going to be able to come up with fairly accurate figures of what we have lost during the last few months. The figures won't be completely accurate because Mrs. L. made no record of our various sales of discarded books, and similar receipts, and we are forced to rely on our memory of such transactions.

Meanwhile, Lorenzo has finished painting the walls and ceilings of the front and back reading rooms, and only has to do the center room to complete our biggest painting assignment. However, he believes now that we should go ahead and paint the insides of the bookshelves, since the dark backs of the shelves look so unattractive and provide such a colorless backdrop for the books. He is, of course, a hundred per cent right about this, and since he will be faced with the job of doing the painting I am glad that the suggestion to paint the shelves has come from him.

    ■   ■   ■   ■   ■

March 4, 1947: We are fortunate to have Mrs. Brown back with us for a few weeks, until the new secretary comes in and learns the job. When she heard that I was without a secretary last week she offered to come in and help out—and there's nobody who could help us more right now than Mrs. Brown who kept things going smoothly at the office for over 20 years, until her husband suffered a stroke that still keeps her home most of the time.

One of the girls saw Mrs. L. downtown this afternoon so she apparently made a complete recovery from her nervous collapse of last week. Called her husband earlier in the day and he said that he had told her that they knew about her money-taking and that this was just the medicine needed to straighten her out. He reported that she had admitted taking our money but he had no idea of how much was taken.

Mrs. Benson and I have finished the job of adding up all the money taken in at the main building and the three branches from September 1st to March 1st, and subtracting all the expenditures from the office. It appears now that we should have cleared $1800 in this six-months period, whereas only $1000 was deposited in the bank. When the bill for the cellarette is added in, we have a shortage of $850 that Mrs. L. and her husband will have to dig up for us. Don't know how they are

going to do it. They haven't yet paid for the $225 wrist
watches they bought for each other at Christmas and a bill for
$167 arrived today for Mrs. L. from one of the smart dress
shops downtown.

Enjoyed talking to 150 members of the Civitan Club at
the Andrew Jackson Hotel this noon. The Library is the only
subject that I can, and like to, talk about—and, as some of the
men remarked, they had never seen anyone so enthusiastic
about his work. Well, the more interested I appear to be in my
work, the more interested they are going to be in the Library.
I wouldn't want to have to talk to them for several hours, but
being limited to 20 minutes I could stick to the highlights—
and any mention of such things as bookmobiles, bookaterias,
phonograph record collections, film libraries, curb library
service, and service to businessmen, is real news to such an
audience. If I had talked in general terms about books and
reading and adult education, I'm afraid I wouldn't have got
anywhere near the attention that I received while talking
about these specific and appealing services that few people
have ever even heard about.

.   .   .   .   .

March 6, 1947: It will be good to get down to real work
again. Spent almost all day yesterday at a meeting of Tennessee librarians in Martha Parks' office in the Division of Libraries of the State Department of Education. Now that the
State has passed the Education bill carrying an appropriation
of $100,000 for regional library service, it is essential that
plans be made now for putting the money to work. Must confess, however, that I didn't contribute very much to the discussion. My work in Nashville is so far removed from the
problems of state-wide library extension that it takes quite a
while to become oriented to all that the Department of Edu-

cation people are saying about instructional materials, county service centers, and all the rest. As I told Miss Parks when I left, running the NPL seems like duck soup compared to the problems that she is up against all the time.

Today, most of my time went to the solicitation of funds for Sewanee (The University of the South). Though I didn't go to Sewanee, I am glad to be able to help out in their campaign to raise $5,000,000 for a new buildings and endowment fund. But the more I learn about Sewanee the more I wish I had gone to school there, instead of going to a large city university. Beautifully located in the Cumberland Mountains, the "Oxford of America" would seem to be a very pleasant place for a young man to spend four years.

.   .   .   .   .

March 7, 1947: Got a letter today from Jack Campbell of The Personal Book Shop expressing considerable interest in our problem of having to purchase over 4,000 books for the Bookmobile in a hurry, and at a low average price. He suggested that I come to Boston—the Book Shop paying all round-trip expenses—and select the books from their shelves. They will give us a discount of 36 per cent on all slightly-used books from their rental libraries. The discounts will apply whether I make the trip or not, but he believes it would be better for me to visit Boston.

As anxious as I am to get the books into the library, so that the catalogers can start to work on them, I wouldn't want to make the trip to New England until I had carefully compiled a long list of the good standard titles that ought to be in this new collection. I've got to make up a good non-fiction list and get from the Children's Department an equally good list of important and readable children's books. Half of the 4,000 Bookmobile volumes must be children's books, and a good percentage of the adult books must be the non-fiction titles available. And if we don't prepare in advance to get all these books for the new collection, we'll run the risk of seeing too much money spent for new publications and "entertaining books". We can't afford to spend too much money on ephemeral literature that will have been forgotten by next year.

Mrs. L. and her husband came in to see me and got the bad news regarding the total amount of the money that must be restored to the Library. Poor Mr. L. must now dig up $958 that his wife appears to have frittered away. He's being very co-operative about it, and believes he can get the money, but it's a mighty tough break for the bridegroom.

.   .   .   .   .

March 14, 1947: Miss Stone, our new Secretary-Bookkeeper, has now been with us a week, but with things mixed up in the office as they are now, it will probably be some time before she feels as if she has things under control. She does, however, seem extremely interested in her new job and appears to like the atmosphere of the Library. She remarked this afternoon on how friendly everybody was, and on how so many of them had dropped into the office Monday morning to welcome her to the library. As she said, nobody would have thought of being that nice to a newcomer in the office where she worked before—all of which made me mighty proud of our little organization.

.   .   .   .   .

March 18, 1947: The County Library program on tonight' Watkins Institute Forum went off rather well. We had a fairly good crowd and the hour's discussion—following the half-hour broadcast—was quite spirited. We had sent announcements of the Forum to all our non-resident borrowers and had called the county magistrates to invite them to the program, and the newspapers had given us splendid publicity.

All of us on the panel enjoyed the show immensely. The group included Frances Cheney, president of the Tennessee Library Association, Martha Parks, director of the Division of Libraries of the State Department of Education, Maxwell Benson, head of public relations for the General Shoe Corp. and me. And the program was sponsored by the Davidson County P.T.A., the Bus. and Prof. Women's Club, the Division of Libraries, the T.L.A. and the Nashville Library Club.

Don't know what will come from the Forum program, but at least it helped to acquaint many people with the library situation in this county and perhaps stimulated some thinking about the possibility of securing county-wide library service. Only one county magistrate, out of the group of 42, was interested enough to attend the meeting, but doubtless others read about the matter in the newspaper or listened to the program over the radio.

•   •   •   •   •

March 20, 1947: Was rather concerned this morning by the article in the TENNESSEAN on the library forum which quoted me as saying that library expansion in the county has been thwarted by a lack of interest on the part of the county magistrates. And last night's BANNER had quoted somebody on the panel as saying that the trouble was due to the "inadequate co-operation of the county magistrates". None of us had made any such remarks; we had simply stated that the magistrates had not yet been sold on the program by the county residents who wanted the service.

I am afraid these write-ups are going to do us more harm than good, by rubbing the magistrates the wrong way just when it is so essential that we have their good will. Nobody gets anything they want by pointing the finger at the people who hold the purse strings. I called one of the leading magistrates, to get his reaction to the story, and found that he had read it with some surprise and annoyance. He accepted my explanation and we parted on friendly terms, but he advised me against calling all of the magistrates. As he put it, most of them probably paid no attention to the articles, and bringing the thing to their attention might only lead to a certain amount of talk that would not help us at all.

Something should be done now to carry forward the program and act upon the interest aroused by the forum discussion, but there is no question but what the job of selling the county magistrates belongs to the county residents who want library service for themselves and their families. The County Court is not going to be influenced by anything we city librarians say, but it wouldn't take very many county people to get them to listen. They will listen carefully to the pleas of much smaller groups for much larger amounts than the number of people who really want and will use a library service that would cost the county a mere drop in the bucket, comparatively speaking.

■   ■   ■   ■   ■

March 24, 1947: The cardboard model of our new bookmobile arrived today and it is a beautiful job. The top is removable, to allow a better look at the bookshelves inside the bus. Don't see how the clever youngster made the thing. Everything is right to scale, with the proper number of windows, a door that opens, and all the rest. It should be a big help to us in trying to sell someone on the idea of giving the money for such a bookmobile named after himself, and it will later make a fine display in the lobby of the main library to call attention to the new service.

■   ■   ■   ■   ■

March 25, 1947: Finally got around to visiting the Tennessee State Library in the Capitol. Their one main room is piled high with books, and the walls are covered with portraits of former Governors and some Confederate generals. They certainly need more room, and a greatly increased staff, and if they can get through the next two years, waiting for the new $1,500,000 State Library and Archives building to be built, they should eventually get everything they need.

Took Miss Stone along with me to the Secretary of State's office, to make a copy of the sections in the new City Charter that pertain to the Library. Copies of the Charter won't be available until May, and we can not wait until then to learn where we stand and begin to work together with the Civil Service Director on the classification of our personnel. It was good to read the new Charter and be reassured that our people are slated to get their pensions, as planned.

I hated to have to write Fremont Rider this afternoon and tell him that we had decided to cancel our subscription to his monumental "Genealogical Index". However, as I explained to him, we just can not afford to spend $50 a year to duplicate a set that is available at the State Library and rarely used here. We have kept a watchful eye on our set the last four months and haven't caught anyone using it yet. Several times I have asked people using the genealogical collection what they thought of the Index, and none of them were acquainted with the set or understood how to use it when the volumes were set before them. Many libraries five and ten times our size, as far as book budgets are concerned, do not take the Genealogical Index, and few cities can boast two sets, so it is perhaps understandable why we do not feel that we can consider this subscription.

We had a young lady from Peabody Library School doing her practice work in the Library last week. We were glad to have her aboard for a week's visit and, while we may not have taught her very much, perhaps we were able to give her a "feel" of what actual library work is like.

■   ■   ■   ■   ■

March 29, 1947: Have been rather busy lately trying to kill a story that the *Tennessean* has been planning to run about the Library. The reporter who misquoted us on the Watkins library forum last week has been trying to dig up some material to sensationalize the discarding of books at the public library. He dropped into my office Wednesday afternoon and started asking questions. Was very vague about what he wanted, and didn't seem to have anything particular in mind. I was still puzzling over this strange visit when Mr. Whitmore, the President of the Library Board, called me to say that this reporter had just visited him and had opened the conversation by remarking that he understood that the Library was going out of business.

We were both concerned by this remark. I called the reporter to find out what he had in mind, and he explained that he had received the idea from some people at Vanderbilt University that the Public Library was going out of business as a research library. He went on to explain that there was a rumor around town that the Library had discarded a great deal of research material, including material that was not available anywhere else in Nashville. I attempted to straighten him out on the matter of our discards and asked for the chance to see his story before it went to press.

The next morning I hurried down to the newspaper office and had a look at the reporter's story. It was full of statements purporting to come from Vanderbilt authorities saying that the Public Library should not discard its valuable newspaper files, its magazine collection, its Tennesseean collection, and its other research material. When I pointed out that the Library had not discarded any such items and had not the slightest intention of doing such a foolish thing, he replied that his article did not say that we had—only that we shouldn't.

I tried to point out the damage such a story would do, and how it would cause needless concern to many people who did not know the facts. Explained that we had been making progress lately at the Library, and been receiving considerable favorable publicity, and didn't want to have anything happen to scare people away from us. Told him that we would be glad to let him, or any other individual or group, go over the records of all our discards and examine the books themselves—most of which are still in the building—and see whether any volume of research value had been withdrawn from the collection. I then pointed out the opportunity for doing a really constructive article on the Library, and asked him to call again on Mr. Whitmore to discuss the matter further.

After lunch, I called on Dr. Kuhlmann—the Director of the Joint University Library—to let him know of the impending story. He was much concerned about the whole thing, and gave assurance of his complete support of our position. Then, too, he certainly did not want the university library to be placed in the embarrassing position of seeming to second-guess or pass judgment on the actions of the public library, particularly since the relations between the two institutions have always been so friendly.

In talking to the people at the university library, we got an inkling of how the whole thing got started. It appears that a Vanderbilt professor was working with the old newspapers in the basement of the public library when one of the girls, doubtless weary of taking the heavy volumes down from the shelves and putting them back up again, remarked that "we ought to get rid of these old things". The professor returned to the campus to tell the librarians that he understood the public library was considering parting with their valuable newspaper collection, and, if so, the university library should take it.

At any rate, the talk of the Library's discarded books flew around town and worried many people who, though they never used the library themselves, felt that none of the old books should be discarded. This kind of a rumor is a hard thing to combat, because we don't want to bring it to the attention of everyone, nor appear to be defending our actions in the face of public criticism.

I mentioned the matter to several other Trustees and they called the Managing Editor, as did Dr. Kuhlmann, to say that the Library Board had voted unanimously to discard the worn out material that was withdrawn from the Library and were completely back of the Librarian and did not want anything to impede the progress that the Library had been able to make in recent months. Several days have now passed, and there has been no further effort on the part of the newspaper to drum up a story on us. It looks, now, as if the whole thing will be forgotten—which is just as well.

. . . . .

April 1, 1947: Am all set to take the train tonight for Boston. The girls have done a great job of preparing lists of the books that we want to be sure and get for the Bookmobile. The children's librarians spent hours together checking the new Children's Catalog and listing their favorite titles. The adult list is made up chiefly of recently published books that we had postponed ordering with the thought of the Boston trip in mind.

A salesman from the Addressograph-Multigraph Company of Cleveland dropped in this afternoon to try to sell us a Multilith machine. Didn't have time to listen to his whole story so told him to drop in and explain the thing to Miss Stone and Mrs. Benson while I was away and see whether we really had enough need for such a machine to warrant the expenditure of $500. Believe we ought to have one next winter when I hope we can do a great deal more direct mail advertising, but probably we don't need one now.

■　　　■　　　■　　　■　　　■

April 7, 1947: It's good to be home after a very busy five days away. I believe the trip was a great success. It's certainly one that I won't soon forget. It was the sort of experience that librarians dream about—and that happens once in a lifetime, if at all.

I arrived in Boston at 8 o'clock Thursday morning and was out at the Personal Bookshop offices an hour later. After chatting a while, Jack Campbell took me over to their large "warehouse"—the first floor of a building next to Boston's Back Bay station—and gave me my first view of the thousands of books which were to keep me occupied for over 20 hours.

It was one of the most fascinating places I have ever been in. New books, all in bright, colorful jackets, were piled on the floor, in bins, and on shelves as far as the eye could see. A hundred copies of one book here, 500 of another there, and sections full of assorted titles all arranged by publisher. The "warehouse" was said to contain 200,000 volumes—and I can well believe such a statement. Such a sea of color! And, as new books will, they smelled as good as they looked.

There must have been sixty people employed there, pulling off the books ordered by their more than 5,000 library accounts scattered over the country and wrapping the shipments for mailing. It was interesting to watch them at work. Couldn't help but admire the organization and efficiency which characterized the operation of this business, or keep from thinking what a pleasant, interesting job these young people had. Perhaps everyone does not consider new books to be as alive and interesting as I do, but certainly they must be thought a more colorful and varied material to handle than most consumer goods.

After introducing me to the people there, Campbell marked off the playing field for me: "Everything from here to that row of shelves over there is 50% off. These are the books that have seen a few weeks' service in our rental libraries—though most of them look as if they had never been used. Everything else in the place is new material—though, of course, not necessarily "new" as regards publication date. The children's books are on this side of the center aisle, and the reprints are over by the office. We'll get you some dollies to pile books on, and you can go to work."

He suggested, however, that before I begin going over these new books I ought to look at a roomfull of books back at the main office building which were available at 70% off. So we walked back to St. James Place and I started to work, finishing with this special collection in time for lunch.

Had a wonderful time all afternoon, back at the warehouse, examining books and picking them off the shelves— one copy here, half a dozen there—and building up the pile on the dolly. Such a wonderful feeling, not having to give a thought to the number of volumes or the cost of the books selected. As a matter of fact, my only concern was that I might not be able to pick off enough books in the time I had to make up the collection that I was there to get. By dinnertime I had plucked only 340 volumes, and it was quite apparent that I would have to step up my pace considerably if I was going to finish the job by Saturday night. I was averaging a book every 40 seconds, whereas I should be picking one off the shelves every 20 seconds to complete the 4,000-book order.

Stayed at the Campbells home in West Newton that night, returning to the warehouse the next morning to continue the fascinating job of handpicking several thousand new books. However, before settling down to work, I decided to hop a cab and run out to Simmons Library School to look into the matter of recruiting some of their students for the Nashville Public Library. Was aware that the students were off doing "practice work" in libraries around the country, but was interested in looking over their records and talking to the placement officer about students interested in public library work.

Spent the rest of the day, and all Saturday, at the warehouse, hurrying over the shelves, racing against time. Worked until midnight Friday night. Never have my eyes been so tired—from the constant jumping from shelf to shelf, and book to book, making a hundred stops or more a minute. My feet were weary from standing all day, but nothing like the tiredness in my eyes.

Was assisted Saturday morning by the Bookstore's expert on children's books who picked out over 500 of the best titles in this collection while I followed along after him—designating the ones that I wanted extra copies of. With this assistance, I was able to complete my slow trip around the warehouse. I felt that we had picked up everything that we needed for both the Bookmobile and the main library—yet my pickings came to only slightly more than 3,000 volumes. However, as I left Boston I had the feeling that the trip was well worthwhile and that we had a Bookmobile collection that couldn't be beat for attractiveness and readability.

.   .   .   .   .

April 15, 1947: Forty-eight boxes of new books were unloaded inside the basement door this morning and carried into the old P.T.A. room that had been made ready for them. Couldn't resist opening half a dozen of them—while the children's librarians stood by and exclaimed over the wonderful books that appeared from each new box. Although I had selected the books myself, and knew all the titles in this big shipment, I had no way of knowing what I would find in each individual box—and the process of opening them was almost as exciting for me as for the rest of the staff who were seeing the books for the first time.

The shelves in the P.T.A. room can hold only half the books from Boston, so we decided to break up the collection—shelving the children's books there and the adult books upstairs in the Catalog Department. Rounded up three girls to get right to work on the shellacking of the books and suggested that the boxes be opened only as fast as these girls could shellac their contents and find the space to set them out to dry.

Everyone seems to be very enthusiastic and completely satisfied with the books that we picked out in Boston—which is indeed gratifying. I had hoped that it would be possible to please everyone, but that is not always the way things work out. It also looks now as if we will have these books ready for the Bookmobile's arrival in early June. The girls are really going to work on them.

. . . . .

April 21, 1947: Had quite a pleasant surprise this morning when I went back to the library after being stuck home in bed since last Tuesday night. Found that all the new books had been shellacked and stamped, and that book cards and pockets had been typed for a good proportion of them. Everybody has pitched in to get this rush job done, and the results are very encouraging.

It's good to see the Catalog Department so full of bright new books, and everything so humming. Would like the place to be like that all the time, but doubtless I am alone in that wish. Guess I just like big rush jobs, and working under pressure, and showing everyone—including myself—what can be done when one really sets out to do a job that has to be done. Such work creates an atmosphere that is very stimulating and yields a sense of accomplishment that is immensely satisfying.

We have tried to streamline our card records for these bookmobile books. In the first place, we are typing only one card for each book—a main entry card—and making this a combination catalog and shelf-listed card. The cards will show only the name of the author, the title of the book, the date of publication, and—at the bottom of the card—the shelf-list number.

We have been doing considerable experimenting with protective covers over the book jackets as we are anxious to have the bright jackets on the books to attract the readers and add color and life to the interior of the bookmobile. We have tried the ''Plasti-Kleer'' cellophane covers—which have a canvas back to give them added strength—and a roll of ''Protektoid'' which gives an adequate cellophane cover to the jacket. The ''Plasti-Kleer'' covers run 6½¢ apiece—in quantity lots—while the ''Protektoid'' averages 5¢. The former, however, appears somewhat sturdier and may last longer. They both take approximately the same length of time to put on a book—10 minutes. Considering the cost of the material and the cost of hiring somebody to put the cellophane around the books, it is apparent that it will cost 15¢ a volume to leave the book jackets on the books and protect them in this manner.

Don't believe we can afford to cover all our books, nor do I think it necessary to do so. In the first place, we could buy 500 more books with the money it would cost to cover all 4000 volumes in the collection, and we probably need additional books more than we need complete coverage. In the second place, I believe that there is little need for covers on the children's books—certainly not the "easy books" and those for children under 12 years old. And probably we could eliminate much, or all, of the adult fiction. That leaves only the adult non-fiction, which we librarians generally consider more worthwhile, and which certainly needs the helping hand of an attractive book jacket more than any other type of book. Our present plans thus call for covers on only the adult non-fiction, but I imagine we will be putting them on most of the volumes with dark, drab, unappealing backs that appear to need some color to fit them for the struggle for readers.

*   *   *   *   *

April 22, 1947: Had a very full and interesting Library Board meeting this afternoon. Was a few minutes late getting to the Board room at the Bank and found 8 of the 9 members in their seats waiting for the Librarian to appear. Equally surprising, nobody made a move to leave until the meeting adjourned over two hours later. It's good to see such attendance on the part of these busy people.

There was some discussion about the matter of the library staff coming under civil service, as some of the members were uneasy about the administrative difficulties which would accompany such a step, but it was pointed out that while the Board did not have to approve the legislation and accept civil service status for their employees, they should expect trouble in getting an increased appropriation from the City should they reject this change. Nobody wanted the Librarian placed under civil service either, but, since it is a matter of accepting all or nothing, everything will go through as written in the new Charter.

I brought up the matter of the three older librarians who left the staff before I took office last year. Although it has been from 11 to 16 months since any of them were on the payroll, all of them have given the City more than the 30 years of labor required for obtaining a pension and thus would seem to be deserving of a retirement allowance. However, as I pointed out to the Board members, nobody could come under civil service or be retired with a pension unless they were on the payroll on this coming June 3rd, and it was up to them to decide whether they wanted to bring these three people back to work next month so as to get them pensions. After some discussion, the Board decided that it would be somewhat unethical to bring back Miss May and Mrs. Brown, but that in the case of Miss Vanderford—who has been on a leave of absence and has always expected to return to the Library—I should explain matters to the Civil Service Director and abide by his decision.

Another interesting question for the Board to decide was the matter of what population groups the new bookmobile should serve. In short, should it serve Negroes as well as Whites. Some of the members remarked that many white people would not want to use books going into colored people's homes and that the program might be jeopardized by trying to serve both population groups with one machine. The general feeling, however, was that while bookmobile service was contemplated for the Negroes, there was such a great need now for service to the white sections of the City that the book-mobile would have more than it could handle taking care of this demand. This is certainly true enough.

Thought I had better check again on the feeling of the Board with respect to naming the bookmobile after the indi-vidual giving us the money for it, and it was fortunate that I did so. One or two of the members didn't like calling the machine, say, the "Jones Branch of the Nashville Public Library", so when I talk to Mr. W. again tomorrow all I can offer him is a bookplate with his name on it in each of the 4,000 books in the collection. Won't be as easy to sell, however, as his name in large letters on the outside of the bookmobile where it would be seen by all passersby and make the "W—Branch" as well known as the name "Carnegie Library".

.   .   .   .   .

April 23, 1947: Went calling on Mr. W. with the model of the new bookmobile, some pictures of similar machines, and a new book with a bookplate in the front of it showing that it belonged to "The W—— Collection". Pointed out to him the tremendous amount of publicity and goodwill that would come from such a gift, and emphasized the great number of people who now use the public library and might be expected to use the bookmobile.

Asked Mr. W. for $6,000 to buy 4,000 books for the bookmobile collection, and $600 additional each year for the next ten years to help keep the collection going. It would then be called "The W—Collection", and every book added to it during the life of the bookmobile would be given a W—book-plate, regardless of whether the book was purchased with his money or the Library's money.

He will think it over and let us know later. I really believe that such a deal would greatly profit all parties concerned. It would mean a lot for the Library—and all the people who would use the bookmobile. And I can not think of a better expenditure of a relatively small amount of money for the W—s. As I pointed out to Mr. W—, the collection would cost him $12,000 over the ten-year period—or an average of only $1,200 a year. That is less than the cost of a single clerk, and such an expenditure of money—making his name almost as well known as the name ''Carnegie''—would mean more to him, his family, and his company, than one clerk more or less in his office. Furthermore, he would actually be spending a good deal less money than that since the gift would be deductible from his income in figuring his tax payments.

    ■   ■   ■   ■   ■

April 25, 1947: Spent yesterday afternoon with the Civil Service Director, talking over the classification of our library people and working up some brief job descriptions. Mr. Worke seems to like the idea of just two professional jobs below that of the Director of the Library, together with a subprofessional position and a ''Library Aide'' job for the part-time high school youngsters. I hope that it will be possible to exempt all our part-time assistants from the civil service so that we won't have to be continually bothering with examinations for page boys, and be handicapped in the employment of such clerical people.

The branch librarians are going to be another problem, since they might fall in either the Librarian I or Librarian II category. We probably ought to have a separate job for them midway between the starting professional grade and the supervisory grade. These positions will probably be filled with young people just out of library school, but we will

doubtless want better people than we can find for the starting
salary of $2220. The difficulty in classifying jobs in an orga-
nization of this size lies in the fact that the individual makes
the job, to such a large extent. For example, if the branch
librarians do no more than check books in and out, as is now
largely the case, the job of branch librarian clearly falls in
the first salary grade. However, if these libraries are operated
by people who are trained to do more than this, and these
people really get out and work and assume responsibility for
building the service of their agency, the branch librarian's job
then becomes deserving of classification on the upper level.
A job analyst classifies jobs, rather than people, but when
he gets into a small organization where he is dealing with
professional people, he is likely to find that his job descriptions are largely expressions of the capabilities of specially
trained individuals who have made different things out of their
job opportunities.

The larger the library, and the more employees in any
organization, the easier becomes the job of classifying positions. More different levels of professional skill and responsibility can be identified, and the greater is the similarity of
background that is found in the workers on any particular
level. Professional work in the larger libraries is pretty well
limited to library school graduates, whereas the smaller library is likely to have a number of untrained people in supervisory positions and many people with considerable experience in the lower positions. Some of the former may not have
the training or the capacity to do the job in which their age and
seniority has placed them, while some of the latter will have
acquired certain skills through years of experience, together
with salary increases, that put them above the classification
level to which their jobs belong. The job of the analyst is
particularly difficult when he is classifying the library's positions for the first time.

I am fairly clear in my mind as to what each member of the staff is worth, relatively speaking, and believe that I could work out a salary schedule that would be fair and acceptable to all—if I were free to set salaries on an individual basis and didn't have to group people of different ability and work habits together in a few salary ranges. There is all the difference in the world between two reference librarians, or two circulation assistants, and when one is obliged to pay them the same salary, despite the fact that one may be far more capable or work twice as hard or show much better initiative or judgment than the other one, it makes a situation that is as unfair as it is hard to defend. As an old job analyst myself, I am strong for such evaluation schemes, but only when it is possible to advance the deserving ahead of the mediocre. Of course, this should be possible to do through a system of employee rating—within the job classification plan—but as the thing is set up in Nashville, salary increases are automatic right up to the maximum of the range. Automatic increases should never carry an employee beyond the midpoint of his salary range, leaving him to advance the rest of the way on a merit basis. It is to be hoped that such a change can be effected here.

Had Mrs. Benson schedule a staff meeting for 8:30 this morning so that the people could ask all the questions I knew they had in mind regarding the forthcoming shift to civil service, and I could have an opportunity to tell them all I knew about it and let them in on some of the things we talked about at the recent Library Board meeting.

Everyone seems happy over the prospect of becoming a civil service employee, largely because of the anticipated increase in library salaries. Even the thought of having their summer vacations limited to the city-wide two-weeks period did not make them unhappy. Since they will not be hampered with the administrative restrictions of civil service status, they have a great deal to gain from the shift and little to lose. We hope that nobody will have cause later to regret the move.

．　　　■　　　■　　　■　　　■

April 28, 1947: The catalogers have been making great progress on the 3,000 bookmobile books. They have regularly rounded up everyone in the place with time to give and put them to work on some aspect of the job of preparing the books for the shelves.

Mrs. Benson had pulled out all the books that weren't already represented in the Library, and these were slated to grace the shelves in the main reading room. It then became my job to go over all these books and decide which titles should be duplicated in the bookmobile collection. Miss Stone followed along behind me, making a list of the books that I had turned down on the shelves. When this list was added to the other order lists that have been compiled since the Boston trip, she had another order of over 1,000 volumes to send off.

I expect that we will have 1500 adult titles in the bookmobile collection, and that includes westerns, mystery stories, novels, the classics, and a varied assortment of nonfiction. Every one of these books is attractive, interesting and readable, and can be counted upon to circulate readily. Most of them have already demonstrated their popularity in a thousand libraries. The non-fiction has been selected on the basis of its ability to satisfy reader needs. More of these titles would have been purchased for the bookmobile if more could have been found to meet the standards of interest and readability established for this collection. Too many non-fiction books gave promise of circulating only five or ten times—in which case it seemed better to lend the bookmobile the copy from the main library. The bookmobile collection will gradually be filled with the best of the new books appearing in the next eight months.

■   ■   ■   ■   ■

<u>*May 7, 1947:*</u> The main lobby is looking much cleaner and more inviting these days as more of it comes under Lorenzo's paint brush. The interior decorator who was called in several weeks ago suggested an interesting color scheme with several shades of beige, but some of the girls were scared to try it for fear it would look too daring to some of their conservative customers. They decided, instead, to proceed with the same green color scheme that has met with such favor in the reading rooms. As a matter of fact, it looks as if the whole building is going to end up with light green walls and dark green trim.

The appearance of the main hall has also been improved by the removal of the heavy pictures from the walls and the busts from the top of the public catalog. The interior of the circulation desk has also been painted, and several of the light fixtures have been changed around for the better.

C H A P T E R **IX**

Campaigning for More Money

May 9, 1947: The circulation figures for last month are quite encouraging. They show an increase of approximately 80% for the Main Library—over the circulation of April 1946. The branches also came up somewhat, so that the increase in circulation for the entire system settled at 50%—the best record so far.

It is unfortunate, in a way, that we made so many changes within such a short period of time. Otherwise, it might have been possible to discover the effects on circulation of a given change. It would have been nice to be able to discern the effects of our increased book purchases, the painting of the reading rooms, the installation of the fluorescent lights, and the additional publicity that the library has received lately. Perhaps if we had taken one thing at a time, with a sufficient wait in between, and had not had the homecoming of many reading veterans to constitute still another and doubtless very important factor, we might have been able to learn something interesting about the use of the library.

■   ■   ■   ■   ■

May 14, 1947: The recruiting situation seems to be looking up. If we can sign half the young ladies we have contacted the last few days we should make out fairly well. My only worry now is that they will all want the same one or two jobs of the half dozen that I mentioned to them.

Will also be relieved when our salary schedule is finally determined, since the salaries that I offered these young people were based on our expectations of what civil service status will mean for us, salarywise. We had to take a chance and offer them more than anyone on the staff is now making, realizing full well the position we would be in should our new salary schedule be postponed for any reason.

The first young lady to apply for a position wrote us from the Grand Rapids Public Library. She sounded very interesting, and appeared even more so when a confidential folder on her—with a nice photograph—arrived the next day from the Illinois Library School. I wasted no time in telephoning her—to explain what we were trying to do and had to offer her in Nashville, and to get a better idea of her interests and personality. Invited her to visit Nashville at our expense to look the place over and so better decide whether or not she wanted to work and live here.

Made the same offer of transportation here to four other girls who were highly recommended by Western Reserve, Emory, and Peabody Library Schools. Most librarians would consider me unnecessarily extravagant for doing this, but I see a great deal to be gained from it. In the first place, I want to see these young people before we definitely offer them a position, and—equally as much—want them to see our library and understand clearly what they are getting into. In the second place, I know that they will be flattered by such an offer, since almost no libraries pay traveling expenses of candidates for any position but that of Chief Librarian, and this will tend to make Nashville rank high in their thoughts. And if they do visit us, at our expense, they will think twice before they decide against employment here. In short, such invitations are designed to give this library a preferred position in the competition for capable young people. And the cost—in each case, only about a week's pay—is certainly little enough if it helps us to get the calibre of people we need.

This recruiting job is the most interesting and important one I have to do, and it is a thrill to learn of a new possibility who seems to have what we want. It's a matter of picking up somebody here, and somebody there, and following up all interesting leads. It all reminds me of the time I was Rushing Chairman of my college fraternity, although the situation here is by no means as hectic.

Mr. Whitmore tells me that the Mayor has found some technicality that might keep us from going under civil service. This comes as something of a shock since everyone on the staff now believes herself to be already under civil service. According to the new Charter, all regular employees of the Library gained this new status at 10 o'clock this morning. Certainly, we will have to get together with the Mayor and straighten things out as soon as possible.

■   ■   ■   ■   ■

June 4, 1947: Took the sketch that Tom Tichenor made of the bookmobile and painted a nice firemen red, around to three of the Trustees. They all approved the inscription "Donated by the W—" that Tom had lettered on the side of the machine. So now we will have another shot at Mr. W. It's really too bad that we have to go around begging for funds that should be forthcoming from the City, but apparently that's the way it's got to be. Perhaps after we once get a few things like the bookmobile in action, it will be easier to get the money we need from the city fathers.

In talking further with these Trustees about the question raised by the Mayor it became very clear that no time should be wasted in arranging an appointment for the four of us with Mr. Cummings. Apparently, both the Mayor and the City Attorney feel that civil service status is out of the question for the employes of the library since they are not city employes. This condition has many times in the past excluded the library people from the City's civil service and pension plans, despite the fact that many law-makers and city officials have tried to secure these advantages for them. Now, with the new Charter expressly putting the library staff under civil service, everyone felt that the goal had finally been reached.

・　　　・　　　・　　　・　　　・

June 5, 1947: After the long meeting with Mayor Cummings this morning we all feel as if we know better what has to be done. It is very clear now that the Library Board must get together very soon and decide what it wants to do with the property and management of the Library. We can't continue any longer in our present position—"half in and half out" of the city administration. The three Board Members present agree with the Mayor that non-city employes should not receive city pensions, so it looks as if we will definitely have to turn the Library over to the city and come into the city family before any of our older people get their pensions.

I feel certain that no one on the Board will object to giving up the Library's corporate status. Most of the members feel that the Library will never receive proper consideration from the City Council until such a change is made. I don't necessarily disagree with this viewpoint, but—on the other hand—I am not too confident that our turning the Library over to the City is going to mean a marked increase in our appropriations from the City. Such a transfer is not likely to make the Councilmen any more interested in library service or inclined to favor the Library over other departments whose appeals for funds they may have a more personal interest in granting. No, I believe the Library will still have a very hard time in getting the money it needs. However, I am in favor of making the Library a responsibility of the City, and a real part of the city administration, because I believe it is the right thing to do from the administrative standpoint. Its present position is contrary to all principles of administration.

The meeting gave us a good chance to acquaint the Mayor with the amount of service that the Library is now rendering and the cost of such service. I'm sure that it came as a surprise to him to learn how many Nashvillians regularly use the Library, and how little our trained librarians make. It was the first meeting in years between members of the Board and the Mayor and those present felt well satisfied with the way the meeting turned out.

Mayor Cummings seems to have some definite ideas, himself, about the future organization and service of the Library. He suggested that the Library come under the Board of Education and that the facilities of the Library be merged as much as possible with those of the school system. He seems to feel that we ought to sell our branches and, in the future, render branch library service through the schools. His thought is that by having branches in the schools we would save the expense of heat, janitorial service, and the like.

I explained that such an experiment had been tried out in other cities, without great success. Pointed out the fact that schools are not open in the evenings, that they are not open in the summer times, that they are less accessible in school buildings and that many adults don't like to visit schools to get their books, but the idea of consolidating two agencies both devoted to educational purposes is one that carries an immediate appeal. I could see that the members of the Board were tremendously interested in the Mayor's suggestion, particularly since one of them is President of the Board of Education. The Mayor seemed to feel that such a consolidation would be making educational history and setting a pattern for other cities to follow.

Mr. Whitmore assured the Mayor that the Board would meet and prepare some sort of plan for his consideration. We all feel that we have reached the point where a real decision must be made. No more coasting along, having to beg for a decent handout from the City and being unable to do the job that needs doing. It's time for the Library to decide where it is going and then get started in that direction, taking whatever steps it can to smooth the way ahead and win support for its efforts.

·   ■   ■   ■   ■

June 9, 1947: It is good to get the circulation figures for May and note an increase of almost 60 per cent—for the entire system—over the same month in 1946. It's rather hard to believe, however, when one looks around the building these days. Circulation really falls off in the summertime, and temperatures in the 90's play havoc with library use. Of course, if we were air-conditioned we would have more visitors, but then we would be drawing people who simply wanted to get out of the heat. Last summer was fairly cool, but this is more what I expected from the South in the summer months. It certainly doesn't make one feel like doing tremendous things.

Had a surprise visit from former Librarian Harold Brigham who held forth here in the late 'twenties. We were all sorry he couldn't stay more than a few minutes. To the old-timers, he is the most wonderful person who ever entered library work—and it is easy to share their enthusiasm for this very likable gentlemen. There is nothing the library profession needs so greatly as more men of his type.

■   ■   ■   ■   ■

June 12, 1947: A special meeting of the Library Board was held this afternoon to hear the report of the meeting that several of us had with the Mayor and decide what should be done about it. After some discussion, the matter was turned over to a committee that was charged with the responsibility of drawing a statement of the conditions under which the Library Board would turn over the property and assets of the Library to the City. Everyone seemed agreed that the City should take over the property, but they felt, too, that the transfer should take more the form of a deal than a gift. In other words, the Library should seek to gain some advantage, such as a promise of increased support, from the offer of property worth some $350,000.

The feeling of the group was that no time should be lost in getting the wheels in motion. They all seemed to appreciate the situation at the Library these days—with several library school students planning to visit Nashville for an interview and the Librarian not knowing how much money he will be able to offer them. If the Library staff gains civil service status, or if the Library is granted an increased appropriation, we will be able to offer the standard starting salary to these new people. Without these developments, the Library can not afford to offer a salary anywhere near enough to interest a trained librarian—unless we were to make up the difference from our Special Fund. My recommendation to the Board was that we offer up to $2400 to get these people, inasmuch as we could not afford to let them go, and take the money from some other budgetary item or the Special Fund—and this course of action they unanimously approved.

The Board also was in favor of keeping on the payroll the two people that we brought back to work last month. We don't want to jeopardize their chances of getting a pension from the City, in the event that the staff comes under civil service, and the only safe course seems to be to keep them on the staff until the situation is clarified.

■   ■   ■   ■   ■

June 18, 1947: Had a meeting today of the special committee appointed to handle the matter of turning the library property over to the City. Both Board members present expressed their belief that this was not the time to make the offer since the new administration had many other fish to try—of a more personal and political interest—and would not be much interested in the library transfer.

In short, the Committee felt that the Library stood little chance of getting a favorable reception from the new crowd at City Hall and would not be likely to gain the increased appropriation it sought in exchange for the offer of this property. They were of the opinion that we should try to hang on for another year and try to get the increased appropriation in July 1948.

My response to this was a very definite assertion that we could not wait another year. A year is a mighty long time, and the Library has already waited 15 years for the City to come through with a real increase in its appropriation. Certainly the staff has waited too long for some salary relief to have any faith in any predictions of what might happen in still another "next year".

As I told the Committee, the Library is now faced with the opportunity of a lifetime. With 40 per cent of the professional staff retiring this summer, we have a chance to build a new and hand-picked organization. Most Librarians dream about being in such an enviable position—but never get there. We are fortunate in having an unusually pleasant group of older people, and we shall miss them all both personally and professionally. Yet, at the same time, their departure offers a unique opportunity to bring in new blood and build a younger and faster-moving organization.

To take advantage of this opportunity we must have more money so that we can offer salaries that will meet the competition of other personnel-hungry libraries. If we are forced to go another year without these additional funds we will have to pass up our big chance. With our present salary schedule we will have to be content with untrained people. Surely no librarian of any ability will consider Nashville at the starvation salaries that our present veteran staff-members are now receiving. And if we once employ an inferior grade of library personnel we are likely to be handicapped for years. We won't be able to trade them in on a new—and professionally-trained—model come the day when such a luxury can be afforded.

The outcome of my plea for at least making a try for more funds this year was a decision by the Committee to see the Mayor again and learn why he failed to put the Library down for an increase in its 1947–48 appropriation. This is the next logical step to take and perhaps it will lead to something else. All you can do in a matter like this is to take one step at a time and keep going. But you do have to make a start—and you do have to keep going!

.   .   .   .   .

June 26, 1947: Just got in from a hearing before the tax-levying committee of the County Court. Was glad to have an opportunity to talk to them about this matter of a county-wide library service for Davidson County. Don't know what they will decide to do about it, but am hoping that they are interested enough to at least have a try at this new service. The contract that I proposed to them was one which would open our doors to all residents of the County, and would bring the Library 25¢ for every volume circulated to members of this group.

Wrote a letter to Dinah Shore this afternoon, trying to interest her in the idea of presenting her home town with a Bookmobile. Sent along a drawing of the machine painted a nice bright red color and carrying the inscription "Donated by Miss Dinah Shore". Explained what a Bookmobile would do for Nashville, and that it would cost only $7900—filled with new books and ready to roll—and much of this amount would otherwise be lost to the income tax collector. Also mentioned that we would like to put a bookplate in each one of the 3300 books, identifying them as belonging to the "Dinah Shore Collection", and that each one of these books might go into a hundred homes. Went on to say that if she were interested in the proposal we would want her to come on here for the christening or dedicatory ceremony.

If she doesn't like the idea we will try Claude Jarman, another Nashville product. In his case, we will write to the Publicity Director at MGM. He ought to warm to the wonderful publicity and good-will value of the thing. The expense of the machine would be almost nothing to Jarman's studio, and the gift would offer news and picture tie-ups that would excite any press agent. What I have in mind is a spread in LIFE magazine about the Bookmobile and its donor. They have never had an article on anything connected with libraries, and most people have never heard of a bookmobile, so perhaps they could be interested in our little venture.

. . . . .

July 14, 1947: The "Sunday" Tennessean" came out with a long and strong editorial yesterday in support of the Library's request for additional funds, and the "Banner" took to its editorial columns to support the Library's cause this afternoon. It is not every day that both newspapers can be found supporting the same program or cause, and doubtless this fact has been noted by some of the city fathers.

Meanwhile, we are all excited over the arrival of our long-awaited Bookmobile. It was driven over from North Carolina on Friday and we got our first look at the new baby this morning. The extended bus body seems to afford more room than we had contemplated and the windows are larger, too. All in all, we are greatly pleased with the machine— though we are equally uncertain, at the moment, just how we will arrange certain interior details. Several problems must be decided first. To begin with, shall we have shelves below the windows on both sides of the Bookmobile—or only on the curb side.

The other problem has to do with the location of our charging desk. Shall we place it behind the driver's seat, which would force the center shelving back one or two feet and reduce its book capacity by one-sixth, or should we follow Evanston's example and place the charging desk back along one side—over the wheel-housing? Such a location for the desk would also cost us book-room, but perhaps not as much as the front position. We seem now to be favoring the location in front of the rear exit.

After a good bit of measuring distances inside the bus body we returned to the Library and set up an experiment with shelves placed different distances apart. Several children were recruited to kneel in the passageway between the shelves and pretend they were looking at the books on one side, while some adults were trying to pass by and examine the books on the other side. As a result of all this experimenting we now plan to have low shelves on both sides of the machine, with the center shelves placed directly in the middle instead of being built off-center. I believe we will also try and get by without any shelving in front of any of the windows. In addition to giving better light and attracting more attention from outside the Bookmobile, it will enable us to have all the windows open on hot summer days and enjoy a much cooler and better-ventilated machine.

We have great plans for our Bookmobile. If it doesn't do more business than any other bookmobile in the country we believe that it will at least be the most attractive one in operation.

■   ■   ■   ■   ■

July 15, 1947: We don't have enough time before the end of the month to stage a complete publicity campaign to sell everyone on our rightful claim to a larger appropriation from the City so we will have to concentrate on the Councilmen and try and get their attention and goodwill.

Had the Circulation Department make a list of the neighbors of each Councilman and check our files to see if they were library users. Wanted to be able to make casual mention of a few names of our readers in talking to each man. Unfortunately, however, it was found that none of the Councilmen, and only 1 of some 80 neighbors, were registered with us. We hope to have one of the girls visit all these homes and introduce the Library to them. We ought to be doing more of this house-calling anyway—to win more readers and keep up with the public's attitudes toward the Library.

In the afternoon I had a visit with Vice-Mayor Ben West. Like everyone else, he didn't know where the Library's money came from, so I was glad of the chance to do a little educating along this line. He wanted to know why I came to see him, since if the Mayor said there was no money for the Library there just wasn't. Explained that last year we got some extra money from the Council after the budget was passed and we wanted to know whether there were any chances this year for the same thing. He was very friendly but said the melon was all cut up and there were no extra slices.

However, when I asked what he thought about my making a report on the library situation before the City Council at their meeting tonight, he said to "Come ahead. We're going to have a busy meeting, but we'll *make* time for you".

Rushed home for dinner and then back in the rain to City Hall. When called on at the meeting, I explained that since both newspapers had been running stories and editorials on the Library's needs we felt that the Councilmen were entitled to know what all the shooting was about. In about eight minutes I had time to emphasize the fact that it was THEIR Library—entirely supported by taxes, the great number of people in their districts who used the Library, the great amount and value of the reading done, the extremely low salaries paid, the inability to get new people at that money, the situation created by the loss of five department heads, and the lack of any pensions for these older people.

Took a few minutes to mention the Bookmobile and what it would mean to their people, bringing an abundant supply of the best books within walking distance of everyone in their district. Explained that the bus would follow a regular schedule, stopping in Mr. Bartlett's neighborhood Monday morning, Mr. Sofge's section Monday afternoon, Mr. Ragsdale's district on Tuesday morning, and so on. I had taken the trouble early in the meeting to learn what name went with each of the Councilmen so that now as I mentioned each one I could look directly at them.

The men seemed to pay close attention to what I said, and when I finished, several had questions to ask. Then Mr. Levine rose to ask that the Library's request be given to the Finance Committee for careful consideration. This motion was quickly seconded, after which Ben West closed the discussion by saying that they were all for the Library and certainly would do all they could to see that the children got their books. I departed with the feeling that whether or not the Library gets the money it is asking for, the session tonight was extremely valuable and certainly opened the eyes of many of the new Councilmen to the true status and worth of the Library.

■   ■   ■   ■   ■

July 16, 1947: One of the members of the staff brought some good news this morning. She reported that she had ridden to work with an influential member of the Council and he had mentioned that I had been at the meeting last night and had made a good impression on the Councilmen. Better than that, he had remarked that the Library was going to get "something". He didn't say whether this would be $2,000 or $15,000—but whatever the amount, it is all to the good and that much better than anybody thought we had any chance of getting. If his prediction is proved true, last night will certainly go down on the books as an evening well spent.

The Managing Editor of "The Tennessean" called to say that he had assigned a special reporter to write a series of articles about the Library, starting next week. Needless to say, we raised no objections to this proposal. Later in the afternoon, "The Banner" came out with a long article quoting me at the Council meeting, particularly where I stated that we would have to close several of the branches unless we received more money from the City this year. On the same page with this was my weekly column, "The Library Lookout", also devoted to the matter of the Library's need for funds. Even though most people will probably not read beyond the headlines of these articles, still they must soon—at this rate—learn that they have a public library in town. And perhaps that is all that we can hope for.

■   ■   ■   ■   ■

July 17, 1947: Councilman Levine called to thank me for my letter and to say that he was on his way down to see the Mayor about the Library's request for more money. Wanted to know whether I'd be content with $12,000, which was the figure he planned to ask for. I told him that we would simply have to knock off most of our expansion program, and be unable to raise our salaries up to the level suggested by the Civil Service Secretary, but that we certainly would appreciate any amount added to our present appropriation.

It does look as if we were getting close to some sort of increase, though we are by no means over the hump. The Mayor still has to be sold on the idea, and while it is my nature to be optimistic it is not easy to imagine Mr. Cummings throwing any money our way. The opinion of most people who know is that the new administration already has more political debts to pay than they have money to pay off with. That doesn't sound too hopeful for our side.

Later in the afternoon I sent a letter to the five Councilmen appointed to the new Smoke Abatement Committee, enclosing a copy of part of an article on Pittsburgh which I ran across in Perry's "Cities of America". It gave a good account of what Pittsburgh was planning to do to rid itself of the smoke menace and ought to be encouraging to our Councilmen. Also

asked them to give me a call some day when they had a free
date for lunch as I wanted to meet them and get their suggestions as to the best possible stopping places for the Bookmobile in their district—in the event that we received the money
to operate the machine.

In the evening, Mr. Lancaster—the Librarian at Peabody College —and I joined Dr. Kuhlman and Mr. Pafford for
dinner on the edge of town. Mr. Pafford is the visiting Librarian of the University of London who is making the rounds of
the libraries in this country and Canada. It is interesting to talk
to these librarians from overseas and learn how they operate.
All of the visitors that I have met from time to time have been
of the highest type.

.   .   .   .   .

July 18, 1947: Showed Mr. Pafford around the building
in the morning and then drove him out to Vanderbilt for the
next step in his sightseeing program. Returned to the library
to meet the reporter from the "Tennessean" who dropped by
to gather a story on the Library for her Sunday column.

Also had visits from two trained reference librarians
who want to work in Nashville and get back into public library
work after trying other fields in the fifteen years since they
graduated from library school. Both of them will go to work
for us for $150 a month—well below the salary demand of this
year's graduates—but I am afraid that neither would bring to
the Reference Department the qualities that are needed there.
I don't want another introvert. I want somebody with some
animation and hustle to bring the place alive and sell its services to the many busy people who ought to use the Department but never have.

On the way home I came across a copy of this week's
"Nashville Good News Weekly", which has a circulation of

over 10,000 copies through the theatres. Found that the Library's request for additional funds had made the headlines and that the main article was a copy of the statement that we had presented to the Mayor. It's not every day that a library makes the headlines of any newspaper, large or small.

.   ■   ■   ■   ■

July 21, 1947: Got the sad news from Councilman Levine today that he had asked the Mayor for $25,000, and then $12,500, and been turned down completely. He says the Mayor doesn't believe we need any more money and that we can get along all right on our $56,000. How he can think that after listening to my report to the Council last Tuesday night is beyond me. However, since that is the way the Mayor feels it doesn't look as if we are going to get any more money after all. The Councilmen will take their cue from the Mayor and, at any event, will not dispute his contention that the City has no more money to give the Library.

The Councilman seems to agree with me that the Mayor is unlikely to change his mind next year and give us the money that we are now asking for and needing. Some of the Trustees are counting on his half-promise to take care of the Library in 1948 but after fifteen years of next-year promises I don't see how they can be so trusting. With one or two of them it may be the easy way out of going to work on the city administration to get some more money this year. At least, it looks as if their trust in the Mayor, and their consequent desire to do nothing to offend him, will keep them from doing anything to help bring about an increased appropriation this year.

It is hard to know just what should be done next, since the Mayor seems to be impervious to any pressure at this time. He, and the Councilmen as well, has four years before he has to think about and plan for re-election. It is too soon after the election for the politicians to worry about what the voters may want. And very few users of the Library will take the trouble to contact their representatives—even though we go ahead and close all the branches. They will grumble among themselves and do nothing. Even the members of the library staff, who stand to gain considerable if we get additional money, can't be bothered to write or call their Councilmen. Everyone seems to be too occupied with the failure of someone else to do anything about the situation to realize that perhaps they might speak up or contact a Councilman themselves. We all suffer from these blind spots at times.

The only encouraging note of the day was another editorial in "The Banner" urging the city fathers to come to the rescue of the Library and enable it to continue to operate without having to close its branches, as would otherwise be necessary. At this point, however, I am wondering how much good all these newspaper articles do. The decision is still up to one man who seems to have his mind made up on the matter of giving the Library any more money this year. I only wish I knew who or what could change that mind.

.   .   .   .   .

July 22, 1947: Had 400 copies of a ward map of the City mimeographed for use in letting people know what ward they live in and who their Councilmen are. The addresses and telephone numbers of these men are listed below the map, since few people would take the trouble to find this information for themselves. Took a number of copies out to Mrs. Miser at the P.T.A. meeting on the Peabody campus.

Mrs. Miser reports that the local P.T.A. groups are all set to start telephoning Councilmen in support of the Library's request for additional funds. The local President has been assured by the State President that the Library is a legitimate responsibility of the P.T.A. group and well deserving of their efforts. So tomorrow the President will contact the heads of the individual school groups who, in turn, will call their telephone chairmen, who have a list of telephoners prepared to make ten calls apiece. Hence, eventually the message gets down to the rank and file who do the contacting of the Councilmen. My only hope is that the story will not be garbled or lost before it reaches the end of the line so that the women do not know what they are calling about. At any rate, it will be interesting to observe such an organization in operation.

Also suggested to our East Branch librarian that she talk the matter up to her regular patrons and let them know that they stand to lose the use of their branch library. She said she hated to say anything—up to now—because she was afraid that her people would be up in arms over the thought of her being forced to retire and of losing her as the librarian there. I told her that that was just what we wanted—for them to get stirred up, and do something about it—now. She has many friends in that neighborhood and ought to be able to do some good in contacting them. She called back several hours later to say that she wished she had started her campaign much earlier as her people were concerned about the situation and she wished she had time to get them to the Council meeting.

Had one of Mrs. Moncrief's friends in to see me about a position this noon. When I heard that she was looking for something to do to make life more interesting—having no children to keep her at home during the day—I immediately called her to say that the Library needed her and that we would like to talk the matter over with her. Though she has never seen a library school, she has the intelligence, enthusiasm, and initiative that we need—and those qualifications could take her, and the Library, farther than nine months of library schooling is likely to take the average professional librarian. I wish we could afford library school graduates and could find the kind of professional people we want. But since we can't, we'll make out very nicely by picking people with the basic educational and personality qualifications and letting them pick up on the job the knowledge they need of library practices.

The reporter from "The Tennesseean" dropped by after lunch for another long interview. We're always glad to see people like her. Libraries need more than the normal amount of publicity since library copy is skipped over by most readers and little of it gets through to the mind of the public.

·   ·   ·   ·   ·

July 25, 1947: The campaign for more money to keep the two branches open seems to be rolling merrily along. The story on the front page of the "Tennessean" this morning, and the afternoon story in the "Banner" seem to have shaken many of the people on the North and East sides out of their complacency. We sent an assistant out to the East branch to handle the regular work so that Mrs. Fleming would be free to spend all her time talking to the people who came in the building. She called late in the afternoon to say that she was afraid that her friends out there were going to get up a petition to have her retained as their branch librarian, as well as one asking that the money be provided to keep the place open. I told her that was wonderful, and that we would be delighted to receive a statement from them that expressed the same high opinion of her that we all felt. She went on to say that she wished that she was a younger woman as she would so much like to stay on and work with me as things were really beginning to move now. I assured her that there was nobody that I'd rather have working at the East Branch than her, but that since we couldn't keep all seven of the older people on—and the Board wanted to treat all of them alike and retire them as a group—it looked as if we would have to settle for none of them. She seems to feel that life is just beginning for her branch, despite the present threatened closing, and hates to have to pass out of the picture when "the fun is just beginning". That certainly must be hard to take!

Earlier in the afternoon she called to tell me of two little ragamuffins who were heartbroken when they learned of the closing of the branch. All they could say was "But where will we go now?" I immediately thought of what a wonderful picture that would make, and told her to hang on while I called the newspaper and arranged for a photographer to go out and get a shot of some youngsters looking sadly at a Closing Notice that we would have made and rush out to the Branch. A picture like that could hit home to thousands who would be slightly concerned by a news story on the branch situation.

Spent most of the afternoon kidding individual staff members into the idea of calling 25 friends and relatives and getting them on the trail of their Councilmen. The immediate reaction of most of them was "I don't know whom to call"— or "I wouldn't know what to say" (in talking to the Councilmen). Told most of them to "go to work on all your kin-folks, the neighbors, your grocer, your liquor dealer, and anybody else you can think of". As to what to say to the Councilmen, I told them it made no difference what points they brought up or what they said, as long as they made it clear that they lived in the Councilman's ward and that they were interested in seeing the Library get more money. Explained that the Councilmen were only interested in knowing whether the voters in their territory cared about the Library, one way or another. The only thing that would mean anything to them would be the knowledge that so many of their voters were interested in the library situation—and they wouldn't give the Library any more money until they had heard from enough people to be convinced that it would be politically unhealthy to vote against the issue.

Most of the staff seemed to feel at first that their desires would mean nothing to their Councilmen, and were afraid, too, that he would find out that they worked at the Library and so disregard their appeal as being motivated by self-interest. I tried to explain that their favor was just as important to a Councilman as the well-wishes of the most affluent citizen— that their vote was as good as the next man's. Pointed out that it made no difference to the Councilman whether they worked in a library or a gambling joint, or didn't work at all, and that he certainly wouldn't take the time to check up on them, anyway, to see what they did for a living. And as far as the self-interest idea was concerned, I reminded them that the majority of a Councilman's calls are so inspired and that he is continually hearing from people who want him to do or get something for them. He expects people to be looking out for themselves, and wouldn't be less interested in the Library's request if he knew that his callers were hoping to get a salary raise out of the deal.

As I explained to each member of the staff, this campaign is their baby. If the Library gets the additional money, "everybody gets a raise, except the Librarian. Most of the money is going to you people. I thought you might like to know that you've got a raise riding along on this deal—so that, if interested, you can go to work to help the thing along and so better make sure that you get this money that you so richly deserve to have." This thought seemed to ring a bell with several of them who threw in the remark that everyone certainly appreciated the all-out efforts of the Librarian to raise the level of their salaries.

This particular reaction, which I earlier sensed, greatly interested me as it recalled something of what I learned in my personnel work in industry. I had a chance to observe a number of supervisors who consistently went to bat for their men and would fight for their "rights" up and down the line. They enjoyed the complete loyalty of their people. It was clear to anyone that such a policy was one of the most effective tools a supervisor could use in building morale and loyalty in his organization. I made a note, at the time, that if I ever was head of an institution or department again I must be sure and obey this management rule. But in trying to raise library salaries, I never once thought of my personnel experiences—until these people commented on my efforts.

　　　·　　　　·　　　　·　　　　·　　　　·

July 26, 1947: I generally don't have anything to write in this library log on Saturdays, but I just had two interesting calls. The first was from a Councilman who had received a number of calls from people concerned about the closing of the East Branch and wanted to know what the story was all about. He was sincerely interested in the entire library situation and we had quite a chat.

The second call was from Miss C who triumphantly reported that she had not only called 30 people to put them on the trail of their Councilmen but had actually called 12 of these distinguished gentlemen herself—to say nothing of the Mayor's wife. She reported a friendly reception from all of them and seemed quite bucked up by her energetic actions. I was delighted to learn of all these Councilmen calls, but was even more pleased at the thought of Miss C stepping out and going after something so wholeheartedly. She suffers from quite an inferiority complex and I'm sure that it did her a world of good to discover how much she really can accomplish by herself and to be listened to with respect by such busy people as these Councilmen. She certainly sounded bucked up by her activity on the telephone, and I must be sure and let the rest of the staff know what she did in their behalf so that they can throw a few more bouquets her way.

.   .   .   .   .

July 29, 1947: The campaign for additional funds seems to be rolling along very nicely. The picture that appeared on the front page of the ''Banner'' today showing a group of children dejectedly reading the ''Closing Notice'' on the loan desk at the East Branch apparently aroused all those who until then had perhaps been somewhat complacent about the matter.

Several more Councilmen called me to talk things over and learn just what the Library would need to keep the branches open. They remarked that their people were ringing their telephones off the wall. I was glad that they called for it gave me a chance to straighten out their thinking about the Bookmobile. There seems to be a good deal of misunderstanding about the traveling library. It's too bad that word of it got out at this time, since many people have taken a stand against it as something new that is being brought in to replace their branch libraries. They are greatly attached to the branches and resent this upstart of a Bookmobile. It is too bad that this new service had to receive such an unfortunate introduction to Nashville.

The meeting of the Library Board this afternoon was not too satisfactory since most of the matters up for consideration can not be decided until we know how much money we will be receiving from the City for the coming year. Most of the discussion, however, centered around the retirement issue. The seven older staff members are expecting to be finally retired on August 1st, but it is a question as to how best to secure for them the retirement income they will be needing very quickly.

The Board decided to act on the assumption that the provisions of the new City Charter with respect to the Library are valid and enforceable, and hence the employees of the Library are now under civil service and entitled to its pensions. The applications for pensions for the seven people retiring have been submitted to the Civil Service Commission and are being considered by them this week. There's no telling what the Commission will do about these applications, but the Library Board feel that they can do nothing but act as if they expected the pensions to be forthcoming.

The members of the Board seem to feel confident that the library people will receive city pensions—although some fear that their payment will be made only after a certain amount of litigation that may take four or five months to be settled. The thought seems to be that the City can do nothing else but pay these pensions, and the right course of action for the Library Board is to submit the seven applications to the Civil Service Commission and do all that they can to follow up the matter and help secure an early and favorable decision.

One member suggested that the seven librarians be kept on the staff until it is known for sure that pensions will be paid them. It was pointed out, however, that the group must definitely retire before application for pensions can be made and, moreover, the Board certainly can not act in such a way as to suggest a doubt on their part regarding the decision of the Civil Service people to come through.

The suggestion was also made that the Library Board provide each of the seven librarians with a small monthly income from its Special Fund until the city pensions are realized. It was felt, however, that this would jeopardize the chances of the seven to receive the larger and permanent city pensions and that they would be in a much better position to inspire quick and positive action from the Commission or the courts if it appeared that they were without any means of support and therefore in desperate need of financial aid.

While the Board meeting was going on, the Children's Department was presenting its second marionette show of the day. The morning performance was given for all the children who had read the prescribed eighteen books that brought them to the end of the Summer Reading Road. Tom Tichenor had painted two scenic Reading Roads winding up to a castle on top of a hill, and these had been set up in the Children's Department to mark the progress of the readers. Each child could move his figure up the road with every book read, and quite a number—in the branches as well as at the main library—made the complete trip and won a ticket to this special marionette show. Prizes for the best book reviews were presented at the conclusion of the show by one of the puppets who performed brilliantly as Master of Ceremonies.

The afternoon show was the first performance of "The Frog Prince" and brought back to the Library many of the children who have seen the earlier productions. We had arranged for a photographer from the "Tennessean" to be on hand to take pictures of the audience—and we are all anxious now to see how they turned out. These marionette shows are fine for our circulation, but they are somewhat of a strain on the staff downstairs.

•   •   •   •   •

July 30, 1947: Mimeographed postcards have now gone out to some 500 people on the North and East Sides with library books that are dated for return to the two branches after August 1st. Signed by the branch librarian, they ask that these readers get their books back before the end of the month since the branches will be closed after that date. As the card states, "We are very sorry to have to make this request . . .

but the library can not operate on the same budget it had 15 years ago, any more than you or I can . . ."

One of the girls took the adult registration book out to the East Branch on Friday, and the children's registration book on Saturday, and addressed all the cards for this branch. The same thing was done for the North Branch borrowers this morning. The mailing of the cards was designed to strike home to these people that the Library means business and that their use of library books is very definitely about to be cut off. Nobody who values library service can receive one of these cards and remain complacent about the present situation.

Word now comes from the East Side that many of the people there have already received their cards and gone into action. A final note on these cards mentioned that the library would be glad to furnish the telephone numbers of the different Councilmen and a number of people have taken advantage of this offer. As Mrs. Fleming states, "The threatened closing of the branches has created the biggest stir on the East Side since the tornado some thirty years ago. People are really concerned about the situation."

Most of the Councilmen assure their callers that they will do everything they can to keep the branches open. However, some of them appear to need a little more education as to what a library is and does and, more specifically, why the Nashville Public Library needs more money at this time. As one Councilman expressed himself: "I don't see why the Library needs more money; it's buildings are built and paid for, and they are already full of books."

Most members of the staff now feel confident that the Library is going to get some additional money from the City Council. For a long time nobody thought we had one chance in a thousand of coming through with anything—but now most of the library people feel that we are definitely going to get something. The most commonly mentioned amount is

$6,000. If it came to a bet, I believe that is the figure that I would put my money on, too. Many times lately at lunch, or at home in the evening, I've worked out different budgets with this additional money added to our present appropriation. It is a fascinating pastime—listing the various members of the staff with the salary that might be paid each one, and then totaling the figures to get the total cost. It is surprising how little one can get by on—if one has to. I'm prepared to go ahead with a staff of only 13 people, exclusive of the janitorial force. That is 7 less than the normal number, and 4 less than the present staff roll. However, I certainly hope that we won't be obliged to trim our sails to any such degree. We've just got to operate our bookmobile—and we've got to build up our staff and go forward!

.   .   .   .   .

July 30, 1947: Meant to spend most of the day out calling on some of the Councilmen who I thought could well stand some further explanation regarding the Library's needs. However, just as I was about to leave the building I received a telephone call from an East Side Councilman who suggested that I send him some figures showing the present expenditures of the Library and indicating how much more money was really needed to keep the branches open. This request made me think that it might be well to send similar sets of figures to all 21 Councilmen.

This job took most of the day. In addition to the figures for our present and proposed budgets we enclosed a list of all the members of the staff, showing the amount of money now paid each one and the amount that should be paid each. These sheets were accompanied by a personal letter to each Councilman which, among other things, was designed to clear up any misapprehension regarding the bookmobile. As I pointed out to them, the bookmobile was (1) ordered seven months ago, before we had any idea that the branches might have to be closed, (2) it was paid for out of the last of the Library's private funds, and (3) it was designed to supplement, rather than replace the branches. Then went on to remark that we had planned to have it go up such-and-such a street and make regular stops at such-and-such a school (or other neighborhood center)—naming, in each case, the chief points in his particular councilmanic district. Each Councilman was thus made to see that the bookmobile was slated to bring books right out to his people and provide them, for the first time, with free library service within one or two blocks' walking distance. In most every case, the bookmobile was planned to drive right by the Councilman's home, and it was made clear to them that the Librarian desired to consult with them regarding the actual scheduled route of the machine, and that the Library wished to provide the service that they felt best for their neighborhoods.

The newspaper stories and editorials continue to appear, keeping the library issue well before the people. It would be hard to find anyone in town who doesn't know that the Library is trying to get more money from the City. Thinking to check on the general public awareness of the situation, in a small way, I casually asked several of the waitresses at lunch whether they thought the Library was going to get any more money. This question set them both off. They made it clear to me—a complete stranger to them —that they certainly thought the Library should get the money it asked for, and that it was a shame that people have to work for so little money.

The East Siders are still as fired up as ever over the threatened closing of their branch library. There's one new development there, however, that is causing us some concern. The East Branch librarian has told a number of people that she would be glad to stay on working at her present salary and save

the Library the expense of replacing her at a higher salary. She
has made it plain that she is very loath to retire and that,
actually, she is not "retiring" but, rather, being dismissed
or discharged.

As a result of her stand, there is now considerable sentiment on that side of town for retaining Mrs. Fleming—if not
all the old employees now slated to retire. Some of the Councilmen now feel that the Library could simply continue along
with these people and do away with the need for additional
funds from the City. In short, the Fleming admission has hurt
the Library's cause by diverting a good deal of attention from
the need for raising library standards and salaries to the matter of retaining the old people who want to continue working.
This situation might be even more serious except for help
from an unexpected source. Two of the East Side Councilmen
who are against giving the Library any more money than they
have to, dropped in at the North Branch (an amazing event in
itself) to see if Miss Schick wouldn't be interested in staying
on as branch librarian there. Her answer, happily, was a very
decided "No", she being the only one of the seven who wants
to retire. She told the Councilmen that she had had enough
years of work and was anxious to get away from it all.

.   .   .   .   .

July 31, 1947: I didn't get much done today. The
thoughts of everyone at the Library were on the Council meeting in the evening which would disclose how much, if any,
additional money the Library would receive in the forthcoming year. It was quite apparent that there would be many disappointed people if the Library didn't get something extra.
Most staff members were betting on an additional $6,000.

Just before I left home in the morning, one of the newspapers called to find out what I was going to say in my noon

talk before the Optimists Club. The reporter wanted to know if I didn't have some notes that she could use for a story. I had to admit that I hadn't yet had time to think about what I was going to tell this group but would drop by her office on the way into town and help her work up something. She asked if I had seen the article in the "Tennessean" this morning where two Councilmen from the East Side reported that they had made a study of the library situation and found that the Library could operate as before—without any extra money—simply by keeping on the seven older librarians. After she had read the story to me over the telephone I really felt like replying to these two misguided gentlemen. One of their statements particularly intrigued me. They asserted that the County should, and doubtless would be willing to provide the additional $25,000 that the Library needed to operate its branches, etc. Perhaps the County *should* do so, but nobody who has tried for years and years to get the County Court to appropriate money for library service—even when every cent would definitely be spent on circulation to county people—can be so easily persuaded that the County will appropriate money for municipal library service.

A reporter from the "Tennessean" dropped in at the Andrew Jackson Hotel to catch my talk to the Optimists Club, but I don't believe I said anything worth noting that hadn't already appeared in one or more news stories. Just before I left the Library, one of the City Hall reporters telephoned to say that he was calling for three Councilmen who wanted to come up to the library and work out with me what amount of money the Library really had to have to keep all its units operating. We arranged a 3 o'clock meeting but the Councilmen went to work with the Mayor in his office and didn't come out until almost 5 o'clock. They never got up to the library, but it probably didn't make any difference in the final outcome.

When I got home for dinner I learned that one of the Councilmen had called to report that they had come out of the Mayor's office with $10,000 for the Library and "it was now all over but the shouting". He had made the remark that they had just about had to sell their souls to the Mayor to get that amount—and that there was absolutely no chance to get another dollar from the City.

After hearing this news, the actual Council meeting was something of an anticlimax. Not that it wasn't without a certain amount of excitement, and lasted almost to midnight. Nor did I feel comfortable until the matter was completely decided. Perhaps I was thinking of the encounter one of the Library Board members had with the Mayor earlier in the day. The Mayor was reported to be quite put out with the Library Board. He seemed to feel that they had no right to close the branches and stir up the public that way. His parting remark was, "We'll fix you".

The "fix" wasn't long in showing itself. It appeared in the reading of the long budget which was awaiting final passage before the new fiscal year began the next morning. For the first time in the history of the Library, its appropriation from the City was broken up into four separate parts. A sum of $6,000 was allocated to each of the three branches, with $48,000 allocated to the main library. This made a total of $66,000—or $10,000 more than the Library had been slated to receive before.

I didn't care for these allocations one bit. When the Chairman asked if anyone in the audience wanted to say anything about the budget I felt obliged to go forward and explain what they would mean to us. I told them how appreciative we all were of the extra $10,000, particularly since we knew how hard they had worked to find the money for the Library, but pointed out that by their allocations they had actually given nearly all of the money to the branches, thus putting the pinch definitely on the main library. Explained that last year we had spent less than $9,000 on the three branches together, and here they were giving the branches a total of $18,000. In short, while we desperately needed the extra $10,000 to raise the general level of library salaries, the Council was giving us $9,000 to raise the salaries of the three members of the staff in the branches and only $1,000 to raise the salaries of the 15 people at the main library. If this was going to be the situation we would be little better off than before since we wouldn't be able to increase the downtown salaries sufficiently to enable us to find any new librarians; I don't intend to use the extra branch money to bring in librarians there at salaries well above those of our experienced people at the main library.

When I finished talking about the allocation matter I invited questions from the Councilmen. The result was a barrage of questions and comments about the retirement of our seven older people. Some Councilmen seemed to feel that they ought to be allowed to stay on as long as they wanted to. My only comment here was that there were doubtless any number of policemen and firemen who would rather stay on the force and draw their full pay than have to stay home on a pension, but that the City retired them at age 65 regardless of their preferences in the matter. Also added that ''when I reach that age I'm sure that I'll feel good for another ten years, and want to stay on indefinitely, but I'm just as sure that you'll tell me that I ought to step aside and give a younger man a chance.''

Several Councilmen stated their conviction that all seven librarians were capable and efficient and asked if I thought that any of them were incapacitated. I replied that they were the grandest bunch of people that I had ever worked with and that while I might feel that some were stronger or more able to carry on than others I certainly would not want to discriminate between them. I certainly could not look any of them in the eye and tell them that they were at the end of the line, or that they were good for only two or three years' more, and I doubted whether any of the Councilmen could do such a thing, either. They must realize that the Library has to treat all these people alike or be responsible for a tremendous amount of sorrow and heartache.

Half a dozen Councilmen felt that the Library should retain these people until the question of city pensions for them was definitely decided. This sentiment will have to be considered by the Library Board. However, the Councilmen can't appreciate the fact that the Board has thought about this matter for months and weighed all its angles while they are giving their first thought to the problem. Nevertheless, we welcome their opinions and will try and find a solution that will meet with their approval.

.   .   .   .   .

CHAPTER X

Budgeting—How to
Spend an Extra $10,000

August 1, 1947: Well, the campaign is all over—and I must confess that I miss the fun and excitement of planning the different moves and following their progress. We couldn't have gotten far without the support of the newspapers, but with their full co-operation it was as simple as it was pleasant to keep things moving along at a good, steady clip. Both papers concluded the affair with a good story about the $10,000 addition. I stopped at the newspaper office last night on my way home from City Hall to give the morning paper a statement, expressing the great appreciation of all library trustees, employees, and users to the Mayor and City Council and handing the new city administration a bouquet for the energetic way they responded to the emergency. Made it clear that the Library still needed the remaining $15,000 of the amount requested but confessed that we have been poor and had to count our pennies so long that we can't help but feel very grateful for the additional $10,000.

The Library seemed different the minute I entered the main hall and then I realized what it was. It was the absence of the four main-library veterans who completed their long work with the Library the afternoon before. The institution will never be quite the same without them.

The dinner-party that the Library threw for these seven retiring staff members at Sherries tonight was one of the nicest library parties I've ever been to. I had suggested the party to several younger members of the staff and they had gone ahead and arranged the whole thing. The Library paid for all the expenses of the dinner, thus enabling the remaining staff members to do a better job of buying gifts for the honored seven. Two of the seven couldn't make the party, but the other five were in particularly good humor and looking very nice in their best outfits, with a gardenia on the shoulder. A look around the table reminded me again what a nice staff we have at the old N.P.L.

.　　　.　　　.　　　.　　　.

August 4, 1947: We are still a bit unhappy over the divided appropriation the Councilmen voted to give us the other night. I am afraid that it will mean a certain amount of needless paperwork and a good deal of time lost in keeping the record of our expenditures for each branch. Having called two of the Councilmen the morning after the meeting to see whether the separate branch allocations had not been designed primarily for home consumption and been assured that they had been put in to assure the public that the branches would not be threatened again, I have no fear that we will be held to spending $6,000 for each branch regardless of the need, or that we will be kept from spending most of the additional money at the main library where it is needed. Nevertheless, I don't like the uncertainty about the whole thing and the possibility, remote as it may be, that we may be required to spend more money on the branches than we really ought to. However, if we ever are held to these allocated amounts we will simply charge the branches for all the work now being done for them at the main library in the way of selecting, ordering, cataloging, and otherwise processing their books. This will mean apportioning part of the salaries of the Librarian, his secretary, and the Catalog Department personnel, to the different branches. These amounts, added to the present cost of branch personnel, and books and equipment for the branches, will not come quite to the $6,000 designated—but then we could operate the Bookmobile and charge a good part of the cost to the two white branches whose services it will, in part, supplement. That would leave only the Negro Branch, to which we might have to give several thousand dollars otherwise spent at the main library.

Stopped worrying about this matter long enough in the afternoon to write letters of appreciation to all concerned in the Library's receipt of the additional money. This meant the newspaper editors, the Mayor, the 6 Councilmen who wanted to give the Library $25,000 (they got a special letter), and the 15 Councilmen who didn't care to give us any more than was absolutely required to get the branches open and the public off their necks.

Knowing that some of the ''city fathers'' were annoyed with the Library for causing all the stir about the branches, I tried to get across to them in these letters the idea that they benefitted from the library matter—as well as the employees and users of the Library. I gave many people an opportunity to know and feel grateful to their Councilman, and it gave the Council a chance to demonstrate that it has only to be told about a real civic need to take the action necessary and desired. Also made the comment that some people had the feeling that politicians had no interest in "libraries and things like that" and that while this might be entirely wrong, still it gave a Councilman a chance to take on added status and stand out in the minds of many people simply by showing a sincere interest in something like the library which stands as a symbol of everything non-political. Many people seem to place more confidence in a man who values books and consider him more "high-class"—whether rightly so or not—than his neighbor who has no feeling for such things.

I really believe that these Councilmen would be playing it smart to show enthusiastic support for an institution like the Library which doesn't ask for much money and has the sympathy—if not the support—of most people. Such a move might compensate to some extent for, and help people to look with more tolerance on their more political maneuvers. I guess my job will be to bring half a dozen of the Councilmen around to this way of thinking, to make them feel that they are due to gain from supporting the Library's requests for funds. However, after going over—one by one—the list of the fifteen Councilmen who voted against the $25,000 request, it is hard to pick out even one soft touch in the bunch. They look like a pretty tough collection of individuals.

.   .   .   .   .

August 5, 1947: Had to hurriedly work out a budget this morning for the special Library Board meeting scheduled for the afternoon. The meeting was called the morning after the Council meeting to consider what the Library could do with the extra money and re-examine the situation with respect to the retirement of our seven older librarians. Since then, I had a call from the principal of the East High School who reported that a delegation of East-Siders would appreciate a hearing before the Library Board—in the interests of keeping Mrs. Fleming on as East Branch librarian.

We waited and waited for the delegation to appear at the meeting this afternoon and finally proceeded to hear the high school principal who was the only "delegate" present. After he had gone and we had settled down to the matter of considering the new year's budget, in walked the delegation; they had been waiting for an hour in the wrong meeting room at the bank. When invited to speak their minds, the leader of the group stood up, pulled out his watch and set it on the table in front of him, stepped back a few paces and started an oration that lasted a half hour or more. To say that the Board members were caught with their mouths open is to put it mildly. It was equally apparent that the rest of the delegation was embarassed by the length and vehemence of their speaker's sermon on the perfections of the East Branch librarian. It was simply a case of poor judgment on the part of the young man making the appeal, particularly so in view of the fact that the Board did not need any selling on the virtues of Mrs. F.—as he well knew. At any rate, the President explained that the Board had a definite policy regarding retirement and that any such program must be completely impartial to be successful. Mr. Whitmore also mentioned that he now had a number of letters on his desk urging the retention of another older librarian and that if the Board made an exception in the case of Mrs. F. they would quickly be faced with similar appeals from all the others.

It is really too bad that the movement to keep Mrs. F. ever got started. The other people seemed fairly well resigned to the idea of leaving the library, until the talk about this one member of the group got under way. Since then, several of the people have remarked to me that they couldn't face their friends if the Library kept Mrs. F. but let them go. They would suffer from a loss of face that is understandable and certainly something to be averted, by all means.

The suggested budget for the year 1947–48 was then approved, along with our plans to reopen the branches this week with temporary student help. It may be a month or more before we can find satisfactory professional replacements for the North and East branches. I hope it won't be too long, but meanwhile we will have to do the best job possible to satisfy our branch patrons.

.   .   .   .   .

August 6, 1947: I am a bit undecided at the moment as to when to give the raises that we want to effect now that we have some extra money. I don't want to hold anything out on the members of the staff, yet I would like to wait a month until we are through carrying—on vacation pay—the older people who have just retired. I must confess, too, that it is a temptation to hold off another pay period or two in view of the amount of money that would thus be saved the Library. For instance, the money we would save by waiting two weeks to increase staff salaries might pay for the cleaning of the back of the building.

There is also a question regarding how high to go with these increases. The matter is definitely complicated by the uncertainty that exists regarding the present status of library employees. I would like to get our salaries up to the accepted library standards whether or not we go under civil service. However, I don't want to raise them all the way up to that level now if there is a chance that the Civil Service Commission will soon be obliged to do that for us. If, for instance, they wrote up a particular library job and gave it a salary range starting at $2400 the City Council, presumably, would have to give the Library whatever amount was needed to bring the salaries of all the librarians in this job up to that minimum figure. If the Library is already paying these people such a salary, there would be no chance of getting any more money from the City. However, if the Library was only paying $2100 for this job—and had no money available to spend on raising these salaries to the prescribed $2400—there would appear to be a reasonable chance of getting extra money from the Council in order to implement the new salary scales.

Don't believe we will try and meet the A.L.A.'s standards right away. Tentative plans simply call for a raise for all members of the staff, effective September 1st. These increases will range from $10 to $40 a month. The people will still be underpaid, yet anyone who has come up from $1320 to $2100 in a year's time ought to feel somewhat better satisfied with their professional life. As a matter of fact, there was never any sign that anybody was dissatisfied at the lower figure. Nobody has ever asked us for a raise—but perhaps they were all just used to their low salaries and didn't envision anything better, or maybe we have just managed to keep a jump ahead of them. I suspect, however, that it is just the difference between library people and the gang that was always after me for raises at United Aircraft.

At any rate, while we won't have the salary structure we want, we will be in much better shape than before and within shooting distance of the desired ranges. In brief, we will get our clerical help up to $100 a month, or untrained circulation assistants up to $125, our professional assistants up to $160, and our department heads up to at least $175. And where we formerly had nobody on the staff making more than $1,800 a year, now the Library can boast a salary of $2,400. And there's always the possibility of doing better next year.

•   •   •   •   •

August 7, 1947: Lorenzo has been doing a tremendous job of brightening up the basement hall and entranceways. He has covered the dark, unattractive walls with several coats of jonquil yellow, and painted the doors and woodwork a gray color. The yellow may be a bit too bright but it certainly makes the basement considerably lighter than it was before—to say nothing of much cleaner. He had to have a plasterer come in for several days to prepare the way for his paint brush in the old entranceway off 8th Avenue.

It looks like his next job will have to be the entire basement floor. If he can finish that job by the end of the month, paint the catalog department the first two weeks of September, do the old P.T.A. room in the latter half of the month (the bookmobile books should be out of there by then), and end up with the Librarian's office early in October, we ought to be finished with the redecoration of the entire main library before the state library association meets here in Nashville late in October.

The circulation figures for last month show that our adult borrowers took home more books from the main library in July than in any month since before the war. This is the first time that I ever heard of library circulation hitting a high point in a hot summer month. Book reading generally falls off considerably in the summer, as anyone would expect. Our last month's high was doubtless due partly to the consistent increase in our circulation and partly, perhaps, to all the publicity about the Library's campaign for more money. No doubt, this led many people to think of the public library for the first time in years, and awakened others to the fact that Nashville had a free library service that they might just as well utilize.

.   .   .   .   .

August 8, 1947: Had a call from an East Side Councilman last night asking for the facts about Mrs. Fleming's retirement. Said a delegation or two had visited his home this week in her behalf; I didn't quite get whether they were more intent upon a securing a pension for her. After hearing the whole story from me, he agreed to wait two months and see what the Civil Service Commission does about the situation in the meantime.

We've now had two applications from local people for the library jobs that must be filled. The first one was from a man of 44 who spends most of his time reading in the library. He recently lost his job with the government and now feels that he could be of value to the Library as its North Branch librarian.

The second applicant was a professional librarian who seems to be having considerable trouble finding a position. Having talked with him several times I believe I can understand what his trouble is. Instead of coming to the point and saying what he wants and what qualifications he has to offer, he rambles all over the place and has no sense of time. One tries to pin him down by questions such as, "Where did you work next?", but he ignores these interruptions and goes into great detail about the size and appearance of the apartment they had, his baby's ailments, the name and cost of the physician they had to have, and a good deal more, all accompanied by a good deal of self-questioning to be sure that all his inconsequential facts were right. What a man! No wonder he has lost several of the jobs he has held. He would try the patience of most of the poor people who might bring their reference questions to his desk.

▪   ▪   ▪   ▪   ▪

August 11, 1947: The story hours haven't worked out as well as we had hoped this summer. We brought in an attractive young lady to develop our story-hour program but, excellent as she was at telling stories to the children, we couldn't seem to get enough youngsters down to the main library to listen to her. We had her experiment with a program at Vanderbilt Hospital and the children there were delighted with her stories. Apparently, she must have gotten in there unbeknownst to the Head Nurse, because when we tried for a return visit we were told that such a visit is against all hospital rules and quite out of the question.

.   ■   ■   ■   ■

August 12, 1947: It's good to see Mrs. Brents taking over the Catalog Department so nicely. She always said that she didn't want the responsibility of being Head Cataloger when Miss Wilkin retired but I felt sure that she could handle the work by herself and that we wouldn't need to bring in a new person as Head of the Department. I sorta figured that she would be both surprised and pleased to discover that she could handle the thing by herself and might get a kick out of being boss of the works.

There's nothing like having your own little show to run. I believe everybody ought to be completely in charge of something, no matter how small, and be made to feel that it's her baby—to plan for, to organize, to develop and continue building, and to take the bows for. Mrs. Brents never had any part of the work that was all hers, or anything that she could see or exhibit as entirely the result of her efforts, since her supervisor didn't believe in playing it that way. But now the place is hers, and she seems thrilled to death. The girls say that she rushed through her afternoon coke and can't wait to get back to her work. And she is certainly pushing the work out. I've urged her to train her typist to do a great deal more than the girl has ever done before and she has been delighted to discover how much of the detail work has thus been taken off her hand.

If she can keep from becoming nervous and worrisome I believe that she will stay with the job. Among other things, it will mean a large salary increase for her and a saving of several thousand dollars for the Library. That leaves only three of the seven retired people to replace: a reference librarian and two branch librarians. We will simply get along without the other four staff members. Don't imagine that we will ever fill these four old positions, though I hope that it won't be too long before we will be able to bring in several new people to fill some entirely different positions that we expect to create. I believe every public library could streamline and reorganize its operations to save replacing people in the lower brackets—if it had to, or really wanted to make the effort.

It looks now as if we will be able to raise salaries and obtain our three trained replacements entirely from the money saved by getting along with four less people than we had before. In other words, we ought to be able to spend all of our extra $10,000 on new services and additional books. The operation of the Bookmobile ought to take half of that amount.

＊　　　＊　　　＊　　　＊　　　＊

August 13, 1947: I often stop at the truck builders on my way to work, to see how things are progressing with the Bookmobile. The shelves were painted a light gray last week to match the rest of the bus' interior, and this morning I found the entire outside of the machine looking very bright in its new red coat. All it needs now is some interior lights, a stronger battery, and it's name painted on the outside. Believe I'll also have them get some attractive linoleum or tile covering to add life to the floor of the bus.

We had planned to have unpainted wood shelves but let Kirby & Woodward sell us on some steel shelves that would go better with the steel body shell. They really do look fine, both in the center and around the wall underneath the windows. They also built a steel compartment alongside the seat over the wheelhouse, which is to be the location of the charging desk. I left the design of the desk, and anything else the girls wanted, up to Mrs. Benson and Mrs. Moncrief. They visited the shop several times and thought they had everything all set—but the light wooden table they wanted turned out to be made of steel, too.

Believe I will leave the finishing touches on the machine until the 1st of September and then bring the bus over to the Library to fill it up with the books that are now jamming the shelves of the Catalog Department and the P.T.A. room. Want to have it ready for display at the Tennessee State Fair which starts the 15th of the month, waiting until October to begin actual operation.

.   .   .   .   .

August 14, 1947: There are any number of ways a Librarian, or anybody else, can get publicity for himself and his institution. I believe the easiest way is to simply express to others the sincere interest and commendation that you may momentarily feel for the things that they have done, or are doing, to say nothing of appreciation for favors done you. I have had three examples of this sort of thing recently. The first time I wrote a letter to the publisher of ''The Banner'' expressing interest in his new book; much to my surprise, the letter appeared on the front page of the paper. My second letter went to the publisher of ''the Tennessean'' congratulating them on the second anniversary of their readable Sunday Supplement; almost the entire letter was quoted the following Sunday on the inside cover of the magazine. The third time it was a letter thanking the "Martha and Ed" radio team for some favorable publicity on the Library's need for more money; I understand they spent most of the following program reading my letter and commenting on it in their usual entertaining manner. None of the letters were written for publicity purposes, but the consequences only reminded me again how seldom people bother to express themselves in such a manner. If such letters weren't so unusual, I'm sure my little notes would never have received this attention.

I finally got a chance in the afternoon to get off a mimeographed list of our holdings of old Nashville newspapers to a select list of large libraries. Asked them to check the material which they would be interested in purchasing on microfilm, at a cost of 7¢ a foot. As I explained to them, we are anxious to get our valuable newspaper files on film but can't afford to do so on our own hook. However, if we could line up a number of libraries interested in buying prints of certain portions of our material we could arrange to handle the cost of the negative and a print for this library, as well. We can get the prints made for 5¢ a foot, so that if we can line up ten libraries to take prints at 7¢ a foot, we will have enough money coming in to take care of the negative and one positive print for the N.P.L. This may remain just a dream but it is certainly worth looking into—particularly as it seems to be the only way we can ever get the newspapers filmed.

■   ■   ■   ■   ■

August 15, 1947: Start on a few weeks of vacation today. Called the Library this morning to arrange for Mrs. Moncrief to write the library column for me this week, and Mrs. Benson to write it the following week. Now I hope to be able to forget about the place for the next seventeen days.

.　　　　.　　　　.　　　　.　　　　.

October 6, 1947: The bookmobile finally got off on its first trip. Didn't expect much business as the schedule published in the Sunday paper wasn't too clear. Only 8 or 10 people at the different stops. Most passers-by thought the bus was just waiting for something or had stopped to pick up somebody. Many wanted to know how much the books cost— apparently don't understand the meaning of ''Public Library.'' The machine carried 1300 children's books and 1400 adult volumes, all new.

.　　　　.　　　　.　　　　.　　　　.

October 7, 1947: Bookmobile was swamped by 500 children at Fehr School. Had called the principal about a bus stop at the corner, and teachers brought children out by classes to go through the bus. Had time only to hand out cards. All children wanted library cards, and wanted to get books. Many had never seen a library or a librarian, or had read anything but schoolbooks. Can see that this one school may clean out the bookmobile a week hence. To prevent this, and to save time of charging books on the bus, I believe we'll have boxes of books prepared for the various teachers and delivered by the bookmobile. The books will be older books from the Children's Department, charged to the school rather than to the individual children.

Had a meeting at Peabody College to plan for the Tennessee Library Association meeting here in two weeks.

.　　　　.　　　　.　　　　.　　　　.

October 8, 1947: Finally finished the cleaning of the back of the building. The cleaning company promised the job done in 2 days—at $50 a day—but it's taken 5 days; 2 days to steamclean and 3 to sandblast the parts that steam didn't clean off. The *Tennessean* gave us a nice picture of the job—half black, half white. Shows the library off as a truly beautiful building. Don't believe we'll have to do all of the building. The back was the most conspicuous, the only side seen from downtown, and by far the blackest (having faced the old Polk Apts. chimney). No longer are we an eyesore.

Have spent the last three days visiting possible stopping places for the bookmobile, driving around to get a better impression of the neighborhood and looking for stores and filling stations at which to plug in for electric current to run the lights and heater if necessary. Believe we now have the City rather well covered, though we will remain open to suggestions of further stops.

Will have many more stops than most bookmobiles because we have fewer branches and much more of the city to cover by the traveling library. Find, however, that we can cover them in four days, having the machine at the main library on the other day for work on the bookstock and records. Planned the free day for Wednesday but had to switch to Thursday to accommodate the Junior Leaguers who will now take 4 mornings and 2 afternoons. Our part-timers will fill out the schedule until we can get a person in charge of the bus.

·   ·   ·   ·   ·

October 14, 1947: Having to send my secretary to help out on the bookmobile. One of the children's librarians went out Friday and ran into a lot of schoolchildren and has been nervous and upset since. Must realize that the girls don't like excitement and a lot of business like I do. They prefer things quieter and more routine. The school rush on the bookmobile is scaring them.

The Superintendent of Schools has indicated that he is happy for all schools to use the bookmobile provided the bus gets off the street into the school yard.

.   .   .   .   .

October 15, 1947: Had planned to have the classical music and two turntables upstairs, and the portable phonograph and popular records in the basement Young People's Room. I'm not sure just what type of records to give the teenagers. I realize that they want the loud and fast, the short-lived and ever-changing records that are so popular in the jukeboxes. However, if we provide such music, it would be more sensible to rent a jukebox for $15 a month and have the music company keep the machine supplied with up-to-date records. This would cost much less than trying to buy the records they want and filling the shelves with ephemeral material. Either way, though, we'd have the library swarming with noisy, uninhibited, jitterbuggers who might offend some of our more serious customers without adding to the use of our book resources. The only arguments in favor of such a program are that it introduces the young people to the library, gets many in the habit of coming to the building, gives them the entertainment they want in the right surroundings, and perhaps keeps some of them from making less desirable use of their time.

At the moment, I believe it would be better to stick to the classical and semi-classical, and some of the better-class popular music, and stay away from the boogey-woogey type. The room isn't large enough to handle the crowd that would descend on us if we went all out on teen-agers music.

.   .   .   .   .

October 16, 1947: Visited the company that has been advertising pre-fabricated housing units in the newspapers.

They are selling a 16' X16' house for $195—F.O.B. the army camp where they are being taken down. Also have a 16' X 48' building for $395. Has a slate roof, many windows, and plain wood floor. The small size could be delivered and set up for $400. Might make us a series of small and unfinished "branches" or stations in public parks and other unrestricted locations.

Have been thinking about the need for such agencies, especially after my meeting last night with the steering committee for the Negro Branch Library. These seven prominent Negroes wanted to hear what the Library was planning for their people, as far as library service is concerned. I told them, among other things, that we were concerned about the little use now being made of the Negro Library and its stations, even the new one in the Ford-Greene school. Told them that we were still interested in selling the Negro Library and, if this could be done, we would put the money into 2 or 3 small prefabricated branches. Each would hold many more readable books than were now available in the entire Negro library system, and enough to meet all possible demand in each of the three colored sections of Nashville. These little branches would be compact and more cheerful and attractive than the present big branch.

Was interested to hear them say that they wouldn't want the new Negro Library—if just one new library was to be built—located out by Fisk and Meharry colleges, in the center of the largest Negro section, but downtown where all Negroes could come to it. They all emphasized that their present branch should not be considered a branch library but a main library, since it was all they had. They felt it ought to be stocked as a main library. As they said, people know they can't find the books they need now on its shelves, and many don't use it because they resent not being able to use the main library at 8th & Union.

Certainly their shelves are bare! Only 1 book in 25 is readable. The others are hopelessly old and worn out and too specialized or hard to read for popular use. A good job of weeding would leave no more than 500 books in the building and perhaps only half that number.

Several of these leading Negro citizens wanted to know in a nice, friendly way why they couldn't use the Main Library. They pointed out that they now use the State Library and the Supreme Court Library. Seemed to feel that the white folks wouldn't mind their using the Library. As they pointed out, only the educated Negroes would use the building, not the masses that people see sitting in front of dilapidated frame houses and all those they picture when hearing the word "negro."

After all, the Negroes pay taxes and should, on that basis, have some claim to the central library. Asked the group how many potential readers there were in the Negro population. They reported (1) some 4,000 Negro college students in Nashville, (2) 400 college teachers and administrators, (3) over 150 ministers, (4) 7,500 children in the public schools, (5) 4 publishing houses, etc.

The outcome was their asking that a committee of Negro citizens meet with the Library Board. They thought it best that they speak for themselves instead of putting me on the spot.

Told them I'd be glad to see about such a meeting and let them know. Didn't encourage their hopes, however, knowing that it will be no easy thing for them to win the right to borrow books from the main library, even if they don't sit down or stay in the building. Of course, it would save us considerable money, as well as increasing Negro reading and improving race relations. If they are not allowed to use the Library, we will be obliged to pour money and books into the Negro Branch to give them their own main library.

The decision is the Board's to make. I'm too much a newcomer to the South to try and influence their thought on the matter. Of course, if they vote in favor of the Negroes, the Yankee librarian will be in for considerable punishment from the small people and the old-time Southerners. I expect to be attacked plenty if this thing goes through. However, if I'm asked to express an opinion for or against, I can only say that it is the Christian, the right, the positive thing to do—to let everyone use the main library who cares to.

■   ■   ■   ■   ■

October 17, 1947: More trouble with our branch buildings! The Negro Branch furnace is ailing and it's almost impossible to get an estimate of the trouble and the cost of repairing the thing that one has any confidence in. It takes weeks to get a firm to send out a man to look at the branch troubles and they always render reports that are so much at variance that I'm darned if I know which one to credit. So we go seeking additional estimates, and wait more time—and it's just a great headache.

The situation at East Branch is one of leaking water pipes. The plumber says it'd be better to replace all the pipes under the building than to try and find the leak under the concrete. They say the pipes are all shot anyway.

Sitting in my office downtown with nobody on the staff to look into such situations for me—no building and grounds staff—and no understanding of plumbing or furnaces or building problems, I feel at a loss to know what decision to make. Finally persuaded the City Water Department to send out a man to look at the trouble spot for me.

Things like this are a great nuisance and mental hazard for librarians. But it's all part of the job. Most of us are cautious and suspicious when the building patchers and repairers put in their frequent appearance and tend to put off taking steps, and parting with some of our meager funds, until the need is obvious and imperative.

.   .   .   .   .

October 24, 1947: Had the bookmobile on display this morning for the TLA delegates. Brought it back in the afternoon to take a group out to tea at Peabody College. Had a marionette show before the public library session in the new Young People's Room. Had 40 in there for the meeting. Groups from Chattanooga, Knoxville, and Memphis were all very enthusiastic over the tremendous transformation of the main library. Kept saying how ours was the most attractive children's department they'd ever seen.

The new room looks wonderful with its light walls, white ceiling and gray floors and shelves. New record shelves and fog blue table and two lipstick red leather davenports and new gray chairs.

.   .   .   .   .

November 5, 1947: Called on the Chairman of the City Council's Finance Committee—to ask him for his advice on the location of bookmobile stops on the north side. Will take his suggestion and move one stop five blocks up the street.

Stopped by the North Branch to congratulate the new branch librarian on the fact that her circulation had doubled over last month and the same month last year. It's great to see her business pick up. Not the least of reasons is the satisfaction I know it gives her, thus helping to insure her continuance there.

Brought back some fine non-fiction—the best in the 100 and 200's. People just won't read adult non-fiction there.

So we'll put these books on the bookmobile and give her more fiction in return. I realize that many librarians say what's the good of circulating a pile of novels—but these people want and need only entertainment and escape. They need some romance and excitement in their drab environment. If we can add anything pleasurable to their lives I'll settle for that. Furthermore, few of these adults are capable of reading nonfiction. It is also to be noted that many of these homes lack adequate light for reading—perhaps only a single 40 watt bulb in the living room, and maybe not a place for everybody in the family to sit down.

■　　　■　　　■　　　■　　　■

November 6, 1947: Staff meeting—our first in the new basement room. Explained why we hadn't yet acquired a bookmobile librarian or an East Branch librarian. Let them in on all our employment problems and the money we had offered and would have to offer to find these people. Nobody seemed to mind our paying the new people $300 more than they now make. Assured them that I was the most eager to get new people since I felt in the doghouse with my hard pressed staff now. This happy meeting, with everyone laughing and putting in her 2¢ worth, was such a contrast with our Brockton meetings where nobody expressed any thoughts or good humor.

　　Took the Bookmobile to City Hall for a picture of the Mayor "christening" it with a 4 ft. cardboard bottle. Gave the Mayor and a few other people there the first of our special 6″ X 9″ cards showing a little man holding a long scroll on which is printed "In appreciation of your interest, you are hereby made a lifetime member of the Nashville Public Library. Also room for his or her name and the card number. Should please and flatter and give people something to display to friends. Will go to all Councilmen, the Junior League volunteers, some newspaper friends, and a few others.

Called at three elementary schools on the East Side. Glenn School principal is delighted with the bookmobile and says all the children are crazy about it. Wants us to stay there two hours to take care of everybody. Warner School wants the machine from 1 to 2, for 5th and 6th graders. Caldwell School has a fairly good library so we might pass them up.

■   ■   ■   ■   ■

November 17, 1947: Went calling on a Councilman and stopped at the North Branch on my way back to the Library. Miss Birdsong reports that her circulation has been averaging 100 books a day this month. This may not sound like very much, but it is certainly better than the average of 40 books that prevailed out here only a few months ago. I believe the North Branch is now circulating more books than either of the other two branches—perhaps for the first time in history.

The great increase in our business at North Branch interests me tremendously. It's such a wonderful illustration of the key importance of proper personnel, and shows so clearly the immense difference between the results that two people may produce. Cases like this should convince anyone that personnel is the most important element in any enterprise. Libraries, just as all other institutions, prosper or fail according to the extent that they are managed and operated by able, or poorly qualified, people.

It looks as if the North Branch may have a future after all. When Miss Birdsong, an experienced Peabody Library School graduate, started there ten weeks ago she went knowing that the branch, and its community, were more or less on trial. If the Branch couldn't do any more business than it had been doing, we would have to consider closing it. On the other hand, if some real interest could be aroused in it, we would do everything we could to help the branch along. Before I left Miss Birdsong this afternoon, I told her I was on my way downtown to make arrangements for some painters to come out and brighten up the gloomy, old reading rooms there.

.   .   .   .   .

November 18, 1947: Had another interesting time of it at the City Council meeting tonight. The Chairman of the Finance Committee—in reporting on the matter of the additional $15,000 for the Library—stated that he was not in favor of any further expenditures from the sales tax receipts, inasmuch as he didn't know where any additional funds were coming from, and added that he did not consider the library situation an "emergency".

I popped up at that point to respectfully disagree with the Councilman, and was invited by the acting President of the Council to come forward and tell the group more about the Library's needs. This I was happy to do, although one of the Councilmen who didn't wish me to be heard, picked up his hat and coat and marched out of the chamber.

There were two or three points that I was particularly anxious to clear up in my listeners' minds. In the first place, I wanted to explain why we had a sizable surplus in our account when the year was a quarter through, knowing that some of the men who didn't want to give us additional money were using the fact of the surplus with real effect. Actually, the explanation is very simple: The salaries that we can afford to pay are so low that we cannot get people to work for us. We simply cannot spend all the money now budgeted for salaries, little as the total amount is, until we can find librarians to replace those formerly on the payroll.

I explained to the group that we had increased professional salaries from $1320 to $1920 a year, but that as far as
enabling us to attract new people was concerned, we might as
well have left the minimum salary at $1320. The higher figure
was no attraction to Peabody Library School graduates who
could go to work for the School Board at $225 a month—$65
more than the public library could offer. If any other city department offered their professional people a starting salary of
$1920, they would soon be showing a surplus in their ac-
counts, too, as many of their positions remained unfilled.
Went on to say that we were still looking for a librarian for the
East Branch; none of the many people that we had contacted
cared for the branch's regular hours of 2 to 8 P.M., to say
nothing of the salary.

Told them that we had been able to find replacements
for only one of the seven people who had retired on August
1st, and that our staff was now reduced from the old standard
20 to a mere 13. On the other hand, as I proceeded to point out,
our business has increased about 50 per cent in the same period—so that many of the staff members are being over-
worked and are sure bets for a nervous breakdown if they
don't get some relief soon.

One of the Councilmen then brought up the matter of
the "old ladies" who had been retired—which gave me a
good chance to bring out the fact that we have been paying
them a regular monthly retirement allowance, amounting to
almost half their final salary, from our fine money—and then
asked about the transfer of the library property to the City.
Told him that the Library Board had voted unanimously, on
several occasions, to give the Library to the City, and had
appointed a committee to sound out the Mayor and other leaders at City Hall on the idea. However, when the Mayor made it
very clear that he didn't want the Library, the Board hesitated
to do anything further about the matter. They have no desire to

embarrass the city administration with an unwlecome public offer of the library property, nor do they want to make an offer that will be ignored or rejected.

I again invited all the Councilmen to drop in at the Library and ask to see any of our records that interested them, adding that we would be happy to have them appoint a committee to study the library situation and make whatever recommendations they saw fit. There was no response to this invitation, however, and the discussion ended on the note that the Library's request would definitely be voted on at the next meeting.

.   .   .   .   .

November 19, 1947: Had a pleasant visit this morning with the Fort Wayne, Indiana, Librarian who stopped in on his way to the Peabody Library School. He comes to Nashville several times a year to sell Fort Wayne to the few Peabody students who are interested in the public library field. His starting salary is so much higher than ours, we really don't mind his invading our back yard to sign up young librarians for his library system. Nevertheless, we are going to try and give him a run for his money in 1948.

It was good to see him. There's nothing I miss more in this business than the opportunity to compare notes and talk shop with other men in comparable positions. It's a big day when one of these fellow librarians comes to call, and there is always a lot to talk about. The chief topic this morning was the large new phonograph record collection that Mr. Potterf was organizing for the music lovers of Fort Wayne. He had just spent $30,000 on this new service and, with 15,000 records now in the process of detailed cataloging, expected to have as fine a collection as exists in any library in the country.

Listening to him, I felt like a poor country cousin. Nashville is a larger city than Fort Wayne, but our library doesn't play in the same league with his. His operating budget is now $342,000 a year (including $79,000 from Allen county), whereas ours is a mere $66,000. Don't believe we will ever see the day when we can afford more than one-tenth of what he has just spent for phonograph records.

Like most visitors, he appeared to be quite impressed with the improved appearance of the main library and the entire marionette show program. I believe everyone on the staff is happy to have something in the library that they can show off to the "visiting firemen" and know that others don't have, too.

■   ■   ■   ■   ■

November 20, 1947: Had an interesting time this morning, helping the librarian at East Junior High observe Book Week in her school. Had Jim park the Bookmobile outside the building while I went inside to talk to an auditorium full of 7th-graders. Talked for twenty minutes and then, after I had answered all kinds of questions about the machine, the teachers lined up the children and marched them outside and through the Bookmobile.

The same program was then repeated for the 8th and 9th-graders. In addition to telling all three assembly groups about the traveling library service, I pictured to them our new Young People's room at the main library which they are invited to help operate and use. After explaining how we would like the teen-agers to help select the books and magazines and records that would go into this new room, I told them that we would be glad to have them do somewhat the same thing for the East Branch Library across the street from them. We would bring out all the new books for their age group that were purchased for the main library and let them look them over and decide which ones they would like us to order for their branch collection. Perhaps, when we have our new East Branch librarian, she can organize such a group of teen-agers to meet regularly to examine, report on, and select the best books of the current crop. It would be a wonderful experience for all concerned.

■   ■   ■   ■   ■

November 21, 1947: Lorenzo has finished painting the Catalog Department, along with the connecting washroom, and everyone is as pleased as can be over the new appearance of the place. The light blue walls and the gray bookshelves, below the white ceiling, certainly look attractive. There is nothing dark or musty about the room now.

Now that Lorenzo has taken care of everything but the upstairs office, it would appear that my turn has now come. However, I can't get interested in the painting of this private office as long as the reading rooms in the branches need brightening so badly. Talked this over with Lorenzo and he is willing to help us out by painting the East Branch, realizing that this will save the Library several hundred dollars. He begs off on the North Branch assignment, however; he seems to feel uneasy about working alone in this particular neighborhood. If that is the way he reacts to this second extra job, I certainly won't press him on the matter. His work on the main library has probably saved us a good $2,000 already, and we shall always be grateful for this contribution from him.

■   ■   ■   ■   ■

November 24, 1947: We picked up two more college boys last week and now have a very nice group of young people on the staff. Two of them are Peabody students, two go to Vanderbilt, and two graduated from Vanderbilt in June. The two graduates are now on the regular full-time staff, with the three fellows and the other girl joining in after school. One of the men has developed into a fairly competent attendant in the Reference Department and holds forth there four nights a week and some Sunday afternoons. Another one is handling the East Branch five nights a week. The third fellow is filling in at the main library's loan desk and substituting, as needed, on the Bookmobile.

It's good having these young people around. I particularly enjoy seeing some men around the place. All of them seem much interested in the Library and the work they are doing, and I hope they will stay with us as long as they are in school. I always have thought that it added to the tone of a library to have some men on hand. Wish we could have a handful of alert young men on the professional staff, but don't believe we could find more than one or two such individuals, even if we could afford them.

One of the girls called my attention to "the four freshmen" at the circulation desk this afternoon. They seemed to be doing very well, and I am sure they looked as good to the average patron as they did to me. The boys are all veterans, and the whole crew is mature enough to handle their jobs properly.

I never stop being mighty pleased with the entire staff that it is my good fortune to be working with. It is an unusual group in a number of ways. It is doubtless the smallest staff of any public library in the country in a city of over 100,000 population, and probably contains the fewest library school graduates and the least number of experienced people. Yet it is different, also, in other interesting ways. For instance, 80 per cent of the professional staff (people actually doing "library work") are married. This percentage may well be the highest of any library in the land; certainly, it is much higher than the normal percentage. Again, the oldest member of the professional staff is still in her forties and at least seventeen years away from thought of retirement. This, also, may put the Nashville library staff in a class by itself, since most libraries are continually beset with the superannuation problem. All this is not to say that married employees are to be preferred to unmarried ones, or that young librarians are more desirable than older ones. It is only to point out a few ways in which the Nashville staff differs from most such groups.

■   ■   ■   ■   ■

November 25, 1947: I believe Mrs. Workman is finally going to take the East Branch position. For several weeks now she has been trying to decide whether she wanted to accept different offers that we have made her, calling for her to work different hours and do different types of work. I had always hoped that I would be able to interest her in taking over the responsibility of the branch and, while working there in the afternoon, devote the remaining hours in the morning to the Bookmobile. If she could help train the Junior League volunteer workers, accompanying them a few mornings a week on the Bookmobile, and do some of the routine work for the traveling branch in her remaining free time at the library, and then run out to the branch for her afternoon work, we would be filling two needs at one time.

This afternoon, while she was in my office puzzling over her proposed schedule, I had a rather fortunate call from our North Branch Librarian. She called to say that she wanted to leave Nashville Thanksgiving Eve to go to Knoxville for the Tennessee-Vanderbilt game on Saturday and would be glad to pay the substitute who would operate the branch in her absence. I told her to go ahead to Knoxville and forget about paying anybody; that the substitute would cost about $8 and I was afraid she wouldn't enjoy her trip if she had that extra expense on her mind. Consequently, we would insist on our paying for her substitute.

I didn't, of course, talk this way to Miss Birdsong for Mrs. Workman's benefit, but perhaps it did help her to see that we wouldn't hold her to a too rigid schedule. At any rate, she agreed to try out this double-barreled job the first two weeks in December and then start to work regularly the 1st of January. All we have to do now is keep our fingers crossed and hope that her new maid doesn't let us all down. As she says, she'll be as good as her maid.

.   .   .   .   .

November 26, 1947: I believe that we are going to get that remaining $15,000 from the City Council. Miss Crocker has talked to most of them the last two evenings and reports a majority in favor of the Library's request. Her calls may have convinced several of the Councilmen that library salaries really were low and that the Library definitely needed the money. Of course, they have heard this story from me many times at the Council meetings, but I am always afraid that they comprehend very little of what is said there. The main reason for putting Miss Crocker up to calling these men, besides finding out how they stood on the matter, was to let them hear directly from a library employee who made only $100 a month. In all my appeals to the Councilmen, she has always been my "Exhibit A"—calculated to best win the sympathy and support of a group of men who care little about the functions or purposes of a library but who have no trouble understanding the need of a family living on $100 a month in 1947.

I simply mentioned to Miss C. that she was due to receive a small raise if the Library got its extra money, and remarked that if she wanted to spend a little time to help insure her getting this salary increase, it might help to let some of the Councilmen know that she was interested in their votes. After all, they are not going to be too concerned about raising the salaries of a group of people who have never expressed any interest in receiving such assistance. We certainly don't want to get into politics in any way, but I don't see any particular danger in Miss Crocker's expressing an interest in the library bill and asking a Councilman what he thinks are the chances of the Library's getting the money. There was no suggestion of a threat or demand in these calls.

.   ▪   ▪   ▪   ▪

November 28, 1947: The Bookmobile is now running along fairly smoothly on its ''permanent schedule''—but it is quite apparent that the traveling library service is going to have to have much more advertising before the adult population will use it to any real degree. The machine is now making 25 stops a week, probably as many as any city bookmobile now operating anywhere in the country. It starts to work at 10:15 four mornings a week—and 12:45 on Thursdays—and is out until 5:30 every afternoon. This gives the driver a chance to clean the bus on Thursday mornings and get some help in putting the collection, and the circulation records, in proper order again.

The Junior Leaguers seem to be holding their interest in the Bookmobile, but they spend so little time on the bus each week and are so rushed while they are aboard, that they have little time for learning, and little success in remembering, the proper methods for handling all the cards that cross their desk. Most members of the library staff feel strongly that we need a full-time Bookmobile librarian to co-ordinate all the activity with regard to this new service and keep everything in good order. I agree with them, for the most part, though dislike doing anything to give our volunteer helpers the idea that we no longer want or need their help. What might be best would be a part-time Bookmobile librarian who would just be on duty in the mornings. She could do work in connection with the traveling branch at the main library on Mondays and Thursdays and go out on the bus with a Junior Leaguer the three mornings they go to the schools. Then, if the morning volunteer workers could take over the afternoon stops, which are less patronized, I believe they could handle the schedule quite comfortably.

■   ■   ■   ■   ■

CHAPTER XI

Library Income Up 72% in 18 Months

December 2, 1947: I really got myself put on a spot this afternoon. I had encouraged the staff to turn out for the City Council meeting this evening, and when I entered the chamber with Mrs. Miser—the Secretary of the Board and the only Board member ever to rally around for one of these meetings—there they were, right in the front row and enjoying every bit of the goings-on. Several of them turned around to whisper to us that Councilman X had advised them that the Librarian would have to agree to spend every bit of the $15,000 for salaries, or the Library would get no money. Perhaps that was the effect on the Councilmen of seeing all the library employees in the audience.

Before we had hardly gotten seated, the library bill was brought up and Councilman D. was on his feet to ask the Librarian how he intended spending the $15,000. I replied by saying that our needs were many and great, but that we were most concerned about providing for the library's personnel—past, present, and future. Explained that this—meaning pensions for those who have retired, salary increases for those now with us, and the employment of new people to fill empty positions—would easily consume the entire amount under consideration.

The Councilman then shot at me, ''Will that enable you to give everyone on the staff a $50 raise?'' When I replied that I thought it would, he demanded to know, ''Will you give everybody such a raise?'' I didn't have a chance to do more than to say something to the effect that I couldn't commit the Library Board to such a course of action, while at the same time giving him the idea that we would do what he asked. I don't even recall whether I made any promise to him or not. I know I didn't want to make any such definite promise, because even though I didn't have time to figure out how this would affect each individual staff salary, I realized that it would mean the over-payment of some people and getting them considerably out of the line in the general salary picture. Moreover, I don't approve of such uniform, across-the-board, salary increases. At the same time, I was thinking of the library staff holding their breath right behind me, and I didn't want to do anything to jeopardize their—and the Library's—cause.

After exacting from me a promise to bring to their next meeting a list of the library employees, showing the amount of money each one made and the increase each was slated to receive, the Councilmen proceeded to vote on the appropriation bill. I believe all of us were surprised when 21 ''Ayes'' were counted—a unanimous vote.

However, neither Mrs. Miser nor I felt very elated as we left the room. When a councilman friend followed us out into the hall, she told him very frankly that she didn't think the

Council had any business in getting into the administration of the Library and saying how library money should be spent. "Even the Library Board would never think of telling the Librarian how he should apportion his funds."

This attitude of the Councilman bothered me, too. In addition to that, I was disgusted with myself for allowing Councilman D. to so put me on the spot, and ashamed of myself for giving him the idea that I had promised to give everybody a $50 raise. I had often been critical of world figures who did the expedient thing, instead of sticking to what was right, and here I was being stampeded into just the thing I despised, while thinking how we could straighten things out later. No, the outcome of the meeting didn't give me much satisfaction.

·   ·   ·   ·   ·

December 3, 1947: Had an interesting experience today. Didn't mean to go out on the Bookmobile, but when its driver called up to say he was home with a cold, it didn't take long to figure out that the poor Librarian was the only person around the premises who could take his place at the wheel. I had Lorenzo go out to the city garage to bring the machine in, but by the time he called in to say that he had been slipped the wrong keys and couldn't move the bus, it was time for the first stop at Falls School. Mrs. Williams, our Junior Leaguer, was already there waiting with several hundred school children.

So the Librarian had to hop into his car and rush out to get the driver out of bed, take his keys and hurry across town to where Lorenzo was waiting forlornly beside the big red bus. It was my intention to let Lorenzo play driver the rest of the day, but when he had some trouble in getting the machine underway, I traded cars with him and eased the Bookmobile along to Falls School, having to go all the way in low when the gears refused to shift properly. We got there just in time to continue on to Howard School where we parked in the school yard and were subsequently boarded by several hundred uninhibited young people.

I stayed around for the length of this stop to see just what the two Bookmobile "librarians" had to contend with—and found that to be quite a good deal. The customers here are older and more rowdy than at the other school stops, being inclined to rock the bus from side to side, slam the rear door, and otherwise squeeze all the fun that they can from the Bookmobile. Yet, at the same time, they carried away almost 200 books. If all the schools continue their present use of the machine, it will mean a total circulation next year of 50,000 volumes from these stops alone. We wouldn't go so far as to say that ALL these young readers will be better off for the books they borrowed from the traveling branch, but many will have gained much in the way of interesting information, inspiration, a broadened vision, and plain good entertainment, and others will have been helped to acquire the reading habit—which means so much in itself, throughout one's lifetime.

When I returned to the Library, after running out to the Montgomery Bell Academy to meet with the Key Club, I soon felt happy to have been away all morning. Apparently, there had been considerable discussion about last night's Council meeting, and many of the staff were still excited over the prospects of getting an additional $50 a month raise. It seems that a minority of the group feels that they should get this amount because I promised the Councilman that I would so distribute the extra money. However, they have apparently taken quite a beating from the majority of the staff—including nearly all the full-time professional people—who realize that I was on the spot last night and shouldn't be held to any promise of a raise.

As soon as I learned of this state of affairs, I had Miss Stone call a special staff meeting for 8 o'clock tomorrow morning. This is the kind of a situation that must be talked out and cleared up as quickly as possible. It isn't the sort of thing that one can let go by default, or that clears up by itself.

.   .   .   .   .

December 4, 1947: Was up until late last night, working out any number of salary schedules and apportioning the $15,000 in a variety of ways. It was immediately apparent that if we were to pay the kind of salaries that I want to pay, and to replace the people who have retired this past year, we would require not $15,000 but a full $25,000. Having only the smaller amount to play with, it appeared that we might have to go easy on some of our salary increases and be content with only three or four staff replacements. I can't say that this makes me too unhappy—in view of the small income that we have been accustomed to working with, and the fact that we will be quite busy as it is making the proper expenditure of the extra $15,000 and expanding our service accordingly.

In planning the expenditure of the money, I first set aside the $390 a month needed to continue the retirement allowances of the seven people who retired on August 1st. Then, after considerable experimenting with salary schedules and the figuring of the individual raises which each would call for, I cut out another $350, leaving $510 for the employment of some of the new people we need on the staff. With the number of full-time members of the professional staff at the main library dropping from 17 to 11 within the last two years, this need is equally as urgent as the other two.

Everybody turned out for the staff meeting this morning, and when all the questions were asked and answered, the air seemed to be considerably cleared. The concensus later was that the meeting had helped a lot; certainly, everyone looked their usual happy selves.

Some of the people knew that I did not approve of the Councilman's idea of giving a fixed amount ($50) to each member of the staff and were a bit afraid that the Library would lose out entirely if such increases were not granted. I told them that while I did not think the Library Board would stand being dictated to by the Councilmen, I felt sure that nothing would be done to jeopardize the receipt of this extra money. Although I felt strongly that salaries should be increased in accordance with a carefully prepared classification and pay plan, I would not hesitate to make a few extra adjustments were I to find, after checking with the Councilmen, that they were necessary to the passage of the library bill.

I told the group something of the theory and practice of job evaluation and tried to get across the idea that any salary structure based on such a logical classification scheme would not only be fairer to the individual employee, more understandable, and more easily defended to outsiders, but would also have much greater permanence. It would be a part of the Library's basic personnel organization. And individual salaries would be protected to the extent that they could not easily be reduced below the minimum figure set for each position.

On the other hand, if we should simply add $50 to each one's salary, these amounts would tend to fall in the same category as the other fixed increases awarded all city employees. These increases were given as cost-of-living adjustments and were promised only for the current fiscal year. The library increases are to correct a situation of long-standing and hence should be incorporated into our basic salary structure with no thought of fixed amounts that might be remembered and subtracted, later, as simply as they were added now.

To clinch the matter, I pointed out that if we were obliged to stick to the $50 basis we would use August 1st—the start of the fiscal year—as our starting point and simply make each salary $50 higher than it was then. However, since everyone on the staff has had a raise since August 1st, nobody would receive the full $50 now. Most of the staff would receive only half that amount, having received the other half in September. For the majority of the group, this would mean a smaller increase than I wanted to give them on the basis of a definite classification and pay plan.

I left it up to the staff to decide which way they wanted the matter handled and they all voted for the more logical and permanent form. One of them then suggested that they give the Librarian something in writing to show their satisfaction with his proposals. This would be a great help to him in talking to the Councilmen. My feeling is that these men will be content with any arrangement provided they know that the people concerned are happy.

Before closing the meeting, I invited everyone to submit a schedule of salaries that they thought right for our different job grades. I suggested that they turn these in to Miss Stone, unsigned, and asked that they not confer with one another in arriving at the figures they wanted to suggest to me. It would be both interesting and helpful to me to know what salaries the members of the staff thought ought to be paid them, but I would rather that they did not get into discussions that might tend to influence the thinking of some of them.

•   •   •   •   •

December 5, 1947: Finally received several suggested salary schedules, from department heads, after some urging. Their figures for the non-professional positions are about the same as mine, but I was interested to see that their be-

ginning salary for trained librarians was well below what
I had quoted at the staff meeting as being desirable. I had
stated that I wanted to establish a minimum professional salary of $2400, but these department heads suggested $2100
and $2160.

That made me think a bit, though I still feel that our
starting salary should be higher than that. To be sure, the
American Library Association is still quoting a minimum
professional salary of $2100 but that figure was first an-
nounced several years ago and salaries—along with the cost
of living—have come up 25 per cent since the summer of
1946. The average starting salary for library school graduates, without experience, is now passing $2500 and no library
is going to get anyone for less than that figure unless they
encounter someone who is obliged to live in that particular
community. As every other library, we must decide whether
we want to try and compete in the open market for trained
librarians or try and get along with the limited number who
want to stay in Nashville or who may marry Nashville men
and come here looking for work.

We will probably settle with a minimum salary of
$2220. However, in raising salaries to this level we will not
kid ourselves that this will facilitate the recruitment of new
librarians. A salary of $2220 is little better than one of $1620
when it comes to attracting young people who can take their
pick of jobs elsewhere for $2520 or more. We don't expect to
draw any trained librarians from outside Nashville, at $2200,
any more than we would expect to lose any of our present staff
if we retained a much lower salary scale. And since the only
people we will attract at $2200 will be those tied to Nashville,
it would probably be possible to get them at a considerably
lower price. But since we don't hold with the policy of paying
people no more than is necessary to get them, we are not much
concerned with such realizations.

▪   ▪   ▪   ▪   ▪

<u>*December 9, 1947:*</u> The Library Board meeting was rather disheartening today. Most of the discussion centered around the idea of opening the main building to Negroes. This possibility was suggested by a letter from the Steering Committee of the Negro Branch. The Negro leaders simply asked for an opportunity to meet with the Library Board to discuss the matter of library service to their community but some of us were aware that their principal interest was in securing access to the collection at the main library.

I simply presented the letter from this Committee, along with a letter from the Richmond librarian telling of their experience in opening the library to Negro readers six months ago. The discussion that ensued was quite spirited. Most of the talking was done by the two members of the Board who felt that such a move was out of the question here. They were sure that the Negroes were not interested in the library's resources but only wanted to break down an old barrier and gain entry into another white institution long closed to them. And, despite the testimony from Richmond which showed that only a handful of Negroes took advantage of the opportunity to enter the library there, these gentlemen felt sure that the Nashville Negroes would overrun the main library once they got their foot in the door.

In the face of the strong feelings of these men, the other members of the Board who might have voted for the opening of the library under calmer circumstances, said very little. It took a certain amount of courage on the part of the minister to remark that he could not help but think of what stand Christ would take if He were there in his place. Certainly no one could doubt what Christ's way—The Way— would be, but if the group thought of this matter they did not let such realization affect their argument. Most of them seemed well aware that such a development was "sure to come", but the vocal element were content with holding out as long as they could and making concessions only when required to do so.

It was pointed out by one of the women that the Negroes use the State Library, are allowed in the Post Office, and circulate freely in the downtown stores where they try on the same clothes that white women have handled—but apparently there is something sacred or special about the public library that does not permit its entry by colored citizens. However, this being the case, it was suggested that the Board be ready with the promise of some sort of mobile service, as well as the assurance of more new books, to compensate this Committee for their disappointment on this main issue. Everyone felt that we should do more for our Negro readers and greatly improve our service to this large population group.

Nobody had any thought of pushing through the opening of the library to Negroes in view of the opposition of at least two members of the Board, but everyone was willing to have this Negro delegation meet with them at the next regular meeting of the Board in January.

Since this was a policy matter for the Board to decide I had carefully refrained from entering the discussion. Once a decision was reached, I barely had time to bring up the matter of our new salary scale before the meeting closed. Explained that the Councilmen were interested in a flat $50 raise for all library employees but that far more desirable was the establishment of a new classification and pay plan and the payment of salaries in accordance with it. As I expected, the group was little interested in the first alternative; they agreed that we should stick to a sound salary schedule and keep the proper relationship between individual salaries.

.   .   .   .   .

December 16, 1947: The Library appropriation bill slipped by the City Council on its second reading tonight, but some of the Councilmen let it be known that they are holding their fire until the matter comes up for final passage early in January. One of the men was not satisfied with the letter we presented the Council, saying how we intended to spend the extra $15,000. It gave our proposed salary schedule but did not list individual salaries—since the Board felt that this was both unnecessary and poor taste. However, the Councilman wasn't content with this since, as he said, he was interested in one staff member and couldn't tell from the schedule of salary ranges how this person was going to make out. He wanted to postpone the vote on the issue until he had the salary list that "Mr. Alcatraz" had promised him, but he let it go through when Mrs. Miser promised that I would get the list to him before the next meeting.

I drove Mrs. Miser to the Council meeting, but in planning our strategy on the way downtown we figured it might be better if she went in alone and presented the letter I had written and she had signed as Secretary of the Board. We felt that it wasn't wise for me to expose myself so often as the sole representative of the Library. It seemed smarter to divert their fire by sending in a representative who wasn't always trying to talk them out of some of their public money. And if I did not put in an appearance they could not ask embarrassing questions—such as why I didn't keep my promise to make available the list of library salaries. So I sat out in the car, happy to have a member of the Board taking over a job that is rightfully theirs and not mine to perform.

·   ·   ·   ·   ·

December 19, 1947: Lorenzo's paint brush has done much in three weeks to transform the appearance of the East

Branch. He has finished painting the ceilings white and the walls Wedgwood blue and has started applying a bright Chinese red color to the backs of the shelves in the Children's room. There is no better expenditure that a library can make than a thorough re-painting job. It makes any building seem so bright and clean and inviting!

I got my first experience as a branch librarian this afternoon. When the person scheduled for the East Branch couldn't make it, Mrs. Benson found that she had nobody she could send out from the main library. When I learned that she was planning to give up her free afternoon to fill the vacancy at the Branch I told her to run along and let me try and handle the job.

Most all of my "customers" were children in the early grades and we got along fine together. A loan desk job—particularly where one deals mainly with children—is just what one makes it. If one really likes his young visitors, likes to kid with them, and has the imagination to learn their names—from their book cards—and talk to them as old friends and share their enthusiasms, it is a full, satisfying job. It would, on the other hand, be a dull affair for all concerned if one were simply to check books out in a mechanical, aloof manner.

■   ■   ■   ■   ■

December 23, 1947: We are closing all day tomorrow, the first year this has been tried. It is a great help to the staff and we certainly will not be passing up much circulation in taking this step.

Had quite a pleasant surprise this afternoon when I walked into the upstairs office and found a beautiful new desk set transforming the top of my big desk. I have always wanted a particularly large desk pad on which I could spread out my work and my arms, and this seems to fit the bill perfectly. In thanking the staff for their Christmas present I told them I suspected that they had picked the desk set to keep me in my office—where I might get some work done—and already I feel drawn to my little-used office and desirous of making real use of the new desk set.

·   ·   ·   ·   ·

January 5, 1948: We were fortunate to get the 78 prize photographs that are now on display inside the front door. They are the product of a nationwide contest sponsored by newspapers in all the leading cities. Believe it is an annual affair, and a very worthwhile one from the look of these wonderful pictures. And it makes the kind of library exhibit that everyone likes to look at.

The personnel situation has straightened out almost overnight. For four months we have been seriously handicapped by the lack of a regular East Branch librarian and a full-time Bookmobile librarian. We thought we had the Branch taken care of a month ago when Mrs. Workman finally found a maid and started to work. However, as most of the staff predicted, the maid proved unreliable and it looked as if Mrs. Workman would not be back with us. We had about ruled her out when she called this morning to say she could be counted on to handle the East Branch job, maid or no maid.

An equally pleasant surprise was the visit of a trained librarian from New England who has just married a Nashville man and settled down her. She has had excellent experience, including a turn as a bookmobile librarian in Vermont, and is interested in continuing her work here. Told her about our need for someone to take over our Bookmobile, co-ordinate the work of all its part-time workers, and make the thing tick. Its business has increased every month but it has a long way to go before we'll be satisfied that it is doing all that it can do. It is difficult to plan a full schedule for such a person since the service time of the machine is now fairly well covered by the Junior Leaguers and I don't want to appear to be crowding them out of the picture or allow them to feel that they are no longer needed. However, as I told Mrs. Chumley, she could easily spend any spare time she had calling on people living near the bus' stopping places or talking about the service to neighborhood groups. It will take every kind of promotional activity to put the Bookmobile across, and I believe we will hear Friday that she is ready to go ahead with the job.

■   ■   ■   ■   ■

January 6, 1948: The library bill was passed by the Councilmen on third reading tonight and we now have the final $15,000 we asked for almost six months ago. That raises our total appropriation from $47,000 to $81,000 in less than eighteen months—a 72 per cent increase.

I had not expected any trouble at the Council meeting—but was relieved that everything went so smoothly, with the library matter being given the unanimous support of the group. We had sent each Councilman a copy of the letter presented by Mrs. Miser several weeks ago, and another letter from me giving the salary of each regular staff member at the start of the fiscal year, together with their present salary and the salary proposed for them, showing the total increase each person would be getting this year. Also added a third letter that I wrote for the staff to sign, expressing appreciation for and satisfaction with the raises that everyone had been told they would be getting in the event that the Library got its extra

$15,000. Told the Councilmen that they realized that their salaries were below those of many other people in similar people, and that they would like to be able to look forward to future increases—as the Librarian saw fit—but that their salaries had been raised higher in the last year than they had ever dreamed of getting and they just wanted to let everyone know how happy they were.

I had Miss Stone take the letter around the building, with instructions that nobody should sign it unless he or she shared the feeling expressed therein. However, everyone seemed enthusiastic about the letter and was glad to sign it. So when I called the Councilman who had asked for the $50 increases, he stated right off that he was satisfied as long as the members of the staff were and that he wouldn't give us any trouble at the meeting tonight. In fact, the long struggle for the increased appropriation might be said to have ended on a very friendly note all around.

■   ■   ■   ■   ■

January 7, 1948: Had a grand time last night and this morning figuring out how to spend our extra money. It looks like we will have $5,000 remaining from the extra $10,000 that we wangled in August, to give us a total of $20,000 to divide up. We won't be able to do any major work on the building—such as putting in a parking strip or punching a new entrance in the side or rear of the library—but we should get everything else that we have long wanted. As I see it, the money will be spent as follows:

$3,000 for salary increases, $3,000 for additional personnel,
$2,000 for pensions, $1,000 for painting the branches,
$1,000 for phonograph records, $2,000 for films,
$2,000 for caulking and repair work on outside of the library,

$3,000 for a Librarian's office on the first floor

$1,000 for a radio-phonograph, a mimeograph machine, and a movie projector, and $2,000 for a mobile unit to serve the colored sections of the community.

We are now paying the retirement allowances from the money we collect in fines and non-resident fees, so when this expense is shifted to the city budget we can count on a sizable amount of money left in our Special Fund for taking care of extra purchases that we want to make. It is good to have this emergency fund to dip into when somebody wants something special.

The nice thing about the expenditure of this additional money is that the greatest part of the money is going into equipment and building improvements that we will always have with us—regardless of the size of next year's appropriation. Only $6,000 of it, not counting the money for pensions, will go into salaries which may either be lost or be a recurring expense in the future. The amount for salaries is figured on a half-year basis, since this year will be half over on February 1st when all raises will be effective. Hence next year we will have double these expenditures for salaries and pensions ($16,000), leaving another $4,000 next year for more equipment or building improvements.

The idea of having the Librarian's office downstairs, next to his Secretary's office, has been in the back of my mind for some time, but I had been thinking of taking over a corner of the first-floor stacks. This would have given me two windows looking out over the parking lot, with only a wall to cut through to get to Miss Stone's office. However, the architect that I had in on Monday to test some of these ideas for changes in the main library quickly pointed out that we couldn't take out this section of the first floor without also removing the stack floor above it—which we wouldn't care to do.

The architect suggested taking out the supply room and making an office that would encompass this space and part of Miss Stone's office. Both offices would then be small, but probably large enough. My office would measure only 10' X 11', but that should allow for my desk, a table, and a few chairs. I'll have only one high window in the office, but I figure that if I top the wall between the two offices with six feet of glass I can take in considerable light coming through the other two tall windows on the front of the building. I am sold on the idea of an office downstairs where it will be more accessible to everyone, including myself. I am sure I shall spend more time in my office—and thus get more work done—if I don't have to go so far to settle down to work, and then be inconvenienced all the time by being so far from my secretary. Another big advantage in such a move is the fact that it will free the space upstairs for other purposes. At the moment, I envision a music or record room on one side of the partition now dividing the upstairs office, and a film library on the other side. We will certainly need space for these new services and I don't know where else we could find or make room for them. Of course, I shall miss the greater space, the quieter atmosphere, the view from the front window, and the better ventilation through the many windows in this upstairs office, but I believe there is much to be gained by centralizing the administrative offices.

The architect also expressed himself on some of the other changes that I have been thinking about. Unfortunately, most of them appear to be costly for us, but we might look forward to a rear entrance that would save walking around to 8th Avenue and having to climb so many stairs. We will put that near the head of the list for consideration next year. It looks as if we are going to be busy enough this year, anyway, making the proper expenditure of our $20,000 and developing the new services thus started.

.   ▪   ▪   ▪   ▪

January 8, 1948: We have all been concerned lately about Tom Tichenor, the Peabody student who makes our posters and puts on the marionette shows. Tom has been out at the V.A. hospital for several weeks now, and we certainly will be glad to see him up and around again. Meanwhile, the girls are clearing out one of the storerooms in the basement, near the Children's Department, to make him an office. He has been wanting a place to work and to keep the drawings he turns out. The preparation of this space is expected to be a nice surprise for him.

Speaking of the basement, I believe we are going to be able to use the central hallway for an auditorium—for our marionette shows now, and our concerts and film showings later. There is nothing that we need more than an auditorium, but it would cost much too much to build one outside the present building and there is no other available space inside the library. The marionette shows are now held in the children's room, but they disorganize the work of the Department as well as not allowing sufficient space to handle the average crowd of children. Tom would have to cut down his stage to get it out of the room, but we believe he could set one up at the entrance to the main hall, rolling it to one side when not in use. We can probably get some chairs or benches that we can keep in position throughout most of the hall, removing enough to make a passage down the middle from the rear door to the stairway to the main floor.

There is also a short passageway around the staircase that we might partition off to make an extra office or workroom. Most people coming into the basement go around the outer side of the stairs and this particular passageway is seldom used. It would only take two sections of plywood to close it off and put it to some real use. One has to utilize every bit of possible space in an old building like this.

.   .   .   .   .

January 9, 1948: We feel particularly well fixed today. First came the news from Mrs. Chumley that she would take the Bookmobile job and start to work next Thursday. Next came two letters from trained librarians asking about the possibility of employment at the Nashville Public Library. Such requests are rare indeed, and we have never before had two in one day—or even one week. And then, while I was marveling at this strange happening and wondering what we could possibly do with one or two more people at this stage of the game, in walked an experienced librarian from Gary, Indiana, to talk about a job here.

Mrs. Gullette had dropped in to see us when she moved to Nashville a month ago but I hadn't wanted to bring up the subject of employment while I knew she was busy getting settled in a new home. She had remarked that she had organized a Young People's Department in the Gary Public Library, so I told her about our made-over room and our plans to organize a Young Moderns room here. I could tell that she was interested in the project and hoped that she would come back and see us when she again had some time on her plans.

So now she was in to see if we had some work for her. I told her she could start to work with the young people any time she wanted to and work as little or as much time as she wanted. The room would be in use by the teen-agers only two hours or more every afternoon during the week, but she would also want some morning time to visit the schools and plan her program. So she took along a booklet listing the best books for young readers—to check for purchasing—and said she would be in to go to work on the 26th. That makes three new people employed this week, and the end of our recruiting problems for awhile!

.   .   .   .   .

January 12, 1948: Posted a letter on the bulletin board, thanking and congratulating the staff for their accomplishments of the past year and telling them of the improvements and new services that I foresee for 1948. They made real progress last year. The circulation figures now coming in attest to this fact, if any statistics are needed to convince the members of the staff. Both the adult department and the children's department at the main library report circulation increases of 45 per cent over last year. The branches won't show much of an increase this year, but all three of them should do a great deal better next year.

We have now set our sights on a circulation of 320,000 vols. for 1948—double that of 1946. We told the Nashville Library Club that we would double our circulation in two years and I believe that we will attain our goal, provided we are not too slow in getting into full swing with the Bookmobile and the branch libraries. We should, at least, be operating at the end of 1948 at a circulation rate twice that at the close of 1946.

.   .   .   .   .

January 14, 1948: Our new bookmobile librarian started to work this morning and was plunged right into the thick of things. Hadn't even had time to introduce her to the rest of the staff before the reporter on the Sunday Tennessean called to say that they would soon be over to get the story on the Bookmobile that I had talked to them about. So we had to drop everything and go out and see that the machine was in proper shape for having its picture taken. This involved carrying many new books out from the Catalog Department to help fill and brighten the shelves.

The Bookmobile left for its first stop with the reporter and her photographer on board and they stuck with it for most of the day. Didn't see Mrs. Chumley again all day, as she apparently rode the bus to the end of the line, but I did hear indirectly from the newspaper people that they thought their bookmobile assignment the most interesting one that they had had in a long time.

Ordered a new mimeograph machine this afternoon. Had been debating for a long time whether to get a Multigraph-Duplicator or a new Mimeograph machine, since our old outfit is pretty well shot. I had my mind set on the more expensive Multigraph-Duplicator but the rest of the staff thought I was being overly extravagent. Miss Stone seemed to prefer the Mimeograph machine so, since she is the person who will have to do the work, I told her to go ahead and get what she wanted. When the salesman came over he had three different machines to offer. When Miss Stone was uncertain whether to get the higher priced one with the extra gadgets I told her she could have the full amount for her office and could decide for herself whether she wanted to throw the whole amount in on a mimeograph machine or get the lower-priced machine and save the rest of the money to spend on something else. With that, she quickly decided on the lowest-priced model—and that problem was settled.

■   ■   ■   ■   ■

January 16, 1948: Work on the East Branch is just about finished, for the time being. Everyone who enters the building is enthusiastic about the re-painting job and remarks on the library's new, fresh look. Most of the people, however, seem to prefer to have the back of the shelves painted red, rather than blue. The branch librarian would therefore like the shelves in the adult room painted again to match those in the children's section, but I hate to ask Lorenzo to do the job over again so soon. Believe we can wait until the blue is partly worn off by the rubbing of the books against the backs of the shelves.

A big improvement behind the desk was the replacement of the six weak lights hanging down from the ceiling on long cords by one florescent lighting fixture in the middle of the ceiling. The painting of the front, exposed end of each stack section, and the addition of new window shades behind the stacks also helped the appearance of the area behind the desk.

Perhaps the greatest single improvement in the minds of most of the patrons is the wonderful job done on the floor covering. The men were able to grind away the blackened surface to expose the distinct pattern underneath. It has been a revelation to everyone to discover how beautiful the floor really is.

.   .   .   .   .

January 22, 1948: Drove out to Old Hickory to look over the library there and meet with its Board of Trustees. I was expecting to find a hopeless collection of books in a bare room above a barber shop, or something along that line, and was greatly surprised and impressed to find a very nice library building located right in back of the public school. Had only a few minutes to survey the collection before the Board gathered at one end of the main room. But a quick glance around was enough to show me that this library had a better book collection (more usable books) than all our three city branches put together.

The Board seemed delighted with my appraisal of their library. I told them that I came prepared to make a dozen suggestions—such as brightening up the place with a little Kemtone—but that I was amazed to find one of the most attractive little libraries that I had ever seen or read about in a city of under 10,000 population. Then proceeded to point out all the essential material that the library already had, and how well it met the accepted standards of the A.L.A. I then tried to pick out places where improvement might be made. For instance, the proportion of library use by adults was too small—due largely to the proximity of the elementary school which pushed up the juvenile circulation—and the members of the Board were concerned about this situation and welcomed all my suggestions for boosting the use of the library by the adult—particularly the male—population of the town.

It is easy to make suggestions and toss out wonderful ideas when one doesn't have to find the time and make the effort to act on them himself. Consequently, I let go with any number of promotional schemes, and the Board members seemed thrilled to death to contemplate all the exciting things that their library could do in and for Old Hickory. However, I made careful to emphasize the fact that their own local librarian was equally aware of all these things but of course had no time to do much about them. She is too busy with the present operation of the library to proceed with these plans and projects for the expansion of library service in her community. I certainly did not want to depart leaving the librarian on a spot.

All in all, it was an interesting and pleasing experience. If all small town libraries were as well founded, and had trustees that were as responsive and appreciative as this one in Old Hickory I wouldn't mind doing a great deal more of this surveying and consulting work.

Stopped at one of the car-trailer dealers on the way out there to see what they might be able to give us for a trailer branch to serve the colored sections of the city. Was interested to see how comfortable and livable most of the trailers now are. Wouldn't mind going to Florida every winter, and the north woods every summer, in one of these apartments on wheels. They ought to be just the thing thirty years from now when I am ready to retire. Meanwhile, I am anxious to learn how much we can get the shell of one of them for, without any of the furniture or equipment now in them. The dealer will try and get us a price on an empty trailer. Believe it will run about $1,000 which—with the cost of the shelves and other expenses—will be well under half the price of our bookmobile.

.   .   .   .   .

January 28, 1948: Called in salesmen from one of the outdoor advertising firms and one of the sign construction companies to see what kind of advertising facilities they might be able to give us. I believe we might well spend a thousand dollars to make the public more aware of their public library and what it can do for them. Some of the things I want to consider are a sign on the top of the library building which can be seen three blocks away on Capitol Blvd. and 6th Avenue, a display case in front of the library, a sign in front of the East Branch that can be seen by all the people driving home from town on both Main Street and Gallatin Pike, and some billboard advertising.

I am not too sold on the billboards for the reason that I am afraid some people will think it wrong to spend public money to advertise a public service. A thinking person would of course appreciate the wisdom of spending a little money on advertising to bring a much greater use of what the public is being taxed to support, but we would doubtless be criticized by some of our less intelligent citizens. However, I was glad to get an estimate of what such advertising would cost. The best deal would seem to be a "quarter panel" which would give us six billboards—two of them illuminated—on important thorofares in different sections of the city. The billboards would be the library's for a three-months period, with the copy changed every month. The total cost of such an advertising venture would be approximately $700.

We may also have to pass up our sign on the top of the library, unless we are content with a simple, painted sign. A neon sign large enough to be seen a few blocks away would run into several thousand dollars. To be sure, the Library Board may not care for the idea of a neon sign on the library. Some people might think it undignified or out of character for a cultural institution.

I trust that we can at least get some kind of a sign on our main library property and a smaller sign on the branch site that will suggest to some of the people driving home from work in the evening the idea of stopping there to pick up a book to take home to their family or read themselves.

■   ■   ■   ■   ■

January 30, 1948: Am sorry to miss the Midwinter meeting of the American Library Association in Chicago this week but am too busy at the Library to leave. Sometime before next Wednesday I have got to find time to turn out my Annual Report. Shouldn't be too big a job, though, since I have decided to make this report as concise, as readable, and as forceful as possible. Few people read long reports of any kind. About the only people who read full library reports are some of the librarians heading institutions of somewhat the same size who are interested in learning how their colleagues are making out in other cities and in perhaps picking up some ideas that they can use in their own situations.

I want to stick to the highlights of the year and keep the report under a thousand words. Hope to have it printed in the form of a folder small enough to fit into an ordinary envelope. All our previous reports have been mimeographed and sent to a comparative handful of city officials and other libraries. This time I believe we ought to have it printed and distributed to 2,000 or more of our leading citizens. If it can be made readable enough it ought to give some of these people a much better picture of their library—its services, accomplishments and problems—than they had before.

■   ■   ■   ■   ■

XII

Letting the Public Select the Phonograph Records for Our New Collection

February 4, 1948: Had a busy morning preparing for the Board Meeting in the afternoon. In addition to nine copies each of last month's financial statement, the docket for the meeting, the minutes of the previous meeting, the Librarian's Annual Report, and a sheet presenting the Librarian's recommended division of our extra $20,000, I had Tom Tichenor prepare two large graphs showing the trend of the library's circulation and appropriation over the last 25 years. The circulation curve rises to an all-time high of 390,000 volumes borrowed in 1933, slides down to 160,000 in 1945 and '46, and then pops back up last year to 210,000. The appropriation curve rises to a high of $55,000 in 1932, drops back to $35,000, climbs back to $47,000 in 1945, and shoots up last year (1947–48) to $81,000.

The meeting this afternoon was the first one held at the library in a long time. The President of the Board had the happy thought that they ought to meet in the library at least once a year, which sounded fine to us. Now that we have an attractive new room in the basement we might as well use it occasionally for our own Board meetings.

Since the meeting at the library would mean a trip of six blocks for our four bankers and lawyers I was a little afraid that we might not have our customary good attendance. It was quite a pleasant surprise when all nine Trustees showed up—only the second time that we have had a full house in many years. The meeting got right underway with a report by one member of a conversation he had had with the Mayor. Apparently, the Mayor had heard that we were planning to transfer the library property to the City and so had called this member of the Board to ask that such a step not be taken. He expressed a fear that the library would become a political football and suggested that the Board wait until the next legislature meets to have the library property transferred to the City by legislative act. This way, the Board could better insure that the library would be properly protected from any future political interference or control. The Board agreed to follow the Mayor's suggestion, so that matter is settled for the time being.

Then, since the meeting was yet young—and my Annual Report only four pages long—I took the opportunity of reading the entire report. It was a story of a very eventful, interesting, and happy twelve months. It might also be said to be an account of new services established and old service records broken. It contained a minimum of library statistics. Just enough to show that 1947 had recorded the greatest circulation increase, percentage-wise, in the Library's history, the largest Children's Department circulation in history, the greatest number of new borrowers and the largest main library circulation since Depression years, and the greatest total circulation since before the war. In addition to all that,

1947 figures showed the largest library appropriation, the highest total expenditures, and the most money ever spent for books. The only thing that was ''smallest'' for the year was the size of the staff which was at its lowest figure in more than twenty years.

The four representatives of the Negro community then came in, and the remainder of the meeting was devoted largely to the consideration of their request. They came to ask if the resources of the main library could not be opened to their people. They spoke with such sincerity and put their request in such a nice way that I was very sorry that they were not going to get what they came for. As their spokesman remarked, ''Our people are allowed to go into liquor stores all day long to get that which destroys one's soul, but they are not permitted to enter the library to get the books that would feed their minds and souls.''

They left without a direct answer, but with the knowledge that the Board would give serious consideration to their plea and let them know later its decision. However, it was clearly apparent from the discussion that followed their departure that the Negroes' request would not soon be granted. The majority of the Board were of the opinion that now was certainly not the right time to make such a move—what with the South already seriously stirred up over President Truman's civil rights program. As far as two members of the group were concerned, the time would never be right.

When everybody had expressed himself sufficiently on this matter, the attention of the Board was directed to the Librarian's recommended apportionment of the extra $20,000 from the City Council. The only expenditures that were questioned were the amount allotted for a new Librarian's office downstairs and the amount that might be spent from our own Special Fund for outdoor advertising. The Board thought it best not to attempt any billboard advertising, and appointed a committee to work with the Librarian on the matter of the office and the question of some signs on library property.

In approving all these expenditures the Board accepted the Librarian's proposed new classification and pay plan, along with all the raises necessary to implement it. That will mean an increase in our starting professional salary of over a thousand dollars—in the next sixteen months. Staff salaries will have been increased anywhere from 42 to 82 per cent in the same length of time. That may set a record for libraries, but the high percentages of increase are easily explained by the fact that our library salaries were so low to start with. Even after being considerably increased, they are still well below accepted salary standards. We are still not completely respectable as far as salaries are concerned, but at least we can now hold our heads up in library circles and *try* and attract new people to Nashville.

At the close of the meeting, the Board asked me to step outside for a minute while they discussed a little matter. The outcome of all this was an additional 10 per cent increase in the Librarian's salary—enough to at least keep up with the 1947 rise in the cost-of-living. Incidentally, that gives him the same percentage of increase in the last sixteen months as the average staff member: 65 per cent.

■   ■   ■   ■   ■

February 6, 1948: We had expected our new Young People's Librarian to start to work this week but she came in to say that her husband was returning to his former job in Indiana and that she would be following him as soon as school was out in June. She figured that we would therefore be no longer interested in her services, so we had to convince her that we would welcome her help even for two or three months. We are anxious to get the new department under way and there is nobody else on the staff who can do the job. Hence, anything that she can accomplish before she leaves here will be all to the good. If she can only get the thing operating right, it shouldn't be too hard to find somebody who can keep it rolling.

I called in Anna this morning to tell her I thought we ought to round off her salary a bit—so she could more easily remember it. As part-time duster of the books she has been drawing the sum of $15.95 every two weeks. Asked her how she would feel about getting $18 every pay day. She thought awhile and then asked, "Is that better'n I'se gettin now"? Apparently, my proposal didn't ring a bell with her. So I then asked her if she would have any objections to our rounding the thing a little further—to $20. From the way she smiled and laughed at that I gathered that she quite approved of the whole deal. Her work may not be too essential but if it is worth anything it ought to bring her at least 30¢ an hour.

.   .   .   .   .

February 7, 1948: I believe that we are going to have to find some office space for the "basement staff". The children's librarians have never been able to get any work done without constant interruption from all the people entering their department. They are forced to spend a good part of their time being charming to people who want to talk. This they do very easily—which is why everyone enjoys visiting with them—but, at the same time, they would much prefer to have some time to themselves to attend to all the behind-the-scenes matters that otherwise pile up on one. It is unfortunate that everyone on that staff must go through this department four times a day on her way to and from work, and that everyone wanting to consult our file of old newspapers across the hall must ask for them here.

Now, with the Bookmobile librarian making her head-quarters in this department, and Tom Tichenor back working on his displays there every afternoon, the place has become too congested for anyone's good. Besides, I believe everyone should have her own desk—some place all her own where she can keep her things, and where she can work and know that she belongs. I think I have found the place to put all these desks, too. It's the corridor connecting the children's room with the staff lounge. We can remove the string of lockers on both sides, which will give us a width of over 5 feet. That is not very much but if we can divert the traffic through this corridor so that the girls can work at their desks without having to make way for people trying to squeeze past them, we might be able to operate that way.

The idea sounds good to the children's librarians but if I read the signs right I don't believe the rest of the staff are too enthusiastic about this proposal. I hope they can be sold on it—but if not, we will have to find some other office space in the basement.

I believe we have finally found someone who can take care of our lobby displays. The assignment was dumped on Mrs. Kling's lap last week and she has since turned out a couple of jobs that top anything that we have shown in the past. It turns out that she studied some art in college, handled all the display work for her sorority, and gets a big kick out of doing this sort of thing. Well, the job's hers as long as she wants it.

•   •   •   •   •

February 10, 1948: It has been only three weeks since the Reference Department set out their new bulletin board and I am sure that they are already sorry they ordered one. However, no one could possibly have foreseen the trouble that stemmed from their first display. It was nothing more or less than three assorted pictures that one of the reference librarians had casually picked out. There was nothing significant about these three colored pictures. Probably few people stopped to give them a close look. Yet there was something about that picture in the middle that sort of got one. It was a picture of a little boy in a bright red suit. It completely overshadowed the colorless picture on either side of it. In short, it had real personality. It was the first thing seen by anyone climbing the stairs to the Reference Department. One's eyes just naturally focused on this little red boy standing there with his arms seemingly pointing into the Department from the bulletin board cutting across the corridor at that point. Even at a distance of 35 feet the little figure seemed to be waiting with a warm welcome for everyone coming his way.

Miss Adams, our No. 1 user and friend of the Library, was the first person to be hit by this fact. She saw immediately that this awkward little red figure was giving the Reference Room a certain new warmth and personality that it never had before. The first few times she enthused to me over him I thought she had gone completely overboard. But then when I rounded the corner at the top of the stairs and got my first look at the little fellow I saw at once what she was talking about. I agreed with her then that the picture should remain there, and that nothing should be put on the same level to detract attention from the central figure. The red boy should be built up as a symbol of the Department, in somewhat the same way as Chessy the Cat represents the Chesapeake and Ohio R.R. to most people.

Unfortunately, however, the reference librarians couldn't bring themselves to share our enthusiasm. To them, the little red boy was just another picture. If anything, they resented him for taking over their new bulletin board. Still, everything would have remained pleasant enough if Miss Adams had not come up with a second promotional stunt that involved the use of this same blackboard.

Not that I blame our patron friend. She really had a good idea and it was indeed kind of her to work it out and offer it to us to help build our reference service. She happened to read in the Wall Street Journal where the idea of the Gibson Girl was discovered in the New York Public Library, and the thought occurred to her that such money-making ideas were there for the taking in any library's reference department. So she found a suitable picture of a girl wearing a Gibson Girl shirtwaist and pasted it on a cardboard. Above the picture she wrote "THE IDEA OF THE GIBSON GIRL WAS FOUND IN THE NEW YORK PUBLIC LIBRARY" and below the picture she wrote "OUR REFERENCE DEPARTMENT IS FULL OF FORTUNES". What a tremendous slogan! What a wonderful word—"Fortunes"! She might have said "Full of information" or "Full of knowledge" or anything else like that—and it wouldn't have carried any punch. People don't react to such words. But everyone is interested in making a fortune. In other words, it's not the books that are important but, rather, the ideas in them and how those ideas can be put to work for someone's benefit.

Well, when she got an enthusiastic response to her idea from me she hurried back upstairs and put her material on the bulletin board outside the Reference Department. Being practically one of the family up there, and always interested in doing things for the Department, it never occurred to her that her reference friends would resent her action. So when one of them came in, glanced at the bulletin board and made some slighting remark about her prized slogan, she broke down and cried. Here she was trying so hard to do something for the Reference Department and they just didn't appreciate it. In fact, they made nasty cracks about her efforts. Such was her state of mind when I came on the scene.

It was easy enough to understand how she felt. It's no fun to come up with what you think to be a wonderful idea and then have the first person who comes along throw cold water on your brainchild. It just happens that she is a very imaginative and enthusiastic person, with a real creative mind, whereas the other girl is a fine worker in every way but simply lacks the imagination and enthusiasm that she has to such an unusual degree.

I tried to straighten things out and make her feel appreciated and that her new slogan was valued by and important to the library. Regardless of what anyone else thought, she and I knew that she had rung the bell and I was determined to use her idea for all it was worth. I had to be loyal to the reference people too, but on this point my sympathies were all with the person with the idea. I just don't believe that anybody has a right to scoff at another's idea—at least, not until they have come up with an idea or two of their own. The trouble with the Reference Department is that they are not doing enough original thinking of their own and they are not showing sufficient initiative. They need all the ideas and all the help that they can possibly get from outsiders. But they will not get such assistance unless they can develop more interest and enthusiasm for the ideas that come their way and become more responsive to every thing and every one around them. I don't mean to criticize the reference librarians. They are good average people and well qualified to do the job generally expected of a reference assistant. Our present situation, however, demands more than that. I'm not interest in operating a reference department as it's been operated here in the past. There is nothing wrong with that type of service, except that it served too few people in too few ways.

I have talked to the reference people, not to criticize them but simply to let them know that I believe Miss Adams' little red boy and her "full of fortunes" slogan have real merit and can be used to build our reference service. I would just like them to get fired up on *some* new idea. I believe they know that I would like to see more life up there, and feel that people were getting a warmer welcome in the Reference Department, but they don't seem to feel that they can do anything about the situation. At the present time, they appear to be suffering from a defeatist complex. I am sure that nobody would be happier than they to get free from this deep-rooted state of mind, which makes me all the more anxious to solve the problem up there. I wish we could afford to have some charming young lady in the Reference Department with nothing to do but greet people at the door, and over the phone, and make them feel welcome and see that they go away satisfied and happy. It would be a wonderful thing—and well worth the expense. I would do it in my own business, but at the library we may have to wait awhile.

The last few days Miss Adams has seemed to have regained her normal good spirits. She has been talking to a number of leading business men about her slogan for the reference department and has apparently gotten a strong positive reaction from all of them. One of them is reported to have offered her $5,000 for the idea, and the others have persuaded her to send it along to Washington to be copyrighted. So, while there may be a lingering coldness in the atmosphere upstairs, I am hopeful that our one little case of unpleasantness has blown away.

.   .   .   .   .

February 11, 1948: The way everybody is ordering books these days I will be might lucky to have any money left for my new office. With two branch librarians, the young people's librarian, and the bookmobile librarian all trying to build up their collections at the same time, the book budget is really taking a beating. We have set aside twice as much money for books this year as was regularly spent during the war years, but no such amount can cover the restoration of the branch collections along with the library's normal current-year book purchases.

We are not going to start holding the different departments and branches to any sort of budgetary allotments until the start of the next fiscal year. Meanwhile, I take delight in being able to accept all the book requests that come in and tell the librarians that we will put their orders through. I know how much they need new books and like to see them show initiative in going after what they need. However, at the moment, I am having some difficulty in getting one of the branch librarians to see that we can't possibly build her long-starved book collection from its present weak state to what it should be, overnight. It would take $5,000 to give any one of the branches the minimum collection it should have. We want to help the branch librarians as much as possible, but the job is going to take time. There is no point in getting impatient, feeling defeated, and begrudging other departments their share of the book money every time a patron remarks on the scarcity of new books in one's branch.

Before going home tonight I typed and stuck on the bulletin board a note attesting to the wonderful job that the Catalog Department has done in putting through all the books that we picked up Monday at the Methodist Book Store's annual sale. I know that everyone will join me in thanking Mrs. Brents and her two assistants for getting these two hundred books ready for the shelves so quickly. Don't know of any other catalog department that could have turned this trick. It is a mighty rare book that stays on Mrs. Brents' shelves for as long as a week—which is proof enough of what an exceptional cataloger we have. She well deserves such a compliment, and she won't be any more pleased to see it on the board in the morning that I was to write it.

These book sales are great fun, but one must be careful not to pick up a lot of material simply because it is selling at a greatly reduced price. It is still no "bargain" if the library can get along just as well without it—which it usually can. Nevertheless, the four buyers from the Library made quite a haul, and managed to avoid any serious duplication of purchases. I left early to take in another sale at one of the department stores. They were selling detective stories from their rental library for 25¢ a volume. Getting there before the rush, I managed to pick out 110 that looked clean and were sufficiently well bound to give service in one of our branch libraries. If we want to have them rebound later, we will gain a sturdy, attractive group of books for a low total cost.

     ■   ■   ■   ■   ■

February 12, 1948: Had a visit this morning with the Mrs. Reynolds who wrote us last month asking if she could write an article about the Bookmobile for a popular magazine. Since we told her to help herself, so to speak, she has visited the machine at two of its stops and composed the start of an article. She confesses that she has never written anything before but wants something to do—now that her husband is working in Washington on a newspaper job—and we can't see any harm in her practicing on the library.

Told her something of the things that needed doing and what we were planning to do at the library and suggested any number of possible news stories. She seemed so interested in the whole thing that I decided to offer her a part-time job doing promotional work for the library. I mentioned that we were thinking of hiring somebody on the paper to do such work for us, and she immediately asked why *she* couldn't do it. So it was quickly agreed that she could start to work any time and put in any hours that she could arrange and wanted to work. When she left my office her arms were loaded with library "homework", chiefly public relations material. There are so darn many things that I would like to do this year that I have been wondering whether I shouldn't try and find a young fellow to take over some of the work. We could offer him a mighty interesting job as an administrative assistant or "Assistant to the Librarian". He would get some wonderful experience that would later be of great help to him in getting an administrative post of his own. And we would profit by having somebody on the staff who could devote all his time to working out some of the things we want to do. For instance, such a person could now take over the trailer branch project, and the phonograph record collection, and get them both into operation. After that, there would be many other interesting jobs to do. I already have someone in mind for this position, but am going slow on the deal for fear that we will not be able to afford an extra thousand dollars for his salary during the remainder of the fiscal year. Furthermore, if Mrs. Reynolds can help us out a bit, we might get by. I would very much like to have another man on the staff but I am just a little afraid that eighteen months from now we will have most of our new services operating nicely and I won't have enough work ahead to keep me really hopping. The main reason that I am now so happy in my job is that I can see so much work ahead and look forward every day to getting to the library and doing some of the things that need doing. I want things to stay that way. Actually, though, I feel certain that there would always be more than enough work for both of us, providing we were fortunate enough to be able to keep such a person in Nashville for more than two or three years.

.   ▪   ▪   ▪   ▪

February 13, 1948: Had Mrs. Chumbley do a little investigating this morning at the telephone, light, and gas companies to learn how their monthly bills are distributed. We had been considering the possibility of having our bookmobile schedules enclosed with the bills mailed from one of these utilities, but don't want them to go to all their customers. Since the bookmobile serves only white neighborhoods inside the city limits we wouldn't want schedules to go to Negro families or residents of the County. Hence we are interested in finding whether any one of the utilities can control the distribution of its bills to meet our needs. We must, of course, arrange for the distribution of our schedules before we tell the printer how many copies to run off.

Miss Adams is all excited this morning about the possibility of one or two of her young friends working for the library. She knows a lot of nice people in Nashville and is always talking about the Library and trying to sell charming young ladies on the idea of devoting their personality to the betterment of the Nashville Public Library. Most of her friends don't have to work for a living, and few of them can picture themselves toiling in a library. Up to now, she hasn't been able to make a sale, but she seemed to feel this morning that she had somebody nicely lined up for the reference department.

This may sound quite silly, considering the fact that the girl who wants to do reference work has never had any professional training. However, if she has warmth and animation and intelligence and is willing to work, I will welcome her and feel confident that after some months on the job she will be able to contribute significantly to the growth of the department. We have got to have friendly, enthusiastic people who can sell the public on library service, and such people—if they are really interested in their work—can learn a lot in a short time. The important thing is to get people who are made of the right material and can be counted on to grow into effective members of the library team. Never again will I take on just the average person—no matter how pressing the need of the moment. The right sort of person is bound to come along, sooner or later, and it pays to wait and keep the position open for the person with something on the ball.

Had some good news today: The Banner is ready to run the library column again. Called the editor to thank him for his kindness and then, on the spur of the moment, told him of our plans for a phonograph record collection and asked his advice regarding the best way of getting the public to participate in the selection of the records. He seemed quite interested and suggested a front-page story about the new service, following which he thought they would be able to publish daily lists of recordings for the public to check, clip, and mail to the library.

So now we have got to step right out and start organizing the record collection. But this is often the way I get things done. I stick my neck out and commit myself to something and worry later about delivering the goods. However, a deadline seems to be the best medicine one can give me; I then settle down and pound out the work.

.   .   .   .   .

February 16, 1948: Things seem to be moving along fine. Tom Tichenor is making great progress with his circus for the children's room. He has already painted and cut out any number of fascinating circus wagons, wild animals, and clowns, and the completed circus certainly ought to warrant a display window in a Church Street department store. Meanwhile, Lorenzo is clearing out one of the storerooms to make an office for Tom and the girls on the bottom floor. The corridor-office idea fell through, but I am convinced that the store-room is the best place after all.

Mrs. Gullette has been having a wonderful time visiting the various city high schools and talking with the principals and librarians about our plans for a young people's room at the Library. Everyone has been so very cooperative and so much interested in the idea that she has been quite overwhelmed by it all. She reports that she will have two representatives from each school at her first meeting next week—and hopes that they will prove to be the "attractive, enthusiastic" young people she is looking for. We don't want any bookworms in this new organization—but I just know that that's the kind of student some of the principals will send us. To them, anything connected with a library calls for the sort of uninteresting individual who lacks the opportunity to do anything more exciting.

The pension checks have yet to come through from City Hall for our six retired librarians, and they are getting quite worried over the delay. The vouchers have been passed back and forth between the Finance Department, the Mayor's office, and the Legal Department, and we have just now been able to pin somebody down to a definite statement. According to the City Attorney we have to get a favorable decision from the Chancery Court before the City can pay these pensions to the former library employees, regardless of the fact that the City Council granted the Library its extra money for the express purpose of taking care of these old people.

It looks now as if we might never get to use our city money to pay the six retirement allowances. Certainly, the matter is far from being solved. Meanwhile, I believe we will have to go ahead and make the checks out from our Special

Fund and pay them immediately for January and February. But we can't continue to do that for more than six months.

.   .   .   .   .

February 18, 1948: Was glad to see that THE BAN-NER ran my long story on the phonograph record collection exactly as I wrote it. I write so slowly that any such effort takes me a long time—and then the newspapers generally cut these articles. Am particularly happy over the treatment of today's story because we had to call the editor yesterday and make our peace with him. We promised to have the copy over there on Friday afternoon—and did so—but the messenger left the envelope at the front desk and nobody has seen it since. Not knowing of this accident I gave the other paper a copy of the story to appear Tuesday morning, and thus the news broke there a day and a half before we got things back under control and saw the story finally appear in THE BANNER.

Hurried over to the Hermitage Hotel at noon-time to tell the Newcomers Club something about their public library. They seemed quite surprised to learn what an interesting place the library was. I was impressed once again with what a great story a librarian has to tell and with what a wonderful opportunity he has to win friends for his library by presenting the library story to the thousands who have no idea of the services a public library offers. All he needs is a nose for what is interesting and newsworthy, and an enthusiastic delivery.

I was interested to see the response to my announcement of our new reference department service. This is the movie information project that the reference assistants now have about ready to go. We have printed some sheets marked off into squares so that they can easily fill in the title of the production at each of Nashville's theatres every day in the week. Then, when somebody asks about a particular movie they can refer from this sheet to a card file which includes information about every picture. Filed alphabetically by title, these cards will give the names of the leading players, a brief summarization of the story, and some opinions as to who ought to see the show and what the critics think of it. I selected this service to represent the work of the Reference Department, figuring that this was a simple use of the library that everyone would understand and respond to, and was delighted to see how they took to the idea.

■   ■   ■   ■   ■

February 20, 1948: Don't know where the time goes. Doesn't seem as if I ever get done the things I have in mind to do when I come to work every morning. Can't recall anything that I did today, outside of writing a letter to LIFE magazine suggesting that they run a picture story of our new Bookmobile. As I told them, probably more people use their public library for more years of their life than any other public service—and more than a million people read LIFE in library reading rooms every week—and yet the magazine has never run a story on library service. It would seem to be about time for one, and no library service has more human interest value than a library on wheels that takes books to thousands of people who have never before enjoyed free library service. Here's hoping that our appeal rings the bell at Rockefeller Center.

Also called the Traffic Commissioner to see if we can get some space marked off along the curb behind the building for the Bookmobile. They won't let the big bus park in front of the building any more, hence Jim must either keep driving around the block looking for a place to park it, or pull it into the staff's parking place for an hour each morning. And since it takes up the space of four cars—leaving only two free places—this alternative is calculated to arouse the ire of those staff members who will be forced to spend money to park their cars in the lot next door.

The Traffic Commissioner isn't at all concerned about the members of the staff who he feels should give up their parking space to the Bookmobile, but he will try to get us some 15-minute curb space for the convenience of library patrons. This will be fine. We can easily park the bus there until it is time for it to go to work. We could leave the machine in the garage until then if it weren't for the fact that the bookmobile librarian needs to go aboard every morning to get the place in order again.

■   ■   ■   ■   ■

February 23, 1948: Attended a meeting this morning of the recreational agencies section of the Council of Community Agencies to tell of our plans to organize a Film Library later in the Spring. Suggested the formation of a Film Council to promote the fullest utilization of educational films in Nashville, and am hopeful that this can be done.

Proceeded from there to the YWCA where Mrs. Miser and I presented the Library's story and needs to the Women's Civic Forum, which includes representatives from many clubs and organizations in the city. Mrs. Miser had some very kind things to say about our accomplishments at the Library, but the part that pleased me the most was her remarks about the present high morale of the staff, and the increased interest in the library on the part of the members of the Board. As long as the staff and the Board remain enthusiastic about the Library it can't help but move forward.

Sent a one-page questionnaire to the Librarians of the 20 cities in the South having a population of over 100,000, along with a letter asking their help in the gathering of a few statistics that all of us could use. The A.L.A. BULLETIN stopped publishing this information in 1944, and while we have no particular use for most of the statistics they collected, we do miss some of them. We would like to know each library's total appropriation, total circulation, main library circulation, beginning professional salary, and top salary.

We have chosen the item of main library circulation because it permits of a fair comparison between all libraries. Comparisons of total circulation favor those libraries which are blessed with county and school library services and show such systems as ours at a disadvantage. Moreover, the opening of a single new library unit may produce a real increase in a library's total circulation while business everywhere else in the system remains the same. An increase in the use of the main library is more significant locally as well as of greater interest to other librarians.

For similar reasons, we have asked only for the two salaries which mean the same thing everywhere. It is difficult to compare the salaries for intermediate positions because titles mean different things in different libraries and there are too many variables in the picture.

.   .   .   .   .

February 24, 1948: The committee of young people had their first meeting today in the library. Two representatives were on hand from all but one of the public schools and everyone seemed interested in the library's new service. They seemed to take to the idea of selecting their own books, magazines, and phonograph records and wasted no time in letting us know what records they would like to listen to at their next meeting. As we hoped, they voted unanimously to include two representatives of each of the city's private high schools—so Mrs. Gullette will now have to do some more calling.

■ ■ ■ ■ ■

February 25, 1948: Had to get downtown early this morning to appear on a "breakfast program" at WSM. "Martha" of "Martha and Ed" had invited me to appear on their program to tell the public something about the library's phonograph record collection, and of course I welcomed the opportunity.

Stopped by downstairs this afternoon to see part of the marionette show—"The Golden Goose". In the audience was a group of students from the School for the Blind, the nicest and most interested bunch of young people that we have had in the building. Before the show, Tom Tichenor brought out some of his marionettes and let the students "see" them by touching the figures and handling the sticks and strings by which they are manipulated. Can't remember when I have met a friendlier, sweeter, more cheerful group of students. It was a real pleasure to show them around the library.

Spent the remainder of the afternoon selecting well-known recordings for listing on the newspaper ballot that THE BANNER had agreed to run. They will publish three ballots each for two days, listing a total of 82 albums or separate records for the public to check, clip, and mail in to the library. The public is asked to help the library start its collection of records by indicating on these ballots the compositions that it would like to see made available.

It was Mrs. Reynolds' starting assignment to persuade the managing editor to run these ballots in the paper. This accomplished, she next called the head of the civic Music

Association to see if he would co-operate in getting a record made of the Nashville Symphony Orchestra that we could then have as a newsworthy addition to the library's collection. He reported that three recordings had already been made of the Symphony, though nothing had been done with them. However, it was his opinion—as well as that of the head of the local musicians association—that we could not put them in the library without Mr. Petrillo's permission. The recordings are supposed to be used only for educational purposes. At any rate, I have just written the Czar of Music and feel sure that he will not stand in our way.

■   ■   ■   ■   ■

XIII

Continuous Flow of Publicity About Library

February 27, 1948: A few weeks ago we had an old storeroom outside the Children's Department, as dark, dusty, and cluttered as could be. Today it is an attractive office for the five members of the staff who work on the bottom floor. The old shelves have come out, the entire place has been painted a light color, and a four-tube fluorescent lighting fixture makes it the brightest spot in the building. Lorenzo built a wide, sloping drawing table for Tom, in the back of the room, and there is room in front for two large desks for the girls. The two children's librarians will share one of them, and the bookmobile and young people's librarians will share the other. This should work out all right since the two owners of either desk will never be in the office at the same time.

.   .   .   .   .

March 1, 1948: Spent a pleasant two hours this afternoon looking over forty religious books that I checked in the Methodist Book Company's catalog and had them send over on approval. This is the only type of material I see on approval. With most of the books that we buy it is possible to tell fairly well from the reviews or short descriptive annotations what they have to offer and I am rarely in doubt as to whether or not we should get them. But with religious books the important thing is not the subject but what the author has to say. There are hundreds of people writing religious books these days but few of these volumes have real meat in them. They are of little help to their readers because their writers have yet to find the answer themselves. Such books are wordy and vague, and more theological than practical.

It isn't enough to read that a new book promises to give the reader a better understanding of the will of God, or is devoted to the subject of prayer, or changed lives, or any other interesting topic. There is all the difference in the world between a little book like Leslie Weatherhead's "The Will of God" and the many other volumes on the same general subject. Any library has plenty of room on its shelves for a book on any phase of practical or personal religion that has something real to say. And while one must examine such books to see whether they are full of ideas or merely words, it doesn't take long to discover which. A reading of a few pages here and there is enough to decide one whether or not to purchase a particular volume. Fortunately most authors are consistent in their writing. If they are concise and clear-cut and have something to offer in a few pages picked at random, they are likely to read the same way through the remainder of the book. And if others are muddled and verbose and deal in the obvious throughout their sample pages, they can also be counted upon to carry through the book in the same manner. In each case you have uncovered the authors style and his writing quotient, as well as the way his mind works. A few religious book authors write only when they have something important to say, and consequently don't let their audience down. The four that I happen to have the most confidence in are E. Stanley Jones, Leslie Weatherhead, Samuel Shoemaker, and Norman Vincent Peale. Their books are the simplest to read and understand because they themselves have gone right to the bedrock of Christian living and experienced the transformation and peace of mind and added power that they write about.

One good thing about religious books is that they are comparatively inexpensive. And the best of them are usually the smallest in size and price. Not one of the four religious books I rate the highest in the library costs over a dollar.

■   ■   ■   ■   ■

March 2, 1948: The Circulation Department's figures for February show that more adult books were borrowed from the main library last month than any time since 1941. The Children's Department report a marked decrease in circulation compared with the same month last year. This is the first time that has happened. The answer seems to lie in the fact that many children who used to get their books downtown are now doing their borrowing from the Bookmobile.

■   ■   ■   ■   ■

March 4, 1948: Ran into a newspaper reporter in the reference room. He was curious as to how books were selected for the library so we went back to my office and talked for some time. Gave me an opportunity to mention our new movie information service and lead into the whole matter of our little-known reference department. He thought there might be a story there so I gave him some highlights of the service and took him back to see some of our reference tools and learn from the reference librarians what kinds of calls came in to them.

Before he left I presented to him the whole picture of our library system with its need for anywhere from two to eight small branch units in areas served now only by our bookmobile. Showed him pictures of two inexpensive types of neighborhood libraries. One was a trailer branch which, with furniture and books included, could be purchased for $4500. The other was a small prefabricated house which could be purchased without any of its customary furniture and equipment for around $2000. It could be fitted out with library furniture and books and be ready to use for a total cost of $6,000, exclusive of the cost of the land on which it would stand.

I told him I thought we ought to be able to get somebody to give these branch units to the library. Many people in Nashville could afford such a gift, particularly when the tax deduction would cut the actual expenditure to such a small fraction of the stated figure. To people in these high income brackets, a donation of $5,000 means an expenditure of only $1,500 or less. And when this amount is spread over the life of the branch, say ten years, it breaks down to a very small annual cost. In short, it is a tremendous advertising or publicity bargain. A few billboards would cost a company ten times as much a year as having its name on one of these library branches. And the library connection would build good will as well as keep a given name before the public.

In my opinion, it should not be too hard to sell half a dozen of these little branches. They should appeal both to business advertisers and people interested in honoring or perpetuating the name of a public benefactor or a late member of their family. Where could one find a better memorial, or one that carried more prestige value for anywhere near that amount of money. If presented to the right people in the right way, they ought to be snapped up.

The reporter was completely sold on the idea and went back to the newspaper office to ask the editor if he couldn't have the job of selling these branches to wealthy Nashvillians. It was my thought that the paper could publish a drawing of the proposed type of branch building along with a story telling of the need for these libraries and offering them to the first bidders.

He later called back to say that the newspaper couldn't take on the offering of these branches as one of its projects but that they would give the story all the publicity that it warranted should the library undertake to sell people on the proposal.

·   ·   ·   ·   ·

March 7, 1948: This has been about the biggest weekend that the library has had, as far as newspaper publicity is concerned. It isn't often that we make the front page two days in a row and rate three feature stories over the weekend. The first to appear was the story announcing the organization of the Young Moderns Council and the opening of the "Young Moderns Den" at the library. They ran it on the front page just as I wrote it, which convinces me that despite all the time that it takes me to turn out a newspaper story I had better continue to present our news stories to the paper already written. It makes things easier for the editorial staff and wins us longer articles than we would otherwise get.

The big article Sunday was the long-awaited feature on the Bookmobile service. As the main article in the Sunday Magazine it was advertised on the front page of the main news section and was doubtless read by many thousands of readers. Another big story Sunday was the feature on the reference department which announced their new movie information service. Was horrified, however, to find our entire reference service classed as "new". This Department is as old as the library itself and we certainly wouldn't want to appear to be taking credit for its services. I had emphasized the fact to the reporter that the only thing new about our reference service was the offer of information about local movies but the story read as if the library was just now entering the reference field so that the public could, for the first time, call there for all sorts of information.

.   .   .   .   .

March 8, 1948: Felt better about the article on the reference department after this evening's meeting of the Nashville Library Club where I had an opportunity to explain the matter to the local librarians, including the former Librarian of the N.P.L.

As a matter of fact, I believe it helped the Library to have this article describe our entire information service as new. Most people were unaware of the existence of this department and it was doubtless better to present this news to them as something new rather than as a little used service that few people knew about. People respond much more to something that is thought to be "new". They have certainly responded to Sunday's news. The reference department's phones have been ringing most of the day. The number of calls for information was six times that of an average day last month. I don't expect this situation to last, as I am sure that many people called out of a curiosity to see whether the library could really come through with what it claimed to be able to do, yet I feel sure that our reference business will never be as low as it was before. The people who call on us this week may not call again for several months but still the contact has been made and they will be likely to think of the library again when they are in need of some facts or figures.

I have been thrilled all day over what has been going on in the Reference Department. Only wish I could slip over there and take some of the calls that I can hear coming in. There is no more interesting assignment in a library than that of rustling up answers to telephone questions when the calls are really coming through. That is, provided one is interested in the people and their needs, takes pride in giving fast, friendly service, and has the imagination to see in each contact a real opportunity to win a new friend and supporter for the Library—and, of course, cares enough about the library and its reputation to care what his callers think about it.

Unfortunately, however, the reference librarians do not seem to share this enthusiasm. They complain that they have been kept so busy answering the telephone today that they have not had time to do any of their regular housekeeping duties. I tell them to relax and rejoice over the additional attention that they are now getting. Made it clear to them that I sympathized with their desire to keep their files up-to-date and everything in neat order, and would not hold them responsible for any lapse in this respect, yet I felt that their service to the public was the all-important factor. They are there to serve the people who call or visit the library and if they can give twice the service by neglecting the clipping and filing and labeling that ordinarily takes so much of their time, let these housekeeping chores go. They are only means to an end.

I hope the girls can find their way to becoming happy over this development in their professional lives. They seem to realize that they *ought* to feel pleased about the whole matter, but from their remarks I am not sure but what they would be happier if there had been no story in the newspaper and their day's quota of telephone questions had remained at 7 or 8, instead of jumping to 61. Don't know why I expect everyone to react to such matters the way I do. The only time I enjoy working at a reference or circulation desk is when the phones are ringing and I have to run to keep up with the people waiting at the desk to see me. If one enjoys working with people, and being of help to them, it ought to follow that the more people the merrier.

      .   .   .   .   .

March 11, 1948: Am having a hard time picking out the right phonograph for our record collection. Believe we ought to get the best machine available so that our recordings will sound sufficiently superior to the playing of the average home machine that people will want to come to the library to hear their favorite compositions. Furthermore, if we go ahead with our plans to have concerts and music appreciation programs in the library we will have to have a machine with the proper volume and tone quality to do the job.

Perhaps my ears aren't sensitive enough to discern differences in the performance of some of the phonographs. At any rate, I don't remember my impressions from one store to another. The Capehart sounded wonderful yesterday afternoon, but so did the Scott machine today. As for the lower-priced machines, I recall liking some of the Philcos and Zeniths but not others of the same make. If I could only hear the same record on all four of the machines I am now considering, at the same time and in the same room, I might be able to make a decision. Even the Consumers Union and Consumers Research Reports are of no help to me this time as they have not made any comparative study of the machines we are interested in.

We called the engineer at the radio station to inquire as to the possibility of building our own machine, with a speaker or two spotted around the walls of the music room. Seemed to be a fairly good idea until I began to think that I might like to move our phonograph, on occasion, into the auditorium that may eventually be built over the main hall. Guess we had better stick to the standard floor model, but I wish we could get a turntable with the sound quality of the Capehart without having to pay for the expensive cabinet, the radio, and the automatic record changer which goes with all good machines nowadays. Don't believe we will have any use for the automatic changer since most people will decide on their recordings and play them one at a time in the library. Moreover, the changers are delicate mechanisms and are apt to be broken, to say nothing of their being somewhat in the way and slowing up the playing of the average machine.

■   ■   ■   ■   ■

March 15, 1948: We are all set now to call in the contractor to go ahead with the new Librarian's office downstairs. The members of the special committee of the Library Board have passed on the matter and expressed their interest in the contemplated changes both upstairs and downstairs.

Looks like we will have to pass up the fine sign that was designed for use on the front lawn. It was to have been a two-sided neon sign with three rows of letters under the metal outline of an open book. On the top line in large letters was "YOUR"; below that in slightly smaller letters was "PUBLIC LIBRARY"; and below that in still smaller letters was the suggestion "TAKE HOME A BOOK". It would have extended out over the sidewalk, at the corner of 8th Avenue and Union Street, where it would have been easily seen by all cars going and coming on both streets. However, one of the men thought that its erection might bring criticism on the library from some people who would feel that the institution was wasting tax money and must have more money than it actually needs. He may be right. Yet, I believe that the sign would do sufficient good with the average citizen to more than make up for the bad taste it might leave with this critical minority.

．　　　．　　　．　　　．　　　．

March 19, 1948: Up until today I thought we were going to get two new rooms out of my office and the old genealogical room on the other side of the partition that runs almost to the big front windows. I had planned to turn my office into the music room to house the phonograph record collection, and make the outer office into our film library headquarters. But now the girls tell me that the old brown partition just has to come out; they don't like its looks and agree that it would look much better to have one big room—as it was originally. I can see how this would facilitate the decoration of the place, particularly around the big half-moon-shaped windows which would otherwise be divided. I don't like to give up the film library space, and am also afraid that it will cost much more to furnish the considerably larger music room, but am letting the girls have their way. I can't help but feel that their judgment in a matter of interior decoration is superior to mine.

．　　　．　　　．　　　．　　　．

March 23, 1948: I have had my fingers crossed the last few days, waiting to hear how the executive committee of the McKendree Church would act on our request to use a small section of their front lawn for a downtown trailer branch. Well, they voted against the idea. This is a big disappointment, but no surprise to us as they have turned down any number of big offers and requests for use of this valuable land. The idea is still a good one—and it is a shame that the people of Nashville cannot enjoy the use of such a convenient library unit.

We could have done a tremendous business from a small, attractive book trailer parked at the edge of this church property. It would have brought the best material now in print within easy reach of the thousands who pass along Nashville's main street but never find their way to the poorly located main library building. The Church is directly across the street from the city's leading department store and in the center of the shopping district. It is set so far back from the street that the trailer branch would be completely removed from it. People would enter this unit from the sidewalk and would go nowhere near the church building. The trailer would measure only 18′ long and 6′ wide and so would not obstruct anyone's view of the church.

It was planned to have the "library" open from 10 A.M. to 6 P.M. from Monday through Saturday, with a possibility of some evening service if such seemed warranted. We would also have been happy to have it open from 10 A.M. to 1 P.M. Sunday morning, to serve the church-goers, if the Church were in favor of such a move. All together, it is quite possible that this downtown branch could have circulated as many books in a given period as the entire main library.

Judge Ewing had arranged for me to call on the minister in the company of a leading member of the Church whom he had interested in the library idea. We had had a nice visit, which I had followed up with a letter outlining our plan in some detail. Apparently, however, the matter was brought before the committee at an inopportune time and just did not have a chance. So many people prefer to say "No" to new ideas when it would be so much more interesting to say "Yes" and see what might develop from them.

.   .   .   .   .

March 30, 1948: We really were lucky today. Mrs.
Workman told us last week that she was going to have to give
up her position at the East Branch to devote more time to her
family and we have been afraid that we would not be able to
find anyone to take her place at this time of the year. However,
I believe we now have a young lady who can step into the job
tomorrow and really grow in it.

The employment agency sent her over this afternoon.
Knowing that there were no trained librarians available in
these parts, I had called everyone I could think of who might
know of some East Side housewife with brains in her head and
time on her hands. I emphasized the point that we would be
content with someone who would work only four afternoon
hours a day, but that there might be more work for them later if
they wanted it. By hiring such a part-time worker we will save
over $1200 a year that we have had to spend every month this
year to give Mrs. W. a full-time job.

The new recruit is a former employee of the employment service who has since worked for American Airlines and
had other good experience serving the public. She seems to
have imagination and ambition and is looking for something
that will command her full attention and interest. She lives
near the branch and can work any hours; she will be content
with the four hours a day but will be glad to take on more work
if and when the need arises. She really appears to be the answer to our prayers.

.   .   .   .   .

April 1, 1948: Work is now underway on the building of
the new Librarian's office downstairs. We had expected a
crew of three or four men to descend on us, but the working

force turned out to be one lone carpenter. However, he has succeeded in knocking down most of the high plaster wall separating the supply room from the secretary's office and would appear to have made real headway his first day on the scene.

Miss Stone has had to move her desk and her files upstairs to get out of the wreckage. She went shopping yesterday for a new desk for my office and rounded up what she thought to be the best buy. I dropped by the store this morning to have a look at it and decided it was what we wanted. Also sat in a dozen different chairs to sample their ''feel'' but couldn't find one that rang the bell. The staff was horrified when I mentioned transferring my present desk and chair to the new office. They have also made it clear that they won't sleep nights if I insist on taking my work table along with me into my new quarters. Looks like this move is going to cost more than one might think.

People keep asking when we are going to open our phonograph record library so we are all impatient to have the carpenters, plasterers, electricians, and decorators get on with their work and present us with an attractive music room ready for public use. The newspaper ran a story on the results of our poll of favorite recordings, listing the 50 compositions that were checked most often by the 160 people who clipped the ballots out of the paper and mailed them to the library. We plan to order these recordings as soon as we can determine which albums are to be preferred in each case. Generally, one has a choice between the Victor and Columbia albums. Looks as if someone is going to learn a lot about music these next few months.

.   .   .   .   .

April 2, 1948: The wall between the supply room and Miss Stone's office is already down and the wall of my new office is on its way up. To be sure, the place is temporarily a mess and Lorenzo may have to repaint both offices, but still there is nothing like progress. A new supply room has been created in the basement by clearing the front of our second old storeroom and it will henceforth be much easier to find what one wants.

Tom Tichenor has finally finished his circus for the Children's Department. Around the walls one now sees large painted cut-out figures of clowns, bareback riders, sideshow freaks, animals in cages, et al. It is wonderful what an attractive display will do for such a department. It gives it real atmosphere and personality.

.   .   .   .   .

April 5, 1948: Had a letter from the young woman in Grand Rapids who wrote us about a job a year ago and then decided to stay there and take a position with a radio station. Now she says her radio programs are taking so much of her time that she doesn't have any leisure. She wants a job where she can take life a little easier. So I wrote back to tell her what we had to offer and to say that we would like to have someone around the place who could put on a few radio programs for us as well as do ordinary library work. It seems to me that she would fit in very nicely, working on her programs in the mornings and taking over the Young Moderns Den in the afternoons—since Mrs. Gullette will be leaving in June. Had to offer a salary beyond anything that we now pay but I feel that she is a good buy for the money and don't know where we could find anybody else with her high qualifications for the same price. As a matter of fact, I didn't make her a definite offer. Just told her that we would be glad to pay the salary she wanted but suggested that she visit Nashville at our expense and look around and let us talk the thing over.

Also wrote the young fellow from Western Reserve to ask if he would be interested in coming to Nashville as a general or administrative assistant. I really believe that it would be valuable experience for him and I could certainly use some help. The members of the Board with whom I checked the matter were strong for the idea of getting such an assistant to relieve the Librarian of administrative details. We still have the smallest professional staff of any city library of our size so no one has any fears of our becoming overstaffed.

.   .   .   .   .

April 7, 1948: It is good to see the branches' circulation coming up this year. Last year was almost entirely a main library year, but 1948 promises to see the three branches make great strides and perhaps catch up with the runaway central library. All three branches spurted ahead this month, but the blue ribbon definitely goes to the North Branch. Over 95 per cent more books were loaned from this agency last month than in April 1947. However, with the warm weather coming along now, we will be lucky if we can get through the next six months without slipping backwards.

I really wish I could be out on the Bookmobile these beautiful Spring days. Nobody ought to be cooped up in a city office with the outdoors filled with such sweet-smelling air. I wish everyone could have been with me this noon when I drove out to the Colemere Club with the Mayor and Mr. Gale, the vice-president of the Library Board. The Colemere Club is the beautiful old home on Murfreesboro Pike, next to the airport, which was recently taken over by a group of local political leaders as a fine social center and clubhouse. Mr. Gale had invited me out once before, with the hope of making some pleasant contacts with the politicians there. As it turned out, we were the only ones there for lunch that day—though we did have a wonderful chicken dinner and enjoyed the excursion in every way.

The trip out there today was equally delightful and it was good to have the opportunity of getting to know the Mayor a little better. Not that I have much in common with the local politicians. They are forever talking about people and cases that I have never heard of. On the other hand, I have a feeling that such men are not too happy about conversing with such serious-minded characters as librarians. I should think they would wonder what to talk about and so say no more than was absolutely necessary. Most people apparently assume that a librarian will want to talk over their heads and that he has no interest in discussing the ordinary things of life that mean so much to them. Consequently, they tend to shy away from us and it is not easy to get chummy with them.

The Young Moderns Den seems to be showing more life these days, but it may be months before the high school crowd uses the department to any great extent. I am giving a book or record to the teen-ager who thinks up the best public relations stunt of the month. This month it goes to the gal who wrote the Night Watchmen's Show to tell about the library's new Den with its phonograph records. The two disc jockies who run this popular program have since told their listening audience—at least four times—about the Library's new service.

Stopped by the East Branch this afternoon to see how Mrs. Hudson was making out on her new job. She seems to have mastered the charging routines in short order, though it will take a much longer time for her to comprehend the many possibilities of the branch and be able to fit each reader with the particular book he or she needs.

April 12, 1948: The plasterer, electrician, & Co., have now finished all their work on my new office, and the carpenter has now started tearing down the partition in my upper office. We can't move in downstairs until Lorenzo gets both rooms painted, which means that Miss Stone and I have no place to work. We've tried the reference rooms and the catalog department but no place is really satisfactory. With all the hammering upstairs we can't stay in the office and get anything done.

We now have 17 questionnaires back from the group of 19 large public libraries in the South. The thing that surprised me is that the two librarians who are holding out on us are both young men, professionally trained. Generally, it is the untrained oldtimers who feel they have little to report who won't supply such information as we requested. And without the facts and figures from the weaker institutions one is likely to reach wrong conclusions and present a distorted picture of the situation. I am going after those two missing forms again, although I can't see why professional people can't take care of such matters more promptly.

■   ■   ■   ■   ■

April 19, 1948: Construction work on the new office is finally completed. The carpenters, electricians, plasterers, and glass fitters have all departed from the scene and one can now get an idea what the new little room is going to look like. Of course the place has yet to be painted, but it is so dark! And with just one window—high as it may be—in one corner of the window I am afraid I shall have a bad case of claustophobia. Already, I want to knock a hole through the front wall for a second window. The fluorescent lighting fixture should give me adequate light but I certainly don't want to have to work under artificial light all the time.

My old office upstairs is now completely separated from the documents room by extending the wall to the ceiling. And the removal of the partition down the middle had doubled its size. I confess I rather like working in this large room, though I believe I shall get more work done in the new and more compact office downstairs.

.   ▪   ▪   ▪   ▪

April 21, 1948: For a long time I have wanted to run a copy of a library registration card in the newspaper, in such a way that people could clip it, fill it out, and send it to the library. It has always seemed to me to be a good way to attract new borrowers from the group who don't realize that library service is free, or have just never thought of taking out a library card, or have simply put off making their first visit to the library. I wanted to see how many people would take advantage of this easy, time-saving, way of securing a library card.

We were able to interest one of the newspaper reporters in the idea and he gave us a fine story in last Sunday's paper, mentioning all the resources of the library that would be made available to anyone interested in using the form printed above the article to register by mail. All anyone had to do was to mail it to the library and the library would send them a library card for their immediate use. So far, we have received over seventy newspaper registration forms.

It seemed rather abrupt, to say nothing of poor public relations, to mail these people their library cards without any accompanying explanatory material, so I have prepared a letter that can be used not only with this group but with all our new borrowers. We are having a thousand copies multigraphed so that when their name and address is typed in at the top each copy will have the appearance of a personal letter.

Each one will be signed by the Librarian. In the future, all new adult cards will be mailed out, instead of being called for at the library by each borrower, so that all new members of the Library Family will have this further introduction to the resources of the main building.

■   ■   ■   ■   ■

April 26, 1948: The Magazine section of the Sunday Tennessean did a good job on the Children's Department. All in all, we have had good newspaper publicity these last twenty months. I have been impressed with that fact this last week as I have been getting our 1947 clippings together to prepare a publicity scrapbook to show at the A.L.A. convention in June. The campaign for additional funds, the new Bookmobile, and the marionette shows, seem to have brought us the most clippings and pictures.

At the present moment, I am home with the flu. Miss Stone has called several times to tell me of the problems the air conditioning people are having in trying to figure out how to install one of their units in my new office. It was rather a setback to learn that the air conditioner would cut off my view out the window. Set above the window sill, it will block off some fifteen inches of window so that anyone sitting at the desk will see nothing of the outdoors but the sky above. I certainly don't want to be shut in like that. I've told Miss Stone to call off the air conditioning people until I have had a chance to try out the room. Want to experiment with a cardboard patch over the lower portion of the window to see how I would like not being able to see outside. I plan to go as long as I can without the air conditioner and then, if it gets too hot and I simply must have the unit, build a framework to support it six feet above the window sill. This will require an expensive glass-cutting operation but I believe it will be worth it to have the machine high enough so that it will neither cut off my view or cast a shadow on my desk.

．　　　．　　　．　　　．　　　．

April 29, 1948: It is good to get Tom Tichenor's long marionette stage out of the Children's Room where, for more than a year, it has blocked access to the bookshelves on one side of the room. He had to take most of it apart to get it through the door but now has it set up again in the basement hall. Last Saturday they had their first marionette show in the hall, just outside the Children's Room, and it was reported to be an improvement over the old arrangement.

The Young Moderns Council voted to have an exhibit at the Hobby Fair sponsored by the Rotary Club at the Fairgrounds. At their meeting this week they assigned members to duty at their booth during the three days of the Fair and arranged to pick each other up to get out there—all in a matter of minutes. These young people really move with dispatch when they start out to do a job. Incidentally, they now have over thirty albums in their phonograph record collection. Many of them will be heard at the Hobby Fair since the Council has been encouraged to bring along their phonographs and add as much noise as possible to the atmosphere there.

．　　　．　　　．　　　．　　　．

May 1, 1948: Miss Ragan was in today from Grand Rapids, to see and be seen before we arranged to have her come to work here. The rest of the staff liked her right away and I was pleased to find that she was as attractive as her photograph and letters gave promise of her being. I took her and Mrs. Moncrief to lunch at the Hermitage Hotel, after showing her around the library in the morning, and then spent the afternoon driving her around Nashville and the prettier suburbs. Stopped by the Y.W.C.A. to see about a room for her when she comes here in July, but found that the dormitories are limited to girls making a good deal less than she will be getting.

Since we were on trial, too, we were glad to hear that she liked the setup here well enough to decide to throw in her fortunes with us. Perhaps some librarians would not think it necessary to spend an entire day—and a Saturday at that—with a young job applicant, but it could be that it was just this personal attention that helped convince her to come here. Certainly a Librarian who showed such interest in a new assistant might be expected to make a more sympathetic and approachable boss than one who couldn't spare the time himself to show a new person around. At any rate, anybody coming all the way from Michigan deserves a great deal of attention, and I don't know how I could have spent the time to better advantage. Building real library interest in a new staff member is as important and productive a job as a Librarian has to do.

．   ．   ．   ．   ．

May 4, 1948: The new office looks great! We finally managed to find a nice carpet for the floor, and with my new desk and that wonderful new chair of mine in position beside the window, everything looks exceedingly snug. I have never sat in a more comfortable chair. It just draws me to the desk. And I am particularly pleased to discover that I can work in there all day long without having to turn on the overhead lights. The light coming in through the window is quite ample, particularly so when the venetian blinds are pulled up. It is very pleasant to work in front of the open window, and I am sure that I am getting more work done now that I have this comfortable office to attract and hold me to my desk.

.   .   .   .   .

May 6, 1948: I feel we really did something constructive this week. It all started with my reading the Election Notice in the newspaper calling attention to the $3,000,000 bond issue that will soon be voted upon. The Notice stated that the money would be used to cover work on streets, sewers, sidewalks, alleys, bridges, etc. There has been almost nothing in the paper about the need for this money. Made me wonder what the facts in the case were, and how people could vote intelligently on the bond issue without knowing what the real needs are and how all the money is to be spent.

I tried our Reference Department, but they did not have the answers. Then asked a number of men in the library what they knew about the situation. They were equally in the dark and did not know how they were going to vote on the issue. By that time I was convinced that there was a real need for the facts, and that the Library ought to go ahead and dig up the answers rather than wait for somebody else to do it. It seemed like a wonderful opportunity to show people that the Reference Department was an active agency with sufficient initiative to go out after the information it needed to supply its patrons when such information wasn't already available.

So I arranged an interview with the Head of the Department of Public Works and called on him the next day at City Hall, armed with some thirty questions that I wanted to have him answer. He was very co-operative and gave quick, frank answers to every question so that I soon had everything that I wanted. He was quite surprised and pleased to find a library taking such interest in a matter of this kind and sent me away with a number of reports that we should have had in the library, but didn't.

It was a simple matter to type up this information in simple question and answer form and have a thousand copies of the two sheets multigraphed. Before multigraphing, we showed a copy to the Public Works Director and he was happy to approve it without any changes. We kept some copies in the library, sent out a few hundred for distribution at the Kiwanis and Rotary Club meetings, and dispatched as many more to the Chamber of Commerce where they provided the information that decided the Chamber's Board of Governors in coming out in favor of the Bond Issue's passage. As a matter of fact, when a delegation from the C of C visited the Mayor to ask for information about the situation the Mayor had his Secretary give them one of the Library's reports. The Sunday Tennessean plans to run the whole thing this Sunday so that everyone will have the information before they go to the polls next week.

All in all, it has been a lot of fun, without being any trouble to do, and perhaps it has benefited the library to some extent. But more than that, it has been heartening to me to see the library doing a job that I have always felt it might do more of—collecting and distributing in neat, intelligible form, needed information that perhaps others should provide but aren't. Another good example would be pre-election information about the various candidates for office, telling something of their qualifications, their past record, and their current campaign platform. This is a job for the League of Women Voters, but seldom are they organized to collect and make available this information. Consequently, thousands of people who should vote, don't, and as many more go to the polls without knowing who the candidates are, what they have done in the past, or what they are likely to do in the future, if elected.

．　　　　．　　　　．　　　　．　　　　．

May 11, 1948: The annual dinner meeting of the Nash-ville Library Club was a huge success last night, due largely to the excellence of the guest speaker—one of the exchange teachers who spent a year teaching in England. All our meet-ings this year seem to have gone off all right, but still I am glad now to be turning the reins over to Dr. Lancaster who will be President this coming year.

．　　　　．　　　　．　　　　．　　　　．

May 17, 1948: We have had a long library article in the Sunday paper so many weeks in a row now that some people are beginning to think it is something planned by the paper. The last three Sundays it has been the Librarian's Annual Report for 1947 (better late than never), the facts behind the Streets and Sewers Bond Issue, and a fine article about the Young Moderns Den. We had a photographer take a picture of the Den with some of the members of the Young Moderns Council dancing, reading magazines, and looking at the books and records on the shelves. It came out very well so we gave it to the newspaper to use with their article. They ran it three columns wide and it really stood out on the page—the clearest picture I ever saw in either newspaper. I presume most everybody in town now knows of the existence of this room for the teen-agers, but knowing young people I am sure that it will take more than that to get them to use the place. High school students don't want to go anywhere unless they expect a crowd there and feel that it is one of the accepted places to go. They would much rather crowd together in Candyland and pay for the privilege of being with the crowd than try some place off the beaten path.

.   .   .   .   .

May 19, 1948: I have finally found the car trailer that I want and can get one from the manufacturer in shell form. It is called a "Trailette" and is one of the smallest units on the market. It is about 16' long and has a completely aluminum exterior, which gives it an attractive appearance. It has seven windows, two on each side and two on the front end, and is particularly light and cheerful inside.

We are having them leave in everything that we can use. This includes a nice closet running the width of the machine above the front windows, the regular trailer stove, venetian blinds on all the windows, and the dinette that fills the front of the machine. This will provide a nice table for the librarian to work on and a comfortable seat for her and as many as three patrons who may want to sit and talk with her. The cost of the trailer, purchased this way, is only $1120, and we ought to be able to add the shelves and some 1200 new volumes and keep the total cost of the trailer branch in the neighborhood of $3,000.

One of the "Trailette's" greatest attractions is its small, compact size, since the smaller the unit the smaller the outlay required to equip and stock it. This machine ought to handle about 1200 volumes and that is all I would want to put into such a unit. We are not expecting any great use of the trailer branch, since the colored population has yet to show that they will do any considerable book reading, and so would not be interested in an average-size trailer that would call for the purchase of many more books to fill it satisfactorily.

.   .   .   .   .

May 21, 1948: Held a quarterly meeting of the Library Board this afternoon, almost four months since our last meeting in January. The chief item of business was the new budget prepared by the Librarian for submission to the City Finance Department.

It looks as if our operating budget the next fiscal year will run $4900 over that of the current year. If the City Council does not grant us an increase on August 1st we will have to watch our pennies even more than usual to get through the year. The biggest reason for the increase is the operation of the two new bookmobiles. We may have to work through the Councilmen of the areas served by these machines to get the money to run these mobile units.

We are also asking for $4500 to build an auditorium on the second floor of the library, $5000 to cut an entrance through the back of the building so that the public could easily enter the main floor from Polk Avenue and save themselves many steps, and an extra $2,000 to permit the much-needed caulking of the main building. The Board also voted to add to the budget a request for the $3900 needed to pay the six retirement allowances for another year. This amount will probably be immediately cut out at City Hall, yet it may serve to bring the matter to the attention of the Councilmen who are interested in the matter of regular pensions for these retired librarians.

Nobody feels at all optimistic about our chances of getting more money this year, yet I do not feel that we could have made our request any smaller, not do I feel that we are demanding more than a library in a city of this size should have. As a matter of fact, we are still asking for only a third of what the A.L.A. prescribes for a city of our population, and smaller Knoxville across the state now receives $50,000 more than we do—and almost twice as much per capita.

Before adjourning, the Board took a look at the drawing of the fine neon sign that had been designed for use at the corner of the library property on 8th & Union. Their first reaction was "That's great. Let's get it." Then somebody brought up the possible reaction of city councilmen who might misinterpret it as a sign that the Library had more money than they needed. The result was to wash the whole idea out, at least for the time being.

■   ■   ■   ■   ■

May 24, 1948: I have been trying to suggest some ideas to Miss Birdsong that might bring more adults around the North Branch library, particularly in the evening. Realizing that she did not feel too comfortable alone there after supper I asked her if she couldn't organize some chess or checkers games, or perhaps a bridge group, that would give her some evening company. The noise would never bother anybody and we would be glad to have people use the library for any decent purpose. Perhaps some new visitor might someday be inspired to take out a book; and even if he never did he might become a friend and supporter of the neighborhood library.

■   ■   ■   ■   ■

CHAPTER **XIV**

Epilog

This diary began the day I assumed the directorship of the Nashville Public Library. With all the things that one could see needed doing, and that I felt sure we would be able to accomplish, I knew that my first two years there would be as interesting and rewarding as any I might experience. I thought it would be good to have a record of this period, but never contemplated going beyond two years with it.

When I reached my second anniversary I put the diary aside and never recorded anything thereafter. By then it constituted 375 pages of double-spaced typing, far more than I ever expected to accumulate. I knew that the thing had no decent ending, but when one simply stops writing on a particular calendar date he is likely to end right in the middle of things, with no conclusion or high point reached.

I never thought anything about this until a reader of the page proofs said to me: "You can't stop there in that in-between place. Your readers will want to know how everything turned out. What happened to the ownership of the library, and to the retirement pay, and to the proposed free service to county residents? And did you ever get an air conditioner in your office, and the neon sign you wanted, along with the booketerias, and was the main library ever opened to the black community?

The answer is Yes, we got all of these things, most of them in the following two years. As to the air conditioning, I managed to get through the first summer without it, though looking back on it later I don't know how I was able to. When the second summer started heating up I called in the engineers and told them they were just going to have to pound a hole through the big stone facing on the front of the building and put an air conditioner in there. Nobody had considered such a drastic move before, but I was desperate. Every summer day in that hot, stuffy little office was like working on a bookmobile with no air conditioning. So the hole was made and my office, and my working life, restored by the wonderful cool air.

At about the same time I decided to propose to the Library Board again that we install that neon sign on the front of the library property, to let everyone know that this old building looming overhead on the corner of two busy streets was their public library. This time, the proposal was unanimously approved, and from then on, everyone driving by the building was invited to "TAKE HOME A BOOK."

Before then, we had our contract with the County Court for free library service to all county residents. We simply started serving these people, being promised 25¢ for every book loaned to them. The county magistrates didn't expect this would cost them very much, but one gentleman was cautious enough to set a maximum payment of $10,000 a year to the Library. That would allow for a circulation of

40,000 volumes. But much to the magistrates' consternation, the circulation to county residents topped 88,000 the first year. We then asked the County to raise their maximum payment proportionally, but they would increase it no more than 50 percent.

For the next nine years, every time we asked the City for an increase in their library appropriation, the councilmen would get very agitated, accuse the County of not paying its fair share of the cost for library service, and swear they wouldn't give us another cent until the County started paying its proportionate share. Several councilmen would always press for the complete cutoff of city funds for the library until the County paid up, but the Mayor was always able to defeat these dangerous proposals. The County made small increases in its payments from time to time, but when county circulation started topping the loans to city residents, the County's appropriation to the library was still less than half the City's.

By 1958, the City Council had had enough of this unfair situation. They cancelled the contract with the County for library service and instructed us to give no more service to county residents. When someone called the Reference Department, the staff member now had to ask where the caller lived. If the person lived outside the city limits, he or she could not be helped in any way. And since the county money had provided all of our book funds, we were then almost completely unable to buy new books. After six months of this intolerable situation, constantly having to deny service to people, the library director gave up the struggle and accepted a directorship in California.

The retired librarians continued to receive their pensions from the library's Special Fund. As the amount of money collected in fines and fees grew along with the greatly increased circulation, the amounts of the individual pensions were also considerably augmented. But the library's entire financial structure wasn't put on a solid and adequately funded base until early in the 1960's when Nashville went on the Metro program and the library became the Metropolitan Library of Nashville and Davidson County, serving a combined population of almost 400,000 people.

Not long after the LIBRARY LOG period, the library had self-service booketerias operating in three Logan Co. supermarkets. Located outside the city limits, far from any library building, they were well positioned to provide a great service to book readers. Since all units operated completely on the honor system, with all borrowers charging out their own books, with no attendant there, some librarians thought all the books would be stolen. Particularly so, since most of the books were new—many being leased from my old friend Mr. McNaughton at the unheard of cost of $1.00 a volume, and all were attractively jacketed. But actual losses proved to be no more than 8 percent of each collection's 800 volumes.

When one compares the value of each unit's book losses against what it would have cost to keep a library assistant on duty the full hours of the supermarket, to protect against losses—which the library would have suffered anyway through the failure to return properly checked out books—it is clear that self-service is an excellent way to operate such a library unit.

In each case, the store gave us a section of shelving about 18 feet long and 5 shelves high. The bottom shelf was a locked bin with an opening along the top wide enough to receive the books being returned. Each unit was maintained by a housewife in the neighborhood who was paid $2.00 a day to come to the supermarket in the morning, unlock the return bins, slip the returned books, re-shelve them, and straighten up the collection. She then stamped a pile of date-due cards with the day's date, picked up the registration cards filled out by new borrowers, counted the fine money that people had deposited in the metal container after figuring what they owed on their overdue books, counted the previous day's circulation from the book cards left in the box, and then arranged all these cards alphabetically and by call numbers in the card tray, which was then locked in the bin on the bottom shelf. In short, the booketerias were a popular, successful, and quite inexpensive library venture. The only thing about them I never understood was why other libraries never copied them, though they were written-up in the *Library Journal*, *Newsweek*, and *Business Week*.

As to the matter of opening the main library to Nashville's black citizens, I was happily able to effect this a year later. At the end of a library board meeting, when I noticed that the two or three men most obstinately opposed to the idea of admitting ''Negroes'' (as they were then called), had left the room, I hurriedly said to the members then in the process of leaving: ''Excuse me. May I say just one thing more. Lately, we've been having a few Negroes come to the main desk asking to borrow a book. Would anybody here mind if we just gave them the books they wanted and let them go on their way?''

Put that way, with no discussion, no emotion, no vote, and nobody there to oppose the idea, the six departing board members said a quick, ''No, go ahead and do it.'' And with that, the bars came down and our main library at long last was open to every member of the community. It was my single most exhilarating moment in Nashville.

I knew some other Southern cities had experienced some pretty rough times over attempts to open up their main libraries. I wanted to avoid that every way I could. So I never said a word to the newspapers about what had transpired, or mentioned it to anyone except library staff members who needed to know. I figured that as the first few black visitors found acceptance, rather than the old rejection, the word would get around pretty quickly through all the black sections of the city.

Things worked out as well as anyone could have hoped. There never was a single article in either of the two local newspapers about the change at the downtown library, and never an editorial mention of it. Things went quietly along, with a slow increase in the number of black visitors. A few months after the board meeting, a desk attendant rushed in to my office to announce that there was a young black man sitting in the reading room. Nothing had been said about letting them do more than borrow some books and then leave. That was earth-shaking enough, as many viewed it. But now we were faced with something more advanced. I could see no harm in the young man's being there in the reading room, so told the young lady to just go about her business and let him stay. So that was the end of that, and I don't recall ever catching any flack from anyone—even the three older gentlemen who had missed that late business at the board meeting—for my part in opening the main library to everyone.

.   .   .   .   .